BTEC First
Early Years

Please return

BTEC First Early Years

Sandy Green

Published in 2003 by:
Nelson Thornes Ltd
Delta Place
27 Bath Road
CHELTENHAM
GL53 7TH
United Kingdom

03 04 05 06 07 / 10 9 8 7 6 5 4 3 2 1

A catalogue record for this book is available from the British Library.

ISBN 0 7487 7164 6

Illustrations by Jane Bottomley; Angela Lumley; Oxford Designers and Illustrators
Typeset by Northern Phototypesetting Co. Ltd, Bolton

Printed and bound in Great Britain by Scotprint

Contents

About the Author

Sandy Green qualified as a nursery nurse in the early 1970s. She has a broad knowledge and experience of Early Years education and care, entering teaching in the late 1980s. Sandy co-ordinated the BTEC National Diploma in Early Years course and the CACHE ADCE for several years, leaving her post in further education to work as an Early Years consultant and freelance trainer. She is also an external verifier for Edexcel.

Introduction

The BTEC First in Early Years is a text book for the course of study of the same title. All eight units of the course, three core and five specialist, have been included, offering a range of reading and self-assessment across the breadth of the qualification.

Links between the units have been indicated, and both case studies and activities have been placed throughout the text to help readers consolidate their understanding. Remember points and definitions have been given where appropriate, with a key terms section and test yourself questions at the end of each unit. Key terms are emboldened in the text the first time they appear. Definitions of each of the key terms can be found in the glossary.

Acknowledgements

Thanks as always go to my husband John for his continuing encouragement and enthusiasm for my work, also to the friends and colleagues who have willingly discussed ideas with me, particularly Lorna Boyd and Gina Ashman. A special mention must be made of my daughter Hannah, who continues to allow me to include photographs and other details of my granddaughter Jasmine's development.

The author and publishers would like to acknowledge the help and advice provided by the reviewers of the manuscript, Jo Irvine, consultant, and Jacky Roe BTEC Early Years Tutor, Barry College.

Photo credits
Photodisc 59 (NT), p. 43; Photodisc 32 (NT), p. 84; Photofusion, pp. 85, 188, 189, 190; Ann & Bury Peerless, p. 92; Photodisc 45 (NT), p. 94; Image Source 2 (NT), p. 148; Digital Vision PB (NT), p. 256 (upper); Photodisc 41 (NT), p. 256 (lower)

Every effort has been made to contact copyright holders, and we apologise if any have been overlooked.

1 Values and interpersonal skills

This unit covers:

- Factors that influence diversity and equality
- Skills required of an Early Years carer
- Responsibilities of the individual Early Years carer

Working with babies and children in partnership with their carers requires an understanding, acceptance and demonstration of the **core values** of **anti-discriminatory** practice, equality and responsibility. This means taking an approach to your work that ensures that you do not treat anyone more or less favourably than anyone else. This means that you do not show favouritism. These values are directly linked to you as a person, and to you as part of a professional team. It includes both your individual actions and practice, and your responses to the actions and practice of others. It requires good interpersonal skills for you to be able to communicate appropriately with the children, parents, carers and others with whom you will be working. It also requires appropriate presentation (your clothing, hairstyle, use of make-up and jewellery) and management of yourself as a person (behaviour, attitude and language use), and as a team member. This sense of values and good working practice requires commitment and enthusiasm, as well as knowledge and understanding.

Factors that influence diversity and equality

The **diversity** of life within our community is affected by many factors. These can be termed social and political factors, and include the following.

Social class

Whatever politicians may say about Britain being a classless society, most people will still recognise that children from wealthier families who live in more secure, spacious and favourable housing, and enjoy a more privileged lifestyle in which they are able to access leisure facilities and enjoy good food, and regular opportunities to socialise (middle income families), are likely to fare better in life than those children whose families are struggling financially, working in lower paid jobs and who have fewer opportunities accessible to them (low income families). In other words, **social class** does matter.

The difference between living on the minimum or basic wage and living on a higher income can directly affect a family in many ways. An example is geographical location. Life within an inner city will offer different experiences than life in the suburbs or in the countryside. Poverty, however, can be found everywhere, with issues such as isolation being a factor both in small rural hamlets and in high-rise city tower blocks, but also accessibility of schools, transport, employment, shopping and leisure facilities will vary considerably. The quality of life will also be affected by the levels of air pollution, which may differ greatly between urban and rural locations.

Activity 1.1

1 Find out about life in the countryside, and in an inner city area, identifying and listing the factors that might lead to isolation.
2 What are the similarities and what are the differences between living in an inner city flat and a rural village? Set out your findings and conclusions in a table.

Remember to consider the viewpoints of different members of a family, i.e. working parents, parents who stay at home, children of school age and pre-schoolers.

Ethnicity

Cultural identity and practice will impact on individuals, affecting time, opportunities and in some cases equality within the workplace.

Activity 1.2

What examples of the impact of cultural identity and practice can you think of?

Gender

Although there have been significant changes in employment practice in recent years, with many women now in managerial roles and men being more easily accepted in what were considered to be 'traditionally female' professions, such as caring and nursing, there is still a long way to go. Equal opportunity policies and monitoring procedures now commonly produced in organisations have helped a great deal, but gender can still affect the level of opportunity faced by an individual.

Activity 1.3

Within the field of Early Years, what examples can you think of where gender may affect equality? An example might be men always being asked to fix broken toys.

Equal opportunities policies have benefited the child care environment

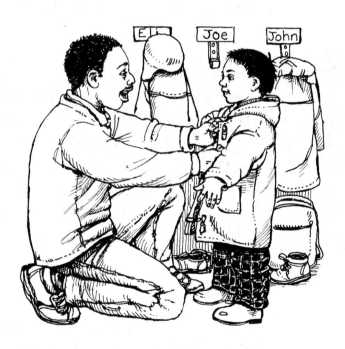

Age

Opportunities can be affected by age, for example due to concerns about a lack of experience in younger people, or about lack of up-to-date knowledge in more mature people.

Family structure

Family structures can vary considerably, with some cultures placing a greater value on family elders and the influence they bring to communities, than in others. There can also be a great deal of difference in the level of support given to children and their parents through the extended family (advice, babysitting and so on), with far fewer families now living near to each other due to increased ease of travel, together with the tendency for people to move to areas of the country where there are more opportunities for employment. The continuing expansion of 'new towns' and urban developments have played a part in this. Additionally, many more women are still working themselves when they become grandmothers, making them unavailable for child care support.

Financial viability

A child born into a family that is financially secure is likely to be able to access a greater range of resources (for example money for a computer or extra books), and opportunities to enhance their life and learning (swimming, piano lessons etc.), than a child born into a family that is struggling to make ends meet. This can cause an imbalance of basic opportunity, affecting issues such as pre-school provision, although since the late 1990s the Government has developed funding for pre-school places for all four year olds, and more recently for three year olds whose families wish to take advantage of it. The Government aim is for all three year olds to have access to a funded nursery or pre-school place. This, of course, is only successful if there are places available and accessible to the families concerned. In many areas of the country pre-school attendance is well provided for, but in other areas there is insufficient provision to meet the needs of the children who live there.

Welfare state

Definitions

Poverty
The basic needs of food, water, clothing and shelter are not met satisfactorily.

The **welfare state** was originally set up with three main aims:
- free health care and treatment for everyone who wants it;
- free education for all children;
- a minimum weekly income for all families that is above the poverty line.

Activity 1.4

1 Many families are still struggling to maintain sufficient food and heating for their children! Make a note of ways in which a lack of food and lack of sufficient heating could affect a child's development.

2 How do you feel if you are cold and hungry?

3 How might your attitude and enthusiasm for learning or work be affected?

Cycle of disadvantage

The diagram below illustrates the cycle of disadvantage. Children can be disadvantaged for many reasons, including their ethnic background, religion, language, social class or gender, but for families who are members of groups also marginalised by society, it is harder to break out of the cycle. As children move through life, they live with the consequences of their families' lifestyle, type of housing, finances and employment opportunities. Some will, of course be able to move on and develop different lifestyles for themselves, but many others will not, and so the cycle of disadvantage is likely to continue through to their own children.

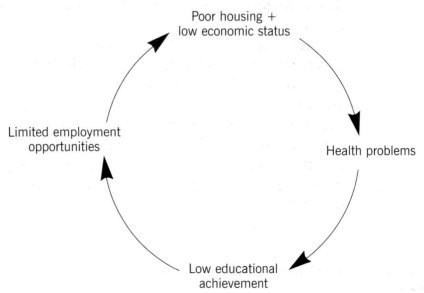

The cycle of disadvantage

Discriminatory practice

To discriminate is to give favourable or unfavourable treatment to an individual because of a specific factor.

- **Discrimination** can be **institutional**, where the policies or working practice of the organisation or workplace result in different groups of people being treated in different ways.
- Discrimination can be **individual**, where the prejudice (an opinion formed in advance) is the prejudice of just one person.
- Discrimination can be **direct**, by telling an individual that they cannot do something because of their race, sex, situation or disability.
- Discrimination can be **indirect**, by excluding individuals who are unable to take part in, or do, something because of their race, sex, situation or disability. This could include items of cultural or religious dress, such as the Sikh turban, the Pakistani hijaab or the Jewish Yarmulka, that may prevent certain activities such as riding horses or motorbikes.

Stereotyping

The pre-judgement of a group of people on the basis of the actions or opinions of one person or a small group of other similar people is known as **stereotyping**. They are labelled because of those actions or opinions. Stereotyped judgements take away the personal identity of an individual. When you make stereotyped judgements, often using phrases such as 'They all …', this prevents you from seeing people as individuals. A stereotyped image can be either positive or negative, and is frequently wrong. They are sometimes built up out of personal experience, but are more likely to have been developed due to the influence of other people.

A stereotyped image can be either positive or negative

Activity 1.5

1 Give four examples of stereotyping.

2 Consider how each of these stereotypes might affect the individuals concerned.

3 Have you included any examples from your Early Years practice? If not, add such an example to your list now.

Definitions

Marginalise
Treat as insignificant or excluded.

Groups of individuals can become **marginalised** by society through prejudice and discrimination. This can result in making them feel unable to initiate change themselves or to make their voices heard. This situation is called disempowerment and its effects can be far-reaching, causing the people who feel disempowered to see themselves as 'less than equal' within society.

Remember !

| *Prejudice* | + | *Power* | = | *Discrimination* |
| *(a pre-formed opinion)* | | *(the practice of the setting)* | | *(certain individuals may not receive equal opportunities)* |

Examples of discriminatory practice

Within society there are a number of groups of people who face discrimination. These include people who are discriminated against on the grounds of their:

- age;
- class;
- disability and differing levels of ability;
- race, culture and religion;
- sexual orientation;
- gender;
- marital status.

Activity 1.6

1 Think of ways in which people in each of the above groups might face discrimination.

2 Explain how the points you have identified can be applied to Early Years settings. Ensure that you have included issues of staffing, access, communication, economics, clothing, cultural practice and diet in your answer.

Unit 3 gives an overview of the laws applying to equal opportunities. You may find it helpful to refer to it at this point.

LINKS TO UNIT 3, page 76.

Remember! Your responses to the actions and practice of others form part of the core values of anti-discriminatory practice, equality and responsibility. You need to consider how you might keep this in mind. The case studies below will help you.

Case study | ***Maxine***

Maxine is an Early Years student on placement in a reception class. She is very creative and enjoys preparing for and supervising children in various art activities. She also likes to help them mix the paints to make new colours. The current topic is 'All about Ourselves'. Maxine has been asked to help each child to produce a portrait of themselves for a large wall display. She has provided a range of colour paints to incorporate all the colours needed to represent the children's clothes, and is encouraging the children to make 'rosy pink' or 'muddy brown' for their faces.

1 Are the terms used by Maxine appropriate?

2 Is discrimination taking place here?

3 What alternative suggestions could you make?

4 Do you think this situation should have been challenged? If so, why?

5 What might be the long-term implications if this situation goes unchallenged?

Case study | ***Claire and Mark***

Claire and Mark work together in the same room of a day nursery. The room supervisor writes the weekly staffing plans. A large amount of Mark's time is scheduled for outdoors play, supervising construction activities and small world play, such as the train set, garage and the road/car mat. Claire is mostly asked to supervise creative activities and the role-play area. Both Mark and Claire are content with what they do.

1 Is there a problem with this?

2 Is discrimination taking place here?

3 What might be the long-term implications of these arrangements if they go unchallenged?

4 If you had the opportunity, what would you do about it?

A large amount of
Mark's time is scheduled
for outdoors play

By exploring issues of stereotyping, discrimination and prejudice you will come to understand the effects it can have more fully. Changing individual opinion is not easy, as this is often based on the earliest learning and the main influences on an individual's development. These influences are described as **primary** and **secondary socialisation**. Primary socialisation is the impact of immediate family and social groups on a child. Secondary socialisation is the impact of social contacts on a child, outside the child's immediate family and social group, including teachers, Early Years professionals and so on. When faced with examples of negative practice that you previously might have found acceptable, you need to explore the alternative views or ideas, re-evaluating your previous thoughts and feelings based on the new information and understanding you have acquired.

Skills required of an Early Years carer

There are many skills required of Early Years workers and one of the most important is communication. As well as being an important aspect of life in general, effective communication is central to good Early Years practice. It involves the giving and receiving of information, both verbally and non-verbally, remembering that the way in which you communicate information sends out a message as to the sort of person you are – your attitude, the way you talk, the manner in which you listen and your approach to a situation at any given time.

Interpersonal skills

Your ability to communicate is directly linked to your **interpersonal skills** (how good you are at getting on with other people, and your sensitivity to their feelings and needs). An individual with good interpersonal skills is able to identify when communication has not been effective by noting the responses of the person they were communicating with, and is both willing and able to adjust their approach accordingly. This is important, as within any Early Years setting there are a variety of relationships both to develop and maintain.

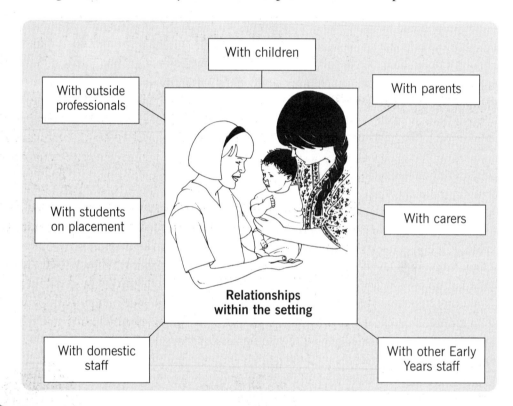

With children

With outside professionals

With parents

With students on placement

With carers

Relationships within the setting

With domestic staff

With other Early Years staff

Activity 1.7

1 Make a note of the different sorts of relationships you might have with each person in the above spidergram, ensuring that you list what are the main aspects of each relationship. For example, one of the main aspects of your relationship with other Early Years staff will be as a team member, working together.

2 Each relationship will involve certain expectations. What might these be?

Remember! Parents are placing their child in your care. These children are extremely precious to them and they will want to know that they can trust and rely on you. Other staff and outside professionals will expect a certain

10

level of knowledge and understanding from you, together with practical skills relevant to your experience and training. Children will simply want you to be there for them, to play, interact, care for and take an interest in them.

Family structures

All families will vary in structure and situation. You should be aware of any personal bias or preconceived ideas you might have about them as this can have an impact on the way in which you interact with them. It is important that you work with families in a non-judgemental way, responding equally and positively to all, respecting their rights and ensuring that your attitude and use of language is always appropriate.

Case study

Monicque

Monicque is the mother of three happy, bubbly children in the primary school where you are on placement. Each of the children has a different father and you have heard that the three dads regularly call round to see the children and take them all on outings.

Monicque works three evenings each week, and the children are looked after by three different babysitters, each of them a grandparent to at least one of the children.

Joan, one of the classroom assistants, remarks to you that she thinks it is terrible 'the way that family lives'.

1   How should you respond to Joan's comment?

'I don't like what she thinks, but I have to accept it is her right.'

Barriers to effective communication

At times communication fails because something gets in the way. A barrier is anything that causes an obstruction or prevents the progress of communication. This can include any of the points set out below:

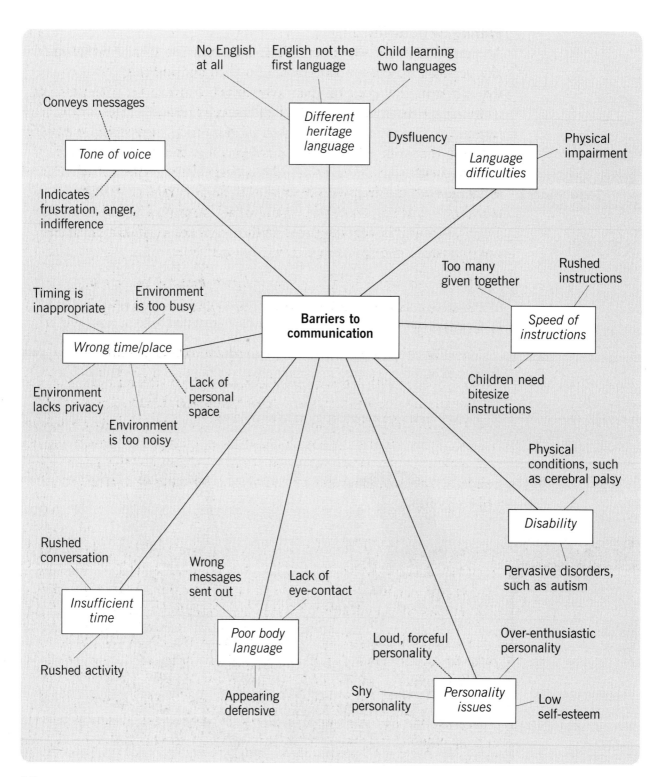

Activity 1.8

1 In a small group discuss all the **barriers to effective communication** listed in the spidergram above.

2 How could you help alleviate each barrier?

Talking with children

It is important that when you talk to a child or group of children that the language you use is appropriate for their age and stage of development. The tone of your voice should convey the same message as the words you are using. Children can be confused if your words are saying yes, but the tone of your voice indicates no. Any stress or anxiety that you are feeling should not be passed on to the children you are working with. Clear communication is particularly important when working with children who have limited English and are perhaps learning English as a second or additional language. They will benefit from learning this new **language within context**, emphasising words and phrases as the appropriate time. For example:

'Here is your drink Asif', as you hand him a beaker at snacktime.

'Let us put your coat on Dipendra', as you help him get ready for outside play.

'Shamilla, where is your shoe?', as you help her dress to go home.

When working with a group of children who have different levels of understanding due to their age or ability you will need to ensure that you are giving sufficient guidance and clarity for those children with the less developed language skills, while offering appropriate stimulation and vocabulary extension to the older or more linguistically able children. This would often be referred to as working with a **mixed ability** group.

Case study

Stephanie

Pre-school leader Heather asks her Early Years student, Stephanie, to organise the children for going out to play in the garden. Stephanie gets the children's attention and gives them the following instructions:

'It is time to go out and play now. You can each take a ball or a hoop or a beanbag out with you. It is very cold, so please put on your coats and do up the buttons. If you need help, please ask. If you have a hat or a scarf or mittens you must put them on. Please check that your shoes are done up properly so that you do not trip. If you need the toilet, go now before you go outside.'

1 How did Stephanie do?

2 How many instructions were there?

3 Do you think the children will have responded to all the instructions? If not, why not?

4 How could you have improved upon Stephanie's instructions?

Remember! Children will focus on what is the most obvious or most exciting thing they hear. In this case the going outside to play, or the taking of a resource with them. It is unlikely that they will have taken in many of Stephanie's instructions. She needed to break them down into smaller 'groups' or preferably give them one instruction at a time. For example, 'Please get your coats on', then 'Who has got a hat or scarf? and so on.

Understanding concepts

As an Early Years worker it will be necessary for you to understand the following **concepts** and their importance to the lives of children. Concepts are thoughts and feelings, which can be expressed through your actions towards others, for example showing sympathy to someone who is crying; or through the actions of others towards you, for example feeling pride when your achievements are praised by another person.

Self-esteem and self-worth

Each of us is happiest when we are feeling good about ourselves. This involves having a good opinion of ourself as a person, feeling that we are admired, respected and valued by others, and being satisfied that we are achieving what we want to achieve. Simply put, **self-esteem** and self-worth are all about liking who we are. This is an equally important feeling for children and is an important aspect of their emotional security and therefore their subsequent development. They need to know that they are liked by other children, and they need the social approval of friends and playmates. As they move into primary school the need for approval of their same sex peers is particularly strong, as this is the stage where such relationships are very important to them.

Belonging

Children need to feel that they belong. This applies both at home and to social situations. Children need the unquestioning love of their family and the security that comes of knowing that whatever happens they will still be loved. They need to know that they are accepted, and that they fit in with their peers. If a child is not accepted, or feels that they are not accepted, it can have a negative impact on both their emotional security and on their behaviour. This can be seen in many ways, such as in this example.

1 A child with low self-esteem will often give up on a task earlier than other children, as they assume that they cannot achieve it.

2 This 'lack of achievement' can lead to disruptive behaviour within the nursery or classroom.

3 The behaviour is declared unacceptable by the staff responsible for the setting.

4 A continuous cycle of lowering the child's self-esteem still further is now in process.

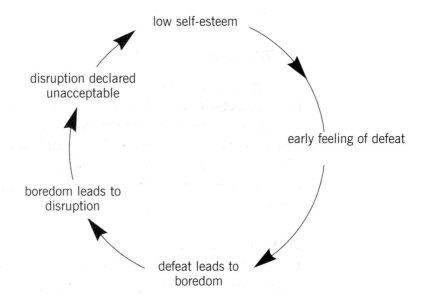

Activity 1.9

1 Can you think of any examples from your work experience linked to the cycle above?

2 Where did this happen?

3 How was it dealt with?

To ensure that children feel valued and maintain (or develop) a good sense of self-esteem, it is important to provide plenty of opportunities to play and learn through 'no fail' activities, such as sand and water play, and creativity. Also, this can be achieved through encouraging manageable tasks and challenges appropriate to the child's age and stage of development. Whenever possible, children should be encouraged and enabled to be independent, to make decisions, however small, and to take on appropriate responsibilities. This all helps to build on their feelings of being competent, and of being valued, therefore building on their self-esteem.

Rights

Rights are the entitlements of each individual to receive the same opportunities as other people. Many rights are linked to standards of service and are protected by legislation (law). **Rights** relate both to you as a worker, and to the children and their families as clients of any setting or provision.

Legislation involves a range of charters and Acts of Parliament, which control and monitor the treatment and behaviour of individuals. Examples of legislation most relevant to your role as an Early Years worker include the following.

- **Children Act 1989** The main principles of this Act are to put the welfare of children first, to protect children from harm and to work in partnership with parents whenever possible. It forms a major piece of child protection legislation.
- **Human Rights Act 1998** This Act focuses on the individual's right to a life free from torture, loss of liberty, unfair punishment and discrimination. It includes respect for private and family life.
- **UN Convention on the Rights of the Child (1989)** This is an international agreement on human rights (for children). Its four main principles are 'non-discrimination', 'children's best interests', 'survival and development of children', and their 'right to participation'.
- **Disability Discrimination Act 2000** This Act guarantees rights for disabled people, helping them achieve fairer treatment, for example when applying for jobs. It also supports the ethos of the Education Act 1993 to provide all children who have a special need with an appropriate education at a suitable school.

You may find it useful to explore these through copies held in your college library or on the internet.

Other legislation, which it would be useful for you to become familiar with, includes:

- Race Relations Act 1976;
- Sex Discrimination Act 1975 and 1986;

- Criminal Justice Act 1992;
- Mental Health Act 1993;
- Equal Pay Act 1970;
- Equal Pay (Amendment) 1983;
- Citizen's Charter;
- Patient's Charter.

Remember! Copies of all government legislation are available from HMSO bookshops and on UK government websites.

Professionalism

To be professional is to be competent, efficient and skilled in your area of work, and also qualified appropriately to carry it out. Most individuals have certain expectations of professional people, such as doctors, solicitors or teachers, regarding what they do and how they go about it. In Early Years you should be aiming to achieve that same level of **professionalism** yourself.

Being professional involves a range of different skills and attributes, including presenting yourself appropriately, paying attention to the following:

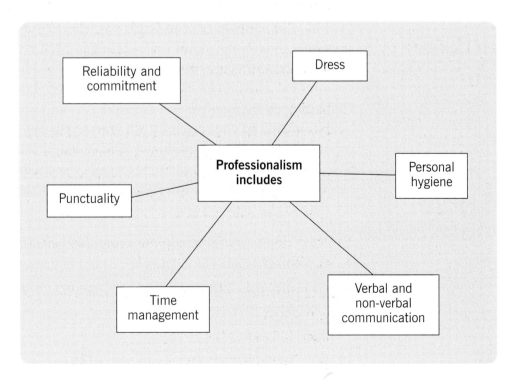

Dressing appropriately

As with any job it is important that what you wear is suitable for the activities and wear and tear you are likely to encounter. Some Early Years settings will have a dress code, setting down rules about the style of dress, the wearing of jewellery and suitable footwear. Some will have a staff 'uniform', usually a sweatshirt or polo shirt with plain trousers. As a student you may be offered items to borrow to help you feel part of the team.

Activity 1.10

1   What clothing do you consider to be suitable for wearing when working with young children?

2   What clothing do you consider to be unsuitable?

3   What are your views on jewellery, make-up and body piercing? Make a note of them.

4   Discuss your answers to questions 1, 2 and 3 with other Early Years students.

Personal hygiene

Anyone who works in the care sector will be in regular contact with other people. It is therefore vital that personal hygiene is given a high priority. You need to ensure that you bathe and wash your hair regularly, keep your nails short, hair well groomed and tied back if long, and clothes should be changed and washed regularly.

Remember! Cotton clothing helps the body breathe more easily. It is absorbent and allows air to pass through its fibres, making it comfortable and reducing the likelihood of body odours.

Children learn by example and therefore it is important that you are seen by the children in your care to wash your hands before food preparation, cooking activities and at mealtimes. It is not sufficient to explain that you have already done so, it is far better to join the children as they wash their hands themselves (even if this means re-washing yours!).

Activity 1.11

1   What might be the impact of a member of staff who is not well presented, or who lacks good personal hygiene?

2   Consider this from the point of view of a child, of a parent and as another member of the staff team.

3 How would you explain the importance of handwashing to children? Give as many reasons as you can.

Communication skills

Remember that you communicate with people both verbally and non-verbally. It is important that you are aware of the messages you are giving out, and also whether those messages are being received in the way you intended.

Time management and reliability

Managing yourself is an important aspect of being professional. This will apply equally to handing in your assignment work in college and to the commitment shown to your work placement experience. Children need stability and routine in order for them to feel secure. A member of staff who takes time off work unnecessarily, or who is unreliable, can have an adverse affect on this.

Activity 1.12

Think about how an unreliable member of staff might affect the workplace.
1 What impact might such a person have on the children?
2 What impact might this have on the planning of the day?
3 What impact might this have on the morale of the staff team in general?
4 How might this affect the long-term professionalism of the worker who is unreliable?

Reviewing own performance

Being professional also means that you are able to review your own performance, noting where your strengths lie, which aspects of your professional practice you still need to develop, and understanding why, when, where and how to seek help when you need it.

Activity 1.13

Use the table below to help you identify what you are good at and what you could improve on for the future.

An evaluation of your current skills

Things I am good at	Things I could improve on
1.	1.
2.	2.
3.	3.
4.	4.
5.	5.

Remember ! Identifying an area of your own practice that you need to work on is not a weakness. It is a strength.

Responsibilities of the individual Early Years carer

Everyone in the work setting has a degree of **responsibility**, and as a student you will too. This may simply be by taking responsibility for your own safe practice within each placement you attend, for thinking ahead and identifying potential problems.

Responsibility

Staff in Early Years settings are responsible for the safety and well-being of all the children within their care. They are entrusted by the children's parents to provide a stimulating, safe and well-supervised environment. This involves providing staff–child ratios that meet or exceed the legal minimums, staff who are appropriately trained both in Early Years care and education, and in health and safety issues. These aspects of Early Years care are set out in more detail in Unit 3. You might find it helpful to refer to them at this point.

LINKS TO UNIT 3, page 110.

Being a member of a team

As an Early Years student you will be under the supervision of an established member of staff at each placement setting you attend. There is a minimum requirement of 200 hours' placement experience during the BTec First programme and if finding a placement is your responsibility it is advisable to arrange this as soon as you can. Leaving this arrangement too late can result in missing out on the best placements and maybe having to accept different types of placement to the ones you had hoped for. In some colleges, a placement officer is employed who sets up the placements on behalf of students. You will be told which situation applies to your course.

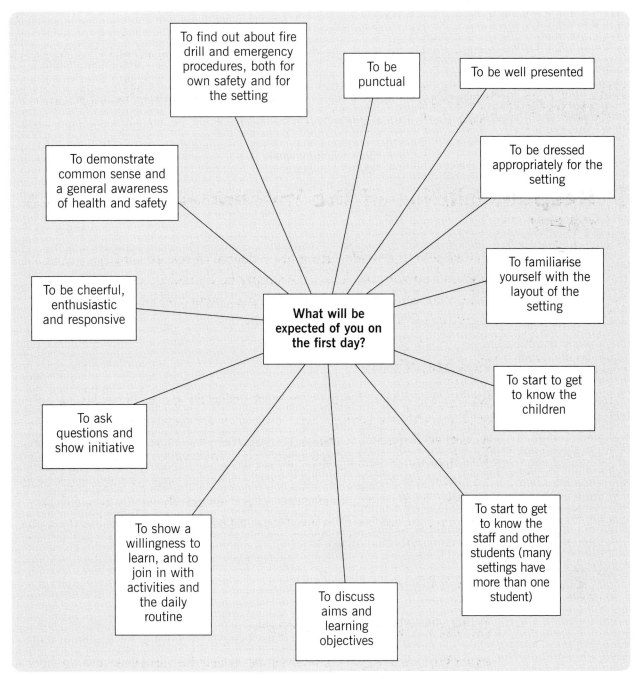

Professional expectations: the first day of a placement

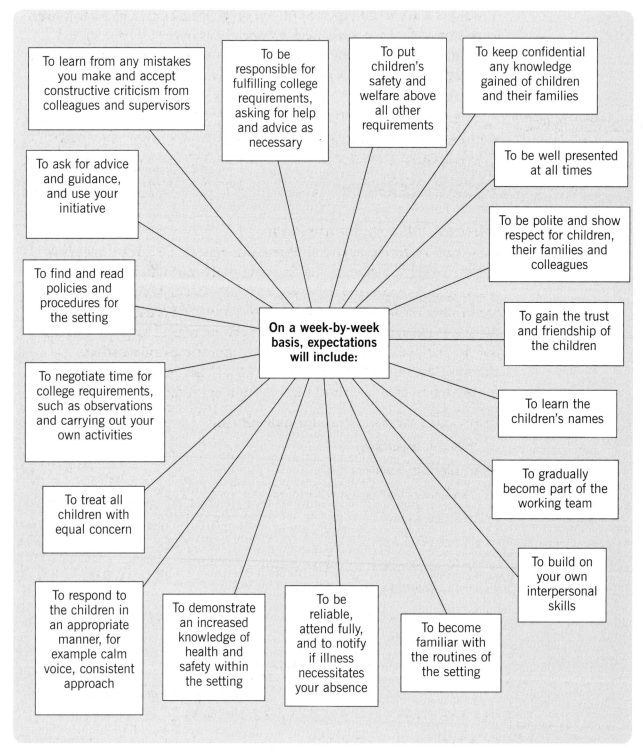

To learn from any mistakes you make and accept constructive criticism from colleagues and supervisors

To be responsible for fulfilling college requirements, asking for help and advice as necessary

To put children's safety and welfare above all other requirements

To keep confidential any knowledge gained of children and their families

To ask for advice and guidance, and use your initiative

To be well presented at all times

To find and read policies and procedures for the setting

To be polite and show respect for children, their families and colleagues

On a week-by-week basis, expectations will include:

To gain the trust and friendship of the children

To negotiate time for college requirements, such as observations and carrying out your own activities

To learn the children's names

To gradually become part of the working team

To treat all children with equal concern

To build on your own interpersonal skills

To respond to the children in an appropriate manner, for example calm voice, consistent approach

To demonstrate an increased knowledge of health and safety within the setting

To be reliable, attend fully, and to notify if illness necessitates your absence

To become familiar with the routines of the setting

Professional expectations: week-by-week

When you join a placement, staff will have certain expectations of you. No one will expect you to know everything straight away, but they will expect you to make an effort to learn, to use your initiative and to show a commitment to your training. The spidergrams above give an overview of what is likely to be expected of you on your first day, and what is likely to be expected of you on a week-to-week basis once you have started attending regularly. Your college will usually provide placement guidelines both for you as a student and for your placement supervisors.

Activity 1.14

Read through the spidergrams above, ensuring that you understand each point that has been set out. If you do not, ask your tutor or placement supervisor.

Different roles within the team

Everyone has different strengths and different skills, and teamwork is about sharing, supporting and learning from each other, as well as working in a complementary way, each member of the team adding to the balance of the overall practice. The sucess of a setting is based on the successful teamwork of the staff. Each individual has a part to play, but no one person can carry the full weight of the organisation, although the nursery owner/manager clearly has overall responsibility for the safety, standards and smooth running of the setting.

In any team there is a need for individuals:

- to work together;
- to identify their own skills;
- to identify their own strengths;
- to share ideas;
- to be reliable;
- to be committed to a shared aim;
- to co-operate with each other;
- to give and take;
- to be flexible;
- to find their 'best fit' within the team.

In a team you will probably find the following types of people.

- Some team members will be good at planning.
- Some will have good ideas.
- Some will be very practical and 'hands on'.
- Some will be good at keeping everyone motivated.
- Some will be good at managing time and tasks.
- Some will be good at finishing off small details.
- Some will be natural team leaders.

- Some will work best under regular guidance from others.
- Some staff will work better together than others; this needs to be accepted.

Opportunities for internal movement of roles and responsibilities will help to ensure that the greatest level of cohesive teamwork is achieved.

All teams need to observe certain rules and guidelines, as shown below.

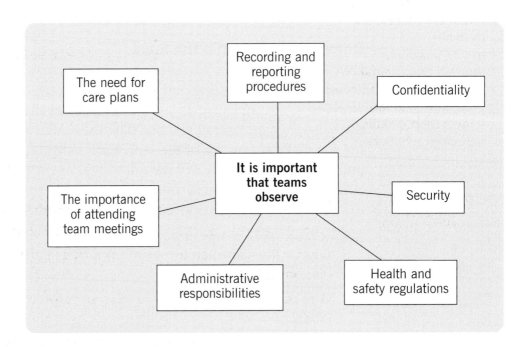

Confidentiality

Definitions

Confidentiality
Keeping information to yourself, not passing it on inappropriately.

Confidentiality is necessary to ensure the privacy of the lives of children and their families. Information should only be passed on on a 'needs to know' basis. For example, if you have a concern regarding the welfare of a child, you would speak to the manager or your supervisor who would take action if appropriate. It would be inappropriate to talk about your concern generally with other staff or fellow students. Similarly, if you hear information regarding a child's parents – such as the fact that they have separated – you must keep that information to yourself. No one else 'needs to know'.

Issues of confidentiality, together with the administrative responsibilities of Early Years workers, care plans, writing records and reports, are covered in Unit 7. Security and health and safety issues are discussed in Unit 3.

LINKS TO UNIT 3, page 110 and UNIT 7, page 303.

Key terms

You should now understand the following key words and phrases. If you do not, read through the chapter again and review them.

anti-discriminatory practice
barriers to effective communication
concept
confidentiality
core values
cycle of disadvantage
direct discrimination
diversity
family structure
indirect discrimination
individual discrimination
institutional discrimination
interpersonal skills
language within context

legislation
marginalise
mixed ability groups
poverty
primary socialisation
professionalism
responsibility
rights
secondary socialisation
self-esteem
social class
stereotyping
welfare state

Test Yourself

1 What examples can you give of diversity within society?

2 What were the three main aims of the welfare state?

3 What is the difference between institutional and individual discrimination?

4 Give one example each of how discrimination can be either direct or indirect.

5 Which groups of people within society are often marginalised in some way?

6 Give an example of how gender may effect equality in Early Years?

7 As an Early Years worker, with whom are you likely to need to build relationships?

8 What barriers to communication can you think of?

9 When working with a child who is learning English as an additional language it is best to help them learn 'within context'. Give an example.

10 Why is it important to give young children instructions in bite-size pieces?

11 Why is a child with a good level of self-esteem likely to achieve better than one whose self-esteem is low?

12 What legislation can you think of that is linked to the rights of individuals?

13 What is meant by the term professional?

14 List three examples of particularly suitable clothing for working with young children, then list three unsuitable articles.

15 Why is good personal hygiene important when working in the Early Years sector?

16 How can poor time management and being unreliable have an impact on the children in your care?

17 What does each member of a team need to do and/or consider?

18 What different sorts of people make up a good team?

19 Give at least three examples of the rules and guidelines that Early Years teams need to observe.

20 Why is confidentiality important in Early Years settings?

References and suggested further reading

Brown, B (2001) *Persona Dolls in Action: Combating Discrimination*, Trentham Books

Burnard, P (1992) *Communicate! A Communication Skills Guide for Health Care Workers*, Edward Arnold Publishers

Dare, A and O'Donovan, M (1997) *Good Practice in Caring for Young Children with Special Needs*, Nelson Thornes

Green, S (2002) *BTEC National Early Years*, Nelson Thornes

Malik, H (2002) *A Practical Guide to Equal Opportunities* (2nd edn), Nelson Thornes

Petrie, P (1991) *Communicating with Children and Adults*, Edward Arnold Publishers

Websites

www.cre.org.uk

www.eoc.org.uk

www.homeoffice.gov.uk

2 Physical, social and emotional development

This unit covers:

- Physical, social and emotional development
- Physical requirements for good health and development
- Emotional development
- Support and management of behaviour

Development is holistic, as each aspect of a person's development (physical, social, intellectual and so on) interacts with other aspects, and can have an effect on them. This chapter focuses on physical development, and also on how children develop socially and emotionally.

Physical, social and emotional development

As you study **growth** and **development** you will look at the processes, and the rate and sequences of change within the body during an average child's life. Growth and development have different meanings, and can be defined simply as follows.

Growth

Growth is most easily defined as the changes in the body that are measurable. This includes height, weight, skeletal frame and shoe size. Each of these measurements can be reproduced on a graph or table and form part of the screening programme (the checking of a child's growth and development) that monitors most children in developed countries. Measurements in the UK are usually plotted on a graph called the **centile** (or percentile) chart. They are found in a child's health record book (often referred to as the 'red book').

A centile chart

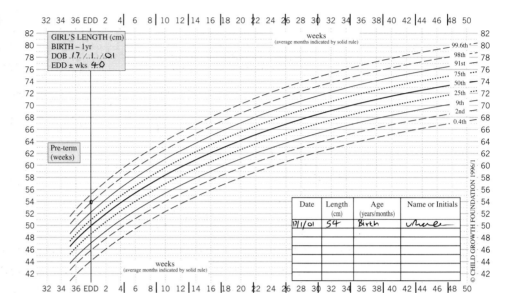

Development

Development is concerned with the changes that occur within the body as it grows, for example, the closing of the fontanelles on an infant's skull and the ossification of the skeleton (where the cartilage in a newborn infant is gradually replaced by bone). Development also concerns the increased physical abilities that develop, such as the infant gaining head control, sitting, crawling, standing and finally walking, together with the patterns of organ and tissue development that mark, for example, the onset of puberty and reproduction in young teenagers and the development of the nervous system, namely the neural pathways in the brain.

Development is often uneven, while remaining sequential, and different areas may be more advanced than others. For example, a child's physical skills may be very advanced, whereas their language is less well developed.

It is important that everyone working with young children understands what is considered to be the 'normal' expectations of a child's development, as this gives a 'benchmark' to guide you in your studies, enabling you to identify if a child's development is delayed or impaired in any way. The terms **normative development** or **developmental norms** are the terms most often used.

Remember! The 'developmental norms' are simply a guideline. Most children are slightly ahead or behind these guidelines in some or all areas of development. It is also important to note that the developmental norms do not accurately reflect all races and cultures.

The continuum of life – from infancy to late adulthood

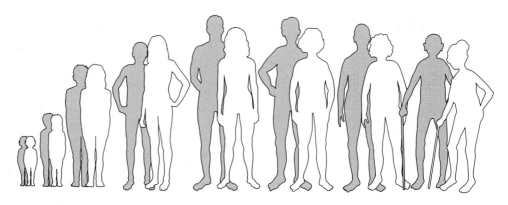

Milestones of development

During an average life-span each person moves through a range of developmental stages, or **milestones of development**, which can be considered in a number of ways. In this book they are categorised as follows:

- **the pre-natal stage**, from conception to birth;
- **the neonatal stage**, from birth to one month;
- infancy, from one month to one year;
- the toddler, from one to two years;
- early childhood, from two to five years;
- middle childhood, from five to twelve years.

This book will focus on the development of children up to the approximate age of eight years. This is the age range mostly associated with the BTec First in Early Years programme.

Milestones of physical development 0–8 years

Physical development includes the primitive reflexes seen in newborn infants. These reflexes are covered in more detail in Unit 8. It also involves motor development and **manipulation**. Motor development can be divided between locomotor skills and non-locomotor skills.

- Locomotor skills involve the body moving forward in some way. Examples of this would be walking, running, hopping.
- Non-locomotor skills describe the physical movements that take place while stationary. Examples are bending, pulling, pushing.
- Manipulation involves actions using dexterity. Examples are throwing and catching a ball, threading cotton reels and placing one brick on top of another.

LINKS TO UNIT 8, page 320.

Different types of physical activity

precise movements

carefree movement

general movement

balance

Physical skills can be gross (large) or fine. They include movement and balance, and can be either precise or carefree. Movement can involve the whole body or just one part of it.

Development becomes increasingly more complex and more difficult as it progresses. The **'maturational' changes** can be described as moving:

- from the simple to the complex – this means that a child learns simple actions, such as learning to stand, before learning the more complex actions of being able to walk;

- from cephalo (head) to caudal (tail) – this can be defined as physical control starting at the head and gradually developing down through the body. For example, head control is attained before the spine is strong enough for an infant to sit unsupported, and sitting unsupported is attained before the child is able to stand;

- from proximal (near to the body) to distal (the outer reaches of the body) – these terms refer to how a child develops actions near to the body before they develop control of the outer reaches of the body. For example, a child can hug and carry a large teddy bear (arm control) before they can fasten their clothing (finger control);

- from general to specific – the more generalised responses of an infant showing excitement when recognising a favourite carer gradually moves through to the facial smile of an older child on greeting the same person.

Physical development

At birth the infant will sleep most of the time, mostly waking for feeds and nappy changing, and often falling asleep during the process of these routines. Sleep patterns change with the infant gradually remaining awake for longer periods as they develop.

There will be a lack of head control due to underdeveloped neck muscles and support is needed during handling to ensure that no damage is caused or undue strain placed on the neck muscles.

All babies are born with dark eyes and permanent eye colour is not established until much later on.

The posture of infants is very flexed and movements tend to be jerky. The extremities (feet and hands) are often bluish in colour due to poor circulation.

A child can hug a large teddy bear before they can fasten their clothing

An infant in flexed pose

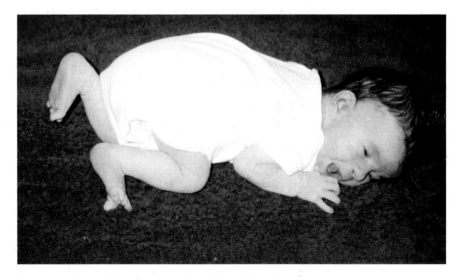

Fontanelles

There are two fontanelles. The posterior fontanelle is a small triangular area near the crown, which closes within a few weeks of birth. The anterior fontanelle is near the front of the head and is diamond shaped. It usually closes over by eighteen months of age and pulsates at the same rate as the infant's heartbeat. Fontanelles are areas of the skull where the bony plates of the skull meet. They enable some movement of the skull during the birth process.

The fontanelles on a baby's skull

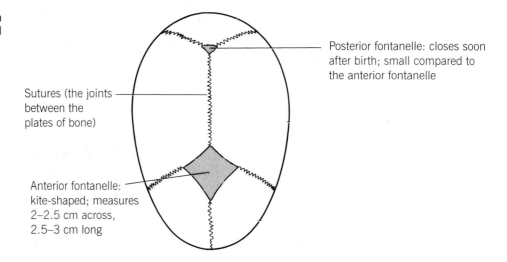

Posterior fontanelle: closes soon after birth; small compared to the anterior fontanelle

Sutures (the joints between the plates of bone)

Anterior fontanelle: kite-shaped; measures 2–2.5 cm across, 2.5–3 cm long

Birth marks

There are various types of **birth marks**, most being neither serious nor permanent. Examples include port wine marks, strawberry neavei (haemangioma), 'stork bite' marks, Mongolian blue spots and CMNs (congenital melanocytic naevus). Details of these can be found in Unit 8.

LINKS TO UNIT 8, page 325.

Reflexes

The term **primary reflexes** can be defined as 'automatic body reactions to specific stimulation' (Bee, H (1992), page 105). These reflexes are explained and illustrated in Unit 8:

- blinking;
- rooting;
- the sucking reflex;
- the palmar grasp;
- the plantar reflex;
- stepping reflex;
- the moro reflex;
- the startle reflex;
- the asymmetric tonic neck reflex.

Some reflexes stay with us for life, for example blinking, but some are lost after the first few weeks (the primitive reflexes). The presence of reflexes are an indicator of how well an infant's nervous system is functioning (their neurological well-being). As the brain gradually takes over the body's responses, these primitive reflexes disappear. If the primitive reflexes are retained for longer than is usual (they start to diminish at around six weeks), it can indicate that there is a developmental problem with the infant that may need to be investigated.

All infants are usually assessed by a doctor at six weeks of age.

The senses
The hearing of a newborn baby is very sharp, whereas their vision is initially limited and their eyes are not always fully co-ordinated. Unit 8 focuses specifically on newborn babies and sets out a useful summary of their senses in the earliest days and weeks.

The senses include hearing, vision, touch and smell.

Posture and motor skills
Immediately after birth, many infants naturally curl into the **foetal position** with their heads to one side.

Limbs are kept partly flexed and are hypertonic (have tension), and they tend to display jerking movements. The head and neck are hypotonic (weak) and there is no head control, so full support of the head and neck area is needed whenever the infant is handled.

A baby in the foetal position

Milestones of physical development

Infancy: 1 month to 1 year

A summary of physical skills (gross motor)

- Movements remain jerky and uncontrolled.

- Head lag gradually decreases and head control is usually achieved by 5 months.

- Rolling over is first seen between 4 and 6 months (from back to side), and then from front to back by about 8 months.

- Reaching for objects begins at about 4 months with the ability to pass toys from hand to hand seen from about 7 months.

- At 4 months the infant discovers their own feet and manages to sit with support.

- Sitting alone commences at about 7–8 months, with gradually greater balance developing.

- Crawling can start from 6 months (commando crawling) and traditional crawling from about 8 months. Some infants bear-walk or bottom-shuffle.

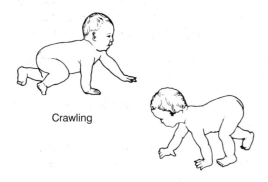

Crawling

Bear-walking

- Some infants miss out the crawling stage, and move straight to pulling themselves up on furniture at around 8–10 months.

- Standing alone can occur any time from 10 months, but is more usual at around a year, when generally balance is more established.

- Walking is normally achieved by 12–16 months.

A summary of physical skills (fine motor)

- Hand and finger movements gradually increase, from the grasping of adults' fingers in the earliest months, through to playing with own fingers and toes, handling and then holding toys and objects from 3–4 months.

- Everything is explored through the mouth.

- At about 7 months, the infant will try to transfer objects from one hand to the other with some sucess. Pincer grasp (index finger and thumb) is emerging.

- By about 10 months, pincer grasp is developed.

- The infant will pick up small objects.

- Toys are pulled towards the infant.

- Pointing and clapping are deliberate actions for most infants by 10–12 months.

- Controlled efforts when feeding, with some successes.

Toddler: 1 to 2 years

A summary of physical skills

- Standing alone is achieved but they are unable at first to sit from being in a standing position without help. They begin to let themselves down in a controlled manner from about 15 months.

- When walking, hands are held up for balance and the infant's steps are uneven, and they have difficulty in stopping once they have started.

- They can creep upstairs on hands and knees quite safely (not advisable without an adult supervising).

- They begin to kneel.

- By 18 months walking is usually well established, and the arms are no longer needed for balance. The toddler can now back into a small chair, and climb forwards into an adult chair.

- Squatting when playing is now common.

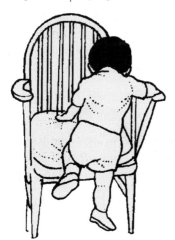

- They can usually walk upstairs holding an adult hand.

- Manipulative skills are developing. Pages of books can usually now be turned quite well, and pencils can be held in a clumsy (primitive) grasp.

Clumsy (primitive)

- By two years the child can usually run safely, starting and stopping at will.

- They are able to pull wheeled toys, with some understanding of direction.

- They are usually able to control a ball to throw forwards.

- Walking up and (usually) down stairs, holding on, two feet to a stair.

- They cannot yet kick a football without falling into it, losing their balance as they kick their foot forward.

- They cannot usually pedal a tricycle.

Aged 2 to 5 years

A summary of physical skills

- Walking up stairs with alternating feet is usually achieved by 3 years. Up and down on alternate feet is securely seen by 3½.

- At 2½ a child can kick a football gently; by 3 years with force.

- Pushing and pulling of large toys is achieved by 2½.

- Locomotor skills (movement forwards, backwards and so on) improve rapidly during this stage of development.

- Use of pedals is often achieved by 3 years, and a child can steer around corners.

- Balance gradually improves and by 4 years a child can usually stand, walk and run on tip-toes, and navigate skilfully when active.

- From 3 years ball skills increase, catching, throwing, bouncing and kicking.

- Manipulative skills (the ability to use their hands and fingers in a controlled manner) improve.

- Scissor control is developing and greater pencil control is achieved by 3 years.

- By 4 years threading small beads and early sewing is achieved.

- Adult pencil control is usually present by 4 years.

Aged five to twelve years
A summary of physical skills

- Physically the body's emphasis is now on practice and further development of the skills already gained. Large motor skills will improve, for example, in how fast a child can run, their stamina when playing group games, and their ability to climb and manoeuvre more difficult objects, and in more challenging circumstances. The ever-increasing ability for balance is seen at this stage too, for example hopping, skipping and climbing.

- Hand–eye co-ordination develops, allowing a more adult level of control when writing, drawing, sewing and so on, and greater skill during ball games and activities involving manual dexterity is seen.

- For girls, the pre-pubescent stage can begin from 9 years onwards. Height develops rapidly here with the thigh bone growing at a faster rate than the rest of the body.

Milestones of social and emotional development

Infancy: 1 month to 1 year
A summary of social and emotional development

- The first **social smile** is usually seen by six weeks.

- Smiling is first confined to main carers, and then in response to most contacts.

- The infant concentrates on faces of carers.

- Pleasure during handling and caring routines is seen by 8 weeks, through smiles, cooing and a general contentment.

- Expressions of pleasure are clear when gaining attention from about 12 weeks and in response to the main carers' voices.

- Social games, involving handling and cuddles gain chuckles from 4–5 months onwards.

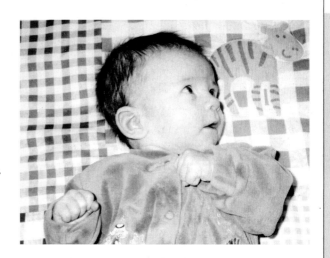

- Infants enjoy watching other infants.

- Sleep patterns begin to emerge from about 4 months onwards, although these will continue to change.

- From about 9 or 10 months the infant may become distressed when the main carer leaves them, temporarily losing their sense of security and becoming wary of strangers. This is a normal stage in development.

- Playing contentedly alone increases by 1 year, but the reassuring presence of an adult is still needed.

Aged 1–2 years
A summary of social and emotional development

- By about 15 months will usually indicate a wet or soiled nappy.

- Co-operates (helps) with dressing, for example, holding up arms for a jumper.

- Dependent on an adult's presence for reassurance.

- Frustration at not being able to achieve their aim – perhaps putting two bricks together, leads to toys being discarded in anger.

- By 18 months feeding self with a spoon is usually very successful.

- Confident handling of a cup, but does not put it back down (gives it to adult).

- Removes hats, shoes etc but can rarely replace them.

- Urgent vocalisations when making a demand.

- Bowel control is sometimes attained by 18 months and is usually attained by 2 years.

- By 2 years the child will play parallel alongside others without actually interacting.

- They can be rebellious and resistive and get frustrated when trying to make themselves understood. Can be easily distracted from their tantrums at this age.

- No idea of sharing is both common and normal, and no understanding of the need to defer their wishes.

- Follows adult around. Needs reassurance when tired or fearful.

- By 2 years can usually put on hat and shoes, and can reposition a cup on a surface.

Aged 2–5 years
A summary of social and emotional development

- At 2½ tantrums are common when needs are thwarted. A child is less easily distracted from them now.

- Very resistive of restraint, for example when having a hand held in a busy shop.

- Mostly still watches others or plays parallel. Occasionally joins in briefly.

- By 4 years a child can eat skilfully and can dress, wash and clean their teeth (with supervision).

- This is a generally more independent age with many children wanting to try things on their own.

- Co-operates with others but can also be uncooperative if wishes are refused.

- Can be very strong-willed.

- At 5 years behaviour is noticeably more sensible and controlled.

- Understands sharing and turn-taking. Now understands the need for fair play.

- Co-operative play is constant at 5 years.
- Chooses own friends and plays well. Very protective towards younger children, pets and distressed playmates.

Aged 5–12 years

A summary of social and emotional development

- Co-operative play is frequent and sustained.
- Gender awareness is strong.
- Co-operative play is mostly with same-sex peers.
- Individual friendships are very important.
- Children make definite decisions about their friends.
- Parents are less openly important, but their continued support is needed.

Definitions

Pre-pubescent
Before the onset of the development of secondary sex characteristics, such as periods, body hair and breast development in girls.

Research has been carried out on social learning, where children observe and copy the actions of others, and examples of this are set out in the following sections.

Social learning theory

Possibly the most well-known example of **social learning theory** was the research carried out by Albert Bandura (1965), who used a film with three different endings to see how children could be affected by what they had seen. The film involved an adult hitting and shouting at a (Bobo) doll and three groups of children were each shown one version of the film.

Group 1. The first film ending showed the adult being rewarded for hitting the doll.

Group 2. The second film ending showed the adult being punished for hitting the doll.

Group 3. In the third film, nothing happened to the adult.

After they had watched their particular version of the film the children in all three groups were given Bobo dolls to play with and were observed by the researchers. The children who had seen the adult rewarded for hitting the doll also showed a higher tendency to hit it. This study could not claim evidence of a direct cause and effect, but it could certainly suggest that children were most likely influenced by the rewarding of negative behaviour.

Remember!

As an adult working with children you need to think about the messages you are giving them. These messages have a direct impact on the social learning of the children in your care. Messages can be portrayed by actions, words, attitudes and non-verbal behaviour. They can be both positive or negative.

Areas of development are not independent of each other. They affect each other in various ways. For example, a child who has unclear hearing will be less likely to develop clear and grammatically correct speech as easily as a child who has perfect hearing. Similarly, a child who has not developed an understanding of social skills such as sharing or turn taking is less likely to be socially accepted by their peers and therefore will be hindered in developing friendships.

Activity 2.1

What other examples can you give to show the links between different aspects of a child's development? An example has been entered on the chart below to start you off:

Development	Effect
Unclear hearing	Poor speech development

Daily routines of care for physical, social and emotional needs

The body needs to be cared for appropriately in order for it to develop and perform to its full potential. The mind also needs care and attention as an unhappy or insecure child will not feel ready to explore and take up opportunities to the same extent as a child who is feeling happy and accepted by their family and peers. Therefore every child needs opportunities for:

- exercise;
- rest and sleep;
- toileting and washing;

• playtime;
• storytime.

Exercise

Healthy exercise is needed for a child to stretch and use all their muscles, limbs and joints, keeping them fit and well. Trying out new skills and consolidating further those that have already been developed allows children to continue to develop healthily.

Healthy exercise is needed for all children

Rest and sleep

Every child needs time to relax as well as time for stimulation and energetic play. This is particularly important during periods of fast growth. At times adults fill a child's day so full that they become over-stimulated, which tires them out and does not enable them to build again on their energy levels.

Toileting and washing

Cleanliness and good hygiene are important both physically in helping to keep the body free from infection and bacteria, and also socially, helping the child to be socially accepted by their peers through smelling nice, looking clean and having hands that feel nice to hold. They are learning the rules of health and hygiene that they will need for the future.

Every child needs time
to relax

Playtime

When planning daily routines for children it is important that an
appropriate balance is struck between times of exercise and times of rest.
Giving opportunities for group activities, both small groups and large,
will help children develop confidence in the company of others. Some
children will respond well to the opportunity to lead and initiate
activities, while others will be happiest playing a supportive role in
group tasks.

Storytime

Storytime is a wonderfully social activity, grouping children together to
share a pleasurable experience. It can be a relaxing experience and also
passive (where the child simply listens), and involve just the storyteller
engaging the children with their voice, and usually illustrations from a
book. Alternatively, it can be a vibrant and active time, incorporating
actions, resources and 'punchlines', and involving both the storyteller
and the children.

Stories can be a useful means of supporting children's emotional
development. Many texts bring sensitive issues into their storylines, for
example, having a new baby in the family, or getting angry and having
tantrums. These stories can help a child understand that the feelings
they are experiencing are usually normal and that other people have
them too, even adults.

Group storytime can be a wonderfully social experience

Physical requirements for good health and development

Physical health is influenced by many factors. These include :

- **fixed factors**;
- **social and economic factors**;
- **environmental factors**;
- our lifestyle;
- the access we have to various services.

Fixed factors

These are aspects of ourselves that we cannot change, such as our genes, our sex and the rate at which we grow, develop and age. Some aspects of our **genetic inheritance** can be identified in advance of birth through antenatal screening, allowing outcomes to be modified and choices made. An example of this would be the identification of the condition Down's syndrome.

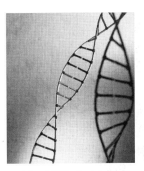

The DNA double helix

Social and economic factors

Issues such as poverty, low income, employment and social exclusion can all affect the health of children, having an impact on the conditions in which they live too. At times this can lead to a higher rate of infections and respiratory disease, and also to depression in parents, which may make them less interested in, and responsive to their children. The access parents have to facilities such as shops, daycare and leisure facilities is often dependent on the levels and types of employment they are in. For some families unemployment drives them to social exclusion as they feel unable to keep up with their former peers, or their self-esteem is lowered and they remove themselves from former social circles. At times disability can also lead to isolation or social exclusion, due for example to lack of access, lack of transport or insufficient carers.

Environmental factors

Poverty, while being an economic issue, can also place environmental pressures on the health of children. Examples would be the effects of a poor diet due to low income or lack of accessible shops.

Poor lighting in the home, lack of suitable heating in winter and lack of safety precautions such as stairgates, cooker guards and so on, raise the levels of potential accidents in the homes of families on lower incomes.

Poor air quality and traffic pollution can affect health, as can a lack of play and exercise space, through living in cramped conditions.

Lifestyle

Depression in parents can increase the levels of family dependency on smoking and alcohol, as these can become comforts to them, with children being exposed to cigarette smoke (passive smoking) and the lethargy that can follow alcohol and depression, often accompanied by associated isolation.

People in general are less active than they were in the past, due to factors such as longer working days for those in employment, greater levels of mental exhaustion and increased travelling times to get to their places of work. This lack of activity in turn can lead to a greater dependency on ready prepared meals and fast foods, lowering the benefits of 'home cooking' skills enjoyed by past generations.

Activity 2.2

1 What facilities can you think of in your area that particularly benefit families with young children?

2 In what ways do you consider that they benefit them?

Importance of health, safety and hygiene practice

In every Early Years setting there is a need for appropriate supervision of the children at all times. The National Standards for Under Eights set out minimum standards (see page 112, Unit 3).

Maintaining a safe and secure environment

Physical health is supported through the safe use of equipment and the maintenance of the environment. Each setting is registered with the appropriate authority, which in turn ensures that it meets the required standards of health and safety. A range of regulations and pieces of legislation need to be met, each adding to the safety of the environment, and therefore contributing to the physical safety needs of children. Examples include:

- Food Safety Act 1990;
- Food Safety (General Food Hygiene) Regulation 1995;
- Control of Substances Hazardous to Health (COSHH) 1994;
- Reporting of Injuries, Diseases and Dangerous Occurrences Regulations (RIDDOR) 1985;
- Health and Safety at Work Act (HASAWA) 1974.

Activity 2.3

1 What are the main requirements of the above Acts and regulations?

2 How do they contribute to the all-round safety of Early Years settings?

3 What might be the results of not having such regulations?

In Unit 3 there are more specific details regarding health and safety of play provision and equipment, both indoors and outdoors, at mealtimes, regarding personal hygiene requirements and the role of the adult in supervising children safely. You might find it helpful to refer to this section now.

 LINKS TO UNIT 3, pages 110–41.

Procedures and policies

Every setting has its own **procedures** for doing things. It will be important that you understand these for each placement you attend, and follow them, as they should be specific about how or what you should do. Procedures ensure that there is a consistent approach by all staff, which enables parents, children and staff to understand and become part of the setting quickly.

Policies and procedures should be readily available for all to read. Most settings will provide parents with a copy of these procedures when they first take up a place at the setting for their child. Parents are usually asked to read them, and sign an acknowledgement that they have read, understood and agree to them. This becomes particularly helpful to staff if an issue arises in which they need to refer to the settings policies or procedures. It can support them as they explain why something is not able to happen, or has had to happen, for example, in supporting staff if there is a need to challenge a racist or sexist remark.

Activity 2.4

1 Ask to read the policies and procedures at your current setting. It is important that you understand them.

2 Test your understanding, by trying to explain them to someone else.

3 If you do not feel you understand them fully, ask your placement supervisor to explain them to you.

The essential components of a healthy diet in young children

A **well-balanced diet** is one that provides all the nutritional requirements for growth, maintenance and development of the body. What we eat helps us to repair and maintain our body tissues, supports the functioning of muscles and organs and helps to prevent infection. It also supplies us with the energy we need in order to function from day to day.

A balanced diet includes foods from the four main food groups:

* proteins, which help growth, development and tissue repair;
* carbohydrates, which provide energy;
* vitamins, minerals and fibre, for general good health and the prevention of illness;
* dairy products, which are high in calcium, enhancing and maintaining bones and teeth.

A fifth food group – fats and oils – are higher energy giving foods, which should be consumed sparingly by adults.

Many foods contribute to more than one food group, for example, meat is a good source of iron, and pulses are a good source of fibre. Look at the illustration below, which indicates where the main benefits of each food lie.

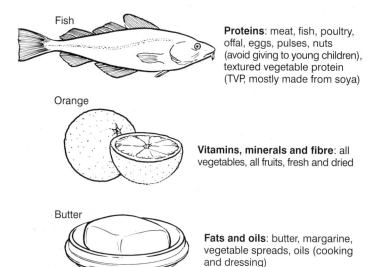

Proteins: meat, fish, poultry, offal, eggs, pulses, nuts (avoid giving to young children), textured vegetable protein (TVP, mostly made from soya)

Vitamins, minerals and fibre: all vegetables, all fruits, fresh and dried

Fats and oils: butter, margarine, vegetable spreads, oils (cooking and dressing)

Carbohydrates: cereals, breads, pasta, rice, starchy vegetables (e.g potato, yam, plantain)

Dairy products: milk, cheese, yoghurt, fromage frais

The food groups

The tables opposite and overleaf set out the benefits of a range of **vitamins** and **minerals**, showing how they help the body, and the problems that may occur if there is a deficiency.

A healthy and balanced diet is one that includes foods from each of the food groups. It is important to encourage children to eat a variety of foods, including:

- foods with different textures;
- foods with different sorts of tastes;
- foods from a range of cultures;
- seasonal foods.

This will help them develop a healthy and diverse approach to diet throughout their lives.

Encouraging a healthy diet and a positive attitude to food

Food and mealtimes should be a pleasurable part of the day and encouraging children to enjoy the social aspect of sharing a meal and conversation with others will help them continue to enjoy this as they grow.

The main vitamins

Vitamin	Food source	Function	Notes
A	Butter, cheese, eggs, carrots, tomatoes	Promotes healthy skin, good vision	Fat-soluble, can be stored in the liver; deficiency causes skin infections, problems with vision
B group	Liver, meat, fish, green vegetables, beans, eggs	Healthy working of muscles and nerves; forming haemoglobin	Water-soluble, not stored in the body, so regular supply needed; deficiency results in muscle wasting, anaemia
C	Fruits and fruit juices, especially orange, blackcurrant, pineapple; green vegetables	For healthy tissue, promotes healing	Water-soluble, daily supply needed; deficiency means less resistance to infection; extreme deficiency results in scurvy
D	Oily fish, cod liver oil, egg yolk; added to margarine, milk	Growth and maintenance of bones and teeth	Fat-soluble, can be stored by the body; can be produced by the body as a result of sunlight on the skin; deficiency results in bones failing to harden and dental decay
E	Vegetable oils, cereals, egg yolk	Protects cells from damage	Fat-soluble, can be stored by the body
K	Green vegetables, liver	Needed for normal blood clotting	Fat-soluble, can be stored in the body

from Beaver *et al.* (2001) page 99

The main minerals

Mineral	Food source	Function	Notes
Calcium	Cheese, eggs, fish, milk, yoghurt	Essential for growth of bones and teeth	Works with vitamin D and phosphorus; deficiency means risk of bones failing to harden (rickets) and dental caries
Fluoride	Occurs naturally in water, or may be added artificially to water supply	Combines with calcium to make tooth enamel more resistant to decay	There are different points of view about adding fluoride to the water supply
Iodine	Water, sea foods, added to salt, vegetables	Needed for proper working of the thyroid gland	Deficiency results in enlarged thyroid gland in adults, cretinism in babies
Iron	Meat, green vegetables, eggs, liver, red meat	Needed for formation of haemoglobin in red blood cells	Deficiency means there is anaemia causing lack of energy, breathlessness; vitamin C helps the absorption of iron
Sodium chloride	Table salt, bread, meat, fish	Needed for formation of cell fluids, blood plasma, sweat, tears	Salt should not be added to any food prepared for babies: their kidneys cannot eliminate excess salt as adult kidneys do; excess salt is harmful in an infant diet

Other essential trace minerals include: potassium, phosphorus, magnesium, sulphur, manganese and zinc.

from Beaver et al. (2001) page 100

Children need a diet that is high in protein and carbohydrates in order for it to meet their high energy needs. Ideally the carbohydrates should be provided in the form of starchy foods, such as potatoes, bread and cereals.

Providing meals that include variation in colour and texture will make them more appealing to children. This will be particularly important if you are catering for a 'fussy' or reluctant eater.

Introducing new foods to children can sometimes be met with resistance. It is important to only introduce one new food at a time, ideally alongside a portion of something they like, encouraging them to eat a little of both.

Giving children a large portion of food can be off-putting for them. It is far better to have them eat all of a small meal, rather than just half of a larger meal. This encourages the good habit of 'finishing' a meal, and lessens any possibility of conflict. The portion size can gradually be increased as the child's appetite grows.

Encouraging children to have a drink of water with their meals is another good habit to develop. Many children will automatically ask for juice or squash, without really considering water. If they have been offered it regularly when very young they are more likely to continue to drink it later on too, which is a healthy recommendation.

Remember ! Children have preferences, just as adults do, and these preferences should be taken into account up to a point. It is, however, important to provide a balance between allowing children to select what they eat and do not eat, and encouraging them to try a range of different foods. A dislike of one food or drink does not automatically mean the child is being 'fussy'.

Cultural and other dietary needs

Many children have specific dietary needs. These need to be clearly understood by all staff in the Early Years setting. This may include a child who is vegetarian or vegan by parental or personal choice, whose culture includes specific dietary requirements, or a child who has an allergic reaction to certain foods, or a medical condition that is affected by certain foods.

Activity 2.5

1 Ask to see the menus for the children in your placement. How are dietary needs incorporated?

2 How many cultures are represented within the menus?

Diet and the unwell child

Children who are unwell are likely to be more selective in what they want to eat, and it is often more appropriate to allow them to eat what they feel like eating, rather than insist they try something they do not want, resulting in little food being consumed. Again, portion size is important. An unwell child will usually require far less food at each meal than usual.

Remember! When a child is unwell it is not an appropriate time to introduce new foods to them.

Activity 2.6

1 Plan a main meal suitable for a young child, ensuring that you include foods from as many of the food groups as you can.
2 How will the meal differ in texture?
3 How will the meal differ in colour?
4 If you have not included foods from all the food groups, what will be missing? Why might this be a problem?

Remember! Processed foods contain many hidden ingredients, such as sugar and salt. Whenever possible, offer children fresh foods and use fresh ingredients in your cooking. Do not provide salt or sugar at the table for children to add to their meals as this can become an expectation and set up bad habits for the future.

Activity 2.7

Collect labels from the packaging of a range of 'fast foods', selecting at least ten products. Examples might be a tin of baked beans, frozen beefburgers and fishfingers, a pizza and a curry from the chill cabinet.

1 What proportions are the ingredients in?
2 How near to the top of the list are sugar or salt?
3 What does this tell you about processed foods?
4 What healthier alternatives could you offer in their place?

Exercise and rest

It is important that all children have sufficient amounts of rest, sleep and quiet periods built into their daily routine. Each child will have different needs and observing when and how often they appear to be 'flagging' will help identify an appropriate balance for them. Sometimes adults try to cram too much into a child's day, resulting in a child who is over-stimulated, over-tired and irritable. In a day care situation, some children attend for a full day, meaning long periods of time in the setting. It should be remembered that if they were at home they would have quiet times, stimulating times, time spent engaged in activity with others and would also have time to play alone. Children need this when in their Early Years setting too. Over-stimulation of children can result in them becoming tired or losing interest, as they are unable to fully enjoy what is being offered to them.

Exercise in the form of both outdoor and indoor physical activity supports healthy physical development, and in turn encourages social development, as much of this type of play will involve actively engaging with others. As a child develops their social skills they grow in confidence as a person, building up their sense of self-esteem, an important part of emotional development. This shows how the areas of development are closely linked and how children develop holistically (as a whole) through play.

In Unit 5 you will find descriptions of a range of activities and equipment, and how they support the physical needs of young children, including those with an additional need.

 LINKS TO Unit 5, page 204.

Emotional development

Emotional development involves children developing a sense of self-awareness, personal identity and security. It involves them learning to understand how they and also others feel, and to learn how to express how they feel to other people. It is much easier for children to explain how they feel physically than how they feel emotionally, although adults should be aware that very young children will often generalise their physical feelings as, perhaps a 'tummy ache', when really the source of discomfort is elsewhere.

Emotions can be both positive and negative, and at times they can also be very intense. Children need to know that it is OK to have strong feelings and to know that, at times, adults have them too. They should also be given opportunities to express their feelings within the safety of play.

Activity 2.8

1 Using the headings 'positive' and 'negative', draw up two lists of human emotions:

Positive emotions   *Negative emotions*
Where would you place the following expressions of emotion?

happiness	curiosity	anger	sadness
love	eagerness	excitement	guilt
disappointment	fright	anxiety	sorrow
fear	hate	suspicion	pleasure
jealousy	contentment	laughter	frustration
delight	distress		

2 Discuss in a small group why you have placed your answers in these columns.

3 Which emotions are common in young children?

4 Which are less common?

5 Would any of these emotions concern you in a young child? If yes, which emotions and under what circumstances would you be concerned?

A range of emotions can be seen on childrens' faces

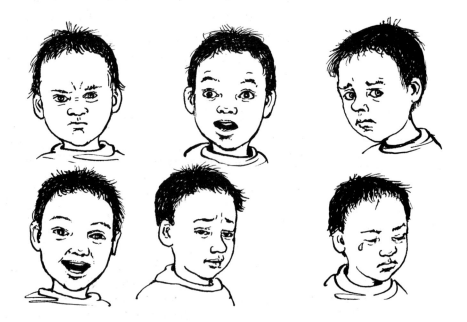

Responding to and encouraging the expression of feelings

Play is an ideal way for children to be able to express their feelings safely, in an atmosphere of support and understanding. A well-planned Early Years setting will offer opportunities for the physical expression of emotions, for example anger or frustration through the use of malleable materials such as clay, dough or plasticine. Alternatively, these emotions can be expressed through physical activity such as woodworking, ball games and activities involving large motor skills.

Emotions such as sadness, confusion and jealousy can sometimes be helped through introducing relevant storybooks, role play and opportunities for creativity. As an adult working with children you should also give children the time to talk, to ask questions and to chat about what is troubling them.

The role of adults in Early Years settings is to encourage the development of positive self-esteem and self-confidence. Children need to feel happy with themselves as a person, they need to have an understanding of what they need to do to achieve their intended 'aim', and they need to have a degree of control within their lives, being able to take the lead, to initiate ideas, and to make choices and manage their environment. It is important that adults consult children about the things that will affect them, giving them age-appropriate choices where possible.

If children have positive feelings about themselves they are more likely to be able to cope with stressful situations than children whose self-esteem is low. It is part of the role of Early Years workers to observe children and note changes in their behaviour. It is also part of your role to identify new children who need help in enjoying and benefiting from what the setting offers them.

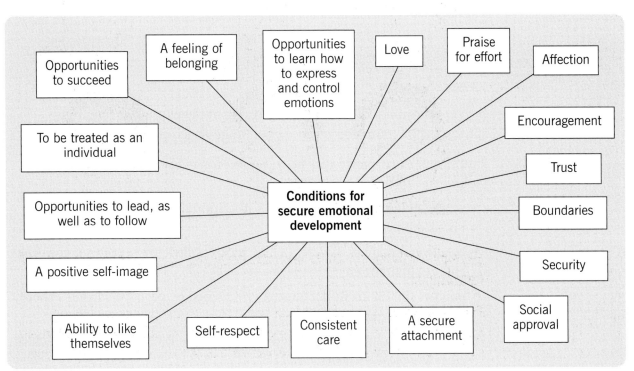

The points indicated on the figure above show what is ideally needed for a child to be secure emotionally. Sadly, there are many children whose lives do not provide these conditions for them. This can, at times, lead to emotional disturbance.

Emotional disturbance

Many children go through periods of mild or temporary **emotional disturbance**, which are not usually serious, and with careful handling are overcome quite quickly. This would include phases such as temper tantrums in toddlers and mood swings during adolescence. These are normal stages of development and are of no real concern. Emotional disturbance as a concern refers to the more worrying behaviours that are occasionally seen.

This might include:

- a child who becomes withdrawn and insecure, clinging to a familiar adult, and lacks confidence;
- a child displaying anti-social behaviour to draw attention to themselves;
- extreme anxiety and phobias;
- physical habits such as excessive hair chewing or nail biting, which can at times indicate a lonely or neglected child;
- tummy upsets, tics and skin irritations, which can also be signs of emotional disturbance.

Remember! Tummy upsets and skin irritations are mostly caused by viral or bacterial infection.

Severe emotional disturbance can result in development remaining stationary, or returning to an earlier stage (becoming regressed).

Emotional disturbance can be triggered for many reasons. These can include:

- physical neglect, where a child's nutritional, clothing or medical needs are not met;
- emotional neglect, where a child receives little or no praise, comfort, encouragement etc.;
- parents unable to understand a child's needs, perhaps through their own limited understanding;
- parents who have not learned how to show love, for example lack of close physical comfort;

- immature parents, where parents are not ready or able to cope with a child's needs and actions;
- a lack of consistent parenting, where no clear boundaries are given to children regarding their behaviour;
- a lack of consistent daycare, for example where children are passed from carer to carer with no regular routine;
- no secure attachment formed between the child and another person, for example where a child has not formed an emotional bond with any adult;
- bereavement, for example loss of a parent or a significant person in a child's life;
- violence in the home, for example either receiving, witnessing or being affected by violence;
- the arrival of a new baby, triggering feelings of jealousy and feeling unwanted;
- a child not ready to cope with a new situation, for example starting nursery or school;
- body image issues, such as disability or physical disfigurement.

Attachment and bonding

It is agreed by modern day theorists that children need a secure **attachment** (a two-way relationship of pleasure and tenderness) with their main carers, not just with their mother, as was thought to be the case in the past by theorists such as John Bowlby (1907–90). Theorists agree that the carers' ability to respond to a child is the most important factor in influencing the attachment process. The quality of the '**bond**' is what counts, and children may have a different sort of attachment to different carers.

The attachment process can be hindered when there is a barrier between the infant and the carer. This may be caused by separation at birth due to factors such as illness or prematurity. It can also be due to a lack of eye contact in a visually impaired infant or carer. What is clearly seen is that a child who has been able to form a strong bond to a parent or carer is usually more secure emotionally than a child who has no secure attachment at all.

Separation and loss

A normal stage of development is seen in infants of around nine months old when suddenly they become reluctant to be with unfamiliar adults.

They are fretful if separated from their parent or carer and visually search for them. Children who are securely attached to their parent or main carer will gradually lose their anxiety with strangers and develop a sense of independence. Children who are not so well attached tend to be less willing to explore and investigate their environment.

Activity 2.9

Part of promoting self-confidence in young children involves them understanding and accepting that at times they will win and at other times they will lose, and most regularly they will need to share and take turns. Opportunities for developing this understanding and acceptance need to increase as the child grows.

1 What commonly found activities within Early Years settings can you think of that encourage an understanding of winning and losing, sharing and taking turns?

2 At what ages would you normally offer them and why?

3 Why do you think it is important for these opportunities to increase as the child develops? Discuss this with a partner.

Support and management of behaviour

Children need guidance and personal example from the adults (role models) around them to help them learn the social rules of the culture and society into which they are born. These rules will vary slightly from family to family and from culture to culture, but mostly they will be based on the same principles. This learning of rules is part of a child's **primary socialisation** – the influences of their closest family and associates.

Activity 2.10

Try reflecting on your own childhood.

1 Who were the most influential people for you?

2 Identify how you think they influenced you.

3 Share your thoughts within a small group, comparing how each of you have been influenced.

Behaviour is influenced by primary socialisation, by individual temperament (an individual's character, disposition and tendencies), and by **secondary socialisation** – the influence of teachers, Early Years staff, neighbours and so on. Behaviour will also be affected by the boundaries that have been set, both at home and elsewhere.

Boundaries

A boundary is a limitation or range of limitations that needs to be agreed and set in advance. Any boundaries set should be reasonable for the child's age and stage of development. Once set it is important that boundaries are adhered to, as otherwise children will continually test them. Boundaries should ideally allow children to explore their environment increasingly as they grow, renegotiating them as children mature to ensure they are age-appropriate. The adult role is to identify risk and balance it against activity, therefore allowing children to explore under supervision, and in safety. It is far better to have a small number of firmly set boundaries that are agreed and adhered to by all adults, and that can be explained and justified to children as non-negotiable, rather than having a larger number of 'desirable' boundaries that are regularly breached. Children will become confused by this, not knowing whether the boundary is in place or not at any point in given time.

Remember! Boundaries = security. Inconsistency = insecurity.

Types of behaviour

In working with children you are likely to see a range of different behaviours. Some will raise concerns for you. At times it is very apparent that a child's behaviour is inappropriate, unacceptable, dangerous and so on, but at other times it will only be identified if you are watching them closely or regularly. This is why observation is such an important part of the Early Years worker's role.

Goodness of fit

To be fully 'one of the crowd' children need to develop something that is known as 'goodness of fit'. This is linked to a child's temperament and is often seen in how 'easy' or 'difficult' it can sometimes be to interact with them. A happy, smiling (easy) child who gladly joins in gives us a straightforward extension of themselves that we can link on to, whereas a child who is constantly fretful and uncooperative makes interactions with them far more difficult. It is the responsibility of you as an adult working with children to find the best way of building a relationship with every child in your care.

Case Study

Anwara and Dillip

Anwara is four years old and has recently moved to the area. She has been attending Sunshine nursery for nearly three weeks.

Although a little shy the first couple of days, Anwara has settled in well, always keen to take part in activities, particularly those involving paint and glue. She chats happily to the adults and likes to show people her pictures and models.

During group activities and circle games Anwara is keen to play a central role (for example being the farmer in Farmers in the Den), and children readily pair up with her in play. During this past week Anwara has volunteered to tell her 'news' at register time, clearly enjoying the attention and opportunity.

Dillip is three-and-a-half and has been attending Sunshine nursery for eight months. He clings hard to his mum's hand when she drops him off, and normally needs to be collected from her by a member of staff, who then tries to engage him in play. Dillip rarely speaks to adults or children, and plays either alone or to the side of a group activity. He cries frequently and needs one-to-one attention to cheer him up again.

Most days Dillip needs to be prompted into selecting or joining in an activity. He is often extremely reluctant to get involved in circle games, needing lots of coaxing.

1 Anwara could be described as an 'easy' child to work with. What makes her so, do you think?

2 Dillip is clearly a more 'difficult' child to get to know. How would you try and build up a relationship with Dillip?

Activity 2.11

Look at the list of behaviours below. A child displaying any of these may be a cause of concern to you at some point. Mostly this is referring to ongoing behaviours rather than 'one-off' incidents, but occasionally a one-off incident may be so out of character that it raises serious concern straight away.

A withdrawn or shy child	An attention-seeking child
An aggressive child	A destructive child
A child who hits others	A child who will not share
A child without friends	A child who bites other children
A child who is constantly anxious	Teasing and bullying
Temper tantrums	A child who finds it hard to settle

Separation anxiety   A child who constantly needs
                                            adult support

Eating issues   Drink/snacktime issues

Jealousy   A child who moves away from
                                            group situations

Repetitive crying   Telling tales

Taking somebody's toy   Rudeness

Defiance   Disobedience

Habits, minor concerns   Habits, major concerns

1 Which behaviour do you think will be the most obvious?

2 Which do you feel might be harder to identify?

3 Why do you consider the behaviours to be unwanted?

4 Who or what is being affected by the behaviour? Using the
   headings below, note where you would place each of the
   behaviours listed. You may find that some behaviours can be
   placed under more than one heading.

Breaches	Affects others' boundaries	Affects the child	Dangerous for child or others

Factors that contribute to behaviour

How well a child's needs are met contributes to the development of
appropriate or inappropriate behaviour. Have a look at the spidergram
on page 60.

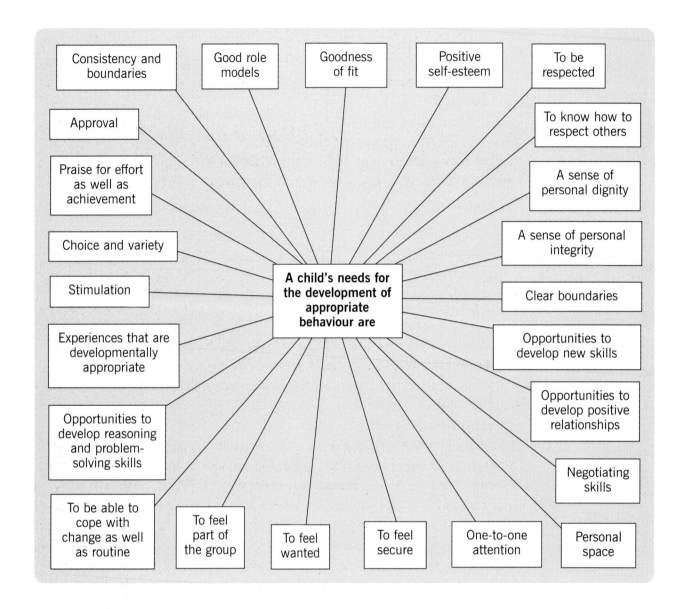

Managing and resolving conflict

The role of the parent or carer in managing and resolving conflict is of course linked to boundaries and consistency. It is about expectations linked to age and stage of development, and it is about understanding. When trying to cope with challenging behaviour or behaviour that concerns you, it is important to ask yourself some questions. Here are some examples.

- Why are you concerned?
- What are you trying to achieve?
- Has the child's behaviour changed?
- If yes, how has the child's behaviour changed?
- How long is it since the change was first noticed?

- Is the change seen in other situations too?
- Are there any known factors that might explain the cause?
- Has a change like this happened before? If so, what was the cause at that time?

Remember ! You will be able to support the management of a child's behaviour better if you understand why it has changed, and why it is not acceptable. Some behaviours will be acceptable at age two, but not at age four.

Activity 2.12

What examples can you think of where certain behaviours are acceptable at one age, but not at another?

Having decided how a child's behaviour has changed, and how they are affected by it, you will need to decide how to deal with it. You may benefit from referring to the behaviour policy of the setting.

Behaviour policies

Each Early Years setting should have a range of policies and procedures, including one on behaviour. These policies should be made available to all new parents, with a request for them to sign that they have read, understood and agreed them. This ensures that everyone works to the same guidelines and can help staff to uphold the rules and boundaries of the setting if their actions or approach are challenged by a parent or colleague. Having something in writing to refer back to ensures that individual decision making is easier.

Strategies to deal with common behaviour

Helping children to cope with change needs sensitivity. A reluctance to try new things or go to new places is common for many children. Most settings allow parents to accompany their children initially to make a visit or to stay for a short while. This usually helps them to settle in. It is often helpful if the same member of staff welcomes the child each day (**key worker system**), particularly in their first weeks of attendance. This helps build security and gives both the child and their parent a focal point where they can say goodbye with limited distress.

Remember ! Parents have separation anxiety too. They should be reassured that their child will be well cared for and given the opportunity to telephone for further reassurance if they wish.

Moving to another setting or a new house can be equally disturbing for a child and helping them to focus on positive things such as what they will be able to do there, rather than what they will miss by leaving their present setting or home, is the best way to help them. Little things such as minor changes in the daily routine contribute to helping a child accept change and flexibility. If their life is based on rigidly set patterns they will be more likely to find coping with new experiences challenging and possibly distressing.

The following strategies are helpful for dealing with behaviour.

ABC strategy

One strategy for managing behaviour is known as the **ABC strategy**, and is based on social learning theory. ABC stands for:

- antecedent – what occurs immediately before the behaviour;
- behaviour – the incidence of behaviour being referred to, whether acceptable or not acceptable;
- consequence – the outcomes following the behaviour, which will be either positive or negative.

This can easily be seen as two 'sums':

Positive antecedent + Positive behaviour = Positive consequence
or
Negative antecedent + Negative behaviour = Negative consequence

Activity 2.13

1 What examples can you think of to explain the ABC strategy?
2 Describe a time when particularly pleasing behaviour has been well rewarded.
3 Describe a time when unwanted behaviour has been challenged.
4 How do you think the adult role in responding to the behaviours could impact on similar situations in the future?

Case study

Jasper

Jasper had been happily using the playdough for almost twenty minutes when Polly came along and started telling him what to do next and interfering with his play. Jasper lost interest and went to play elsewhere. Staff have observed Polly acting in this way on several occasion. What could you do to help the situation?

Case study

Maisie

Maisie continuously splodges paint on to the paintings of other children. She seems to find it very funny, but the other children do not. What could you do to help the situation?

Children respond best to behaviour that is given consistent and appropriate responses. For example, a child who regularly causes disruption in the classroom or nursery should be actively praised when they are concentrating well or being particularly kind or helpful. They are being given attention for doing something positive, rather than for doing something negative. This is **positive reinforcement**, which will hopefully encourage the child to act in a similar manner more often. Similarly, if disruptive or unkind behaviour (negative behaviour) is unchallenged by adults, or is only challenged occasionally, this can be described as **negative reinforcement**, as the actions of the adult do not give a consistent message to the child that their behaviour is unwanted. The result is likely to be a more frequent display of the unwanted behaviour.

Case study   *Paula*

Paula is a very content and placid child who enjoys playing, joins in happily and makes no demands on staff. You realise that you haven't spoken to Paula for days.

1 How does this make you feel?

2 How do you think might Paula be feeling?

Remember!   It is important to praise and reinforce the behaviour of the quiet, 'never a problem' child. They deserve to know that they are noticed and valued too.

Case study   *Freddy*

Freddy gets upset whenever Billy comes near him. Observation shows that Billy tries to dominate Freddy's play. What could you do to help this situation?

To sum up, this is how to put the ABC strategy into effect.

- Where behaviour is identified as being triggered by a specific person or event it is important to observe and try to pre-empt its occurrence.

- Noting and responding to antecedent behaviours is a good way of starting to manage children's behaviour.

- Your role as an Early Years professional is to intervene in a situation before the antecedent (in this case Billy) is put into effect.

- Sometimes a child can be anxious due to the larger size or louder personality of another child. The adult's role here would be to join in and help show the 'wary' child that they can play or work on equal terms with the other child.

Containment

At times a child's frustration or anger overwhelms them and they are unable to deal with it themselves. At this point a sensitive adult can step in and '**contain**' their emotions for them, holding them calmly and preventing them from losing control. Talking to the child reassuringly will gradually ease them back into a state of calm.

It is important for you as the adult to remain unflustered when coping with a child in these situations, offering them examples of how to behave another time by explaining alternative actions they could have taken, where you feel it is appropriate. An example could be suggesting that a child asks to use something rather than simply snatching it away from another child, or asks to join in rather than just watching unhappily. Children do not always realise that other people are being affected by their behaviour. As an adult you may have to help children to understand this.

Remember! Clear explanations must always be given to a child as to why their behaviour is not acceptable.

Some children will benefit from taking 'time out' of the activity, to calm down, relax and compose themselves once again. 'Sanctions' should be used only as a last resort, and if sanctions are indicated to a child, they need to be carried through (part of setting boundaries for the setting).

Sometimes, children need opportunities to express anger, and providing them with clay, wood working or a similar activity can be helpful. Distracting a child away from whatever is being the problem can work well. This is an especially helpful strategy with younger children. If children continually have negative interactions with others, it may be helpful for an adult to join them in their work or play and help to direct their interactions, demonstrating a more positive way to play or work with others.

Setting goals for behaviour

There are many ways of encouraging good behaviour, and using reward stickers and star charts has become a popular approach, particularly in primary schools. If children are secure and feeling confident they are less likely to display unwanted behaviour. The same applies if they receive rewards when they are working or playing well. Some rewards are specifically aimed at building self- esteem. Examples of such rewards include stickers saying:

'I have good thinking skills'
'I am a kind person'
'I have done really well today'

Others will be direct rewards, aimed at acknowledging achievement:

'Good work'
'Well done'
'A kind act'

Whole class rewards are given in some schools by using 'Golden Time' or something similar. Golden Time is often on a Friday afternoon and children are given lots of opportunities for freedom and greater choice regarding what they do. In some schools children can even change to another class for the Golden Time session.

The effects on a child of inappropriate behaviour by others

Activity 2.14

Consider the following situations.

a) Imram's family are asylum seekers. They have recently moved to the area and he is learning English as a second language. Caleb refused to allow Imram into the role-play corner because 'you don't speak properly'.

b) Tracy refused to allow John into the role-play corner (currently a hospital) because 'we're nurses, and you can't be a nurse – you're a boy'.

c) Padraich refused to allow Daniel into the role-play corner shouting, 'Get out, or I'll chuck you out – and don't you come back here.'

1 How would you deal with each situation?

2 How might Imram, John and Daniel be feeling?

3 What might have influenced the actions of Caleb, Tracy and Padraich?

Sometimes you will need to explain to children why their actions are unacceptable and how they are affecting other people. It is important to remember that at times you will be dealing with children acting out scenes they have perhaps seen at home. This needs careful handling, ensuring that you are not making a direct judgement about their family, while ensuring that inappropriate actions within the setting are stopped.

Remember ! If you are ever concerned about the implications of any actions a child is portraying, it is important that you speak to your placement supervisor.

Legal framework of child protection

The abuse of children harms their development in many ways. Abuse is always wrong and it is important that adults act to protect children if ever they are concerned about their safety. Abuse can take the following forms.

Physical abuse; any harmful actions directed against a child, often resulting in bruises, burns, scalds, head injuries, poisoning or fractures.

Neglect; the failure of the child's carers to properly safeguard the health, safety and well-being of the child. This includes their nutritional needs, physical needs and social needs.

Sexual abuse; any involvement of a child or developmentally immature adolescent in sexual activities, including viewing photographs and pornographic videos.

Emotional abuse; the continuous rejection, terrorising or criticising of a child.

Every local authority has drawn up a set of definitions regarding the abuse of children. It is important that you gain access to a copy of this and read it carefully. Your placement will have one. If you do not understand anything, ensure that you ask your placement supervisor or course tutor for clarification.

The main aspects of law that help to protect children are those set out in the Children Act 1989. This Act has brought together all the legislation relevant to children. There are a variety of legal steps that can be taken to help keep a child safe from harm, as follows.

Police protection

A child may be taken into **police protection** for up to seventy-two hours, during which time an emergency protection order (EPO) can be applied for.

Child assessment order

A **child assessment order** can only be applied for through the courts by the local authority or the NSPCC (National Society for the Prevention of Cruelty to Children). It is applied for when a child's parents are unlikely to give permission for an assessment of their child's state of health or level of development to be made, when a concern is raised that a child is already suffering harm, or is likely to suffer significant harm. A child assessment order lasts for a maximum of seven days.

Emergency protection order (EPO)

An application for this short-term order can be made by anyone, and if the order is granted, the applicant subsequently takes on parental responsibility for the child for the duration of the order. The order is usually issued for eight days, with one extension opportunity of a further seven days. An applicant taking on parental responsibility:

> *'must take (but may only take) action which is reasonably required to safeguard or promote the child's welfare...'*
>
> Children Act 1989, Guidance and Regulations, Volume 2

This might include an assessment of the child, or decisions about how much contact or who has contact with the child.

An **emergency protection order** is always followed by an investigation by the local authority.

Recovery order

This is an order designed to provide a legal basis for recovering a child who is the subject of an EPO, a care order (see below) or who is in police protection. It is used in situations where a child has been unlawfully taken away or is being kept away from the person who has parental responsibility for them. It also applies if the child runs away from the 'responsible' person or is considered to be missing.

The **recovery order** directs anyone who is in a position to do so, to produce the child concerned if asked to do so, or to give details of their whereabouts. The child will then be removed by the local authority. Police are authorised under the order to enter and search any premises as is necessary, using reasonable force.

Supervision order

On occasions a child is placed under the supervision of the local authority (for up to one year) if it is not felt that sufficient co-operation between the parents and the authority will ensure that the child is fully protected. Although the child continues to live at home, the local authority has a right of access to the child. The **supervision order** can be extended if deemed necessary.

Care order

As with the supervision order, a child continues to live at home under a **care order**. The local authority has a shared responsibility for the protection of the child, and its decisions hold the greater balance of power in any disputes between the authority and the parents. At any time the authority can remove the child from the parents' home without the need to apply to the courts for any other order. The care order can last until the child reaches the age of majority (eighteen years old).

Area Child Protection Committee (ACPC)

Under the Children Act 1989, each local authority area is required to have a joint forum for developing, monitoring and reviewing child protection policies. This is the responsibility of the **Area Child Protection Committee** (ACPC). ACPCs are made up of those persons who have contact with a child whose case comes before them, for example:

- social workers;
- police officers;
- medical practitioners;
- community health team workers;
- school teachers;
- voluntary agencies.

An interagency approach to each case ensures that relevant information is passed on to all who need it. This means that there is an exchange of information between different professions, such as teacher, GP, police officer and social worker. This helps to reduce situations where communication breakdown can have tragic consequences.

Referral procedures

Investigations into cases of abuse or suspected abuse, or where there is a concern that a child may be **at risk**, are carried out following a **referral**. Referrals can be made to the police, social services departments or to the NSPCC. Anyone can make a referral, and the impetus to do so can follow on from the disclosure by a child to the individual person making the referral, or their representative (Early Years settings and schools have a designated person who takes on this responsibility). It may also result from the concern of an individual or a group of people represented by one individual. Referrals are also made by neighbours, family members and concerned members of the public. It is always preferred if individuals identify themselves when making a referral, but anonymous referrals are also accepted and investigated as necessary.

It is a misconception that following a referral the 'authority' goes immediately to the family and takes away the child. This only happens on rare occasions when there has been a clear case of abuse and the child faces imminent risk of further abuse. Most cases go through a set procedure to establish if a concern is justified, to explore the concerns raised with all those who are in contact with the child, or who might have relevant information, and to establish the level of risk to the child. A situation in which immediate action may be needed to remove the child to safety would be if physical violence is likely to continue or increase following the referral being brought to the family's notice. If a child is not allowed to leave voluntarily, an EPO can be obtained.

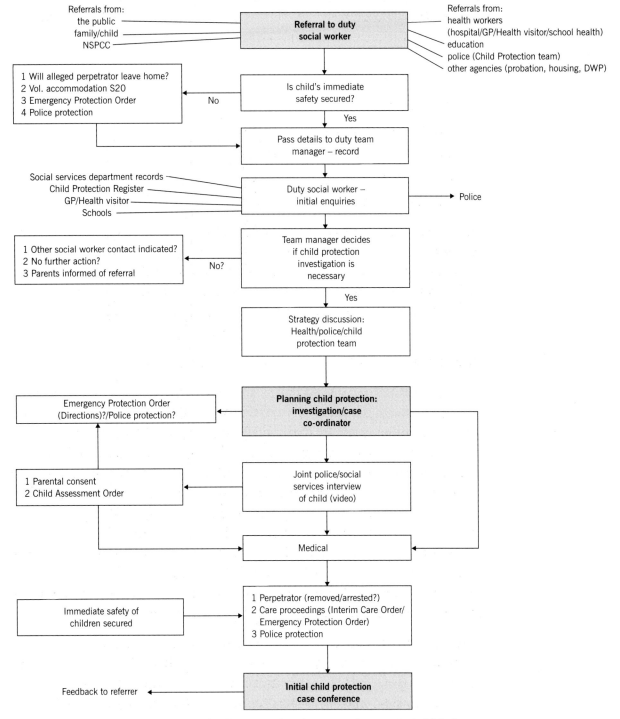

The investigation procedure in cases of suspected child abuse

If during your placement experience you are concerned about a child for any reason, you should talk to your placement supervisor or, if you do not yet feel comfortable doing this, talk to your college tutor. They will help you explore your concerns further and take action appropriately.

Remember! It is never appropriate simply talk to your friends about a concern, as confidentiality is of utmost importance in all cases, and information about any suspected case of abuse should only be discussed on a 'needs to know basis'.

Activity 2.15

Think about how you might feel if you had concerns about a child. What range of emotions would you expect to feel regarding:

a) the child you are concerned about?

b) the perpetrator of any abuse?

c) the prospect of making a referral?

Thinking this through now will hopefully give you some preparation if you are faced with the situation for real.

Keeping records

In Early Years settings, clear record keeping and report writing help to provide all the details that may be asked of the setting in the event of an inquiry. Each setting should have an accident book, where all accidents and incidents are recorded, witnessed and signed by at least two members of staff. Many settings use 'body maps' to record marks and bruises that have been identified, adding a date to them. This can form a useful piece of supportive evidence in a case involving physical abuse. It is important that staff are able to identify signs and symptoms on different skin tones.

Building up good relationships with parents is important in order to provide the best possible care for their child. If the setting has a policy on child protection, which states what will happen in light of any concerns, this lets parents know that you are making the welfare of their child of **paramount importance**, as set down by the Children Act 1989 (the paramountcy principle). The setting's policy could include a clause stating that any child arriving in the setting with an injury will have it noted in the accident/incident book. This will offer added safety for the child, and added safety for the staff, avoiding the situation that a parent may question an injury to their child, when the child had arrived with the injury earlier that day.

A body map

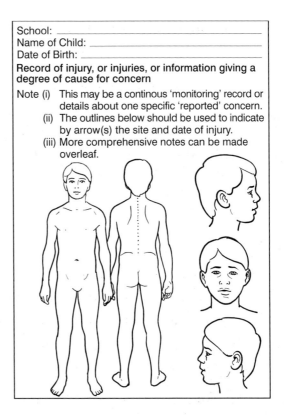

School: _____
Name of Child: _____
Date of Birth: _____

Record of injury, or injuries, or information giving a degree of cause for concern

Note (i)   This may be a continous 'monitoring' record or details about one specific 'reported' concern.
      (ii) The outlines below should be used to indicate by arrow(s) the site and date of injury.
      (iii) More comprehensive notes can be made overleaf.

Each setting should have a child protection procedure, which follows the guidelines provided by the local authority.

Activity 2.16

1 Ask to see a copy of the child protection guidelines and reporting procedures from both your local authority and from your placement. There may be a charge made by your local authority. Try to locate the guidelines from your local authority website.

2 Try explaining the guidelines and procedure to another person. If you can explain them clearly then it is likely that you understand them.

3 If the guidelines are not clear to you, ask for an explanation.

Child protection register

In the mid-1970s **child protection registers** were first set up within each local authority. A child's name is put on the register if there is concern about the safety of that child or their family. At times an unborn baby may be placed on the register, if there is a known abuser in the family.

The register contains relevant information (see below) about the child, so that the child's situation can be monitored and appropriate action taken when necessary. The child's case and inclusion on the register is reviewed regularly.

If a senior professional has a concern about a child they can ask for a check to be made of the register for the name of that particular child or their family. These registers are now computerised and held centrally, enabling a fast checking facility. The information is not readily given out, and professionals wishing to consult them have their details and authority to apply to the register checked before information is released to them.

De-registration

De-registration can take place when a child's case is reviewed, if it is thought appropriate. De-registration can occur if:

- the original points that led to registration no longer apply;
- the child reaches the age of majority (eighteen) and is no longer termed a 'child';
- the child dies.

Contents of a child protection register

The information held on a child protection register includes:

- the child's name (and any other names they are known by);
- their address, gender, date of birth, culture and any known religion;
- the name and contact details of their GP;
- the name and details of their main carer;
- details of any school or other setting the child is known to attend;
- if applicable, the name and details of any person who has parental responsibility for the child (if different from above);
- outline details of any court orders;
- an outline of the alleged or confirmed abuse that has previously occurred;
- the date the child was placed on the register;
- the name and details of the professional responsible for the child's case (the child's key worker);
- the date of the proposed review of the child's situation.

Key terms

You should now understand the following key words and phrases. If you do not, read through the chapter again and review them.

ABC strategy
Area Child Protection Committee (ACPC)
attachment and bonding
birth marks
boundaries
care order
centile
child assessment order
child protection register
containment
cultural and dietary needs
development
developmental norms
emergency protection order (EPO)
emotional abuse
emotional development
emotional disturbance
environmental factors affecting health and development
fixed factors affecting health and development
foetal position
food groups
genetic inheritance
growth
keeping records
key worker system
locomotor skills
maintaining a safe and secure environment
manipulation
maturational changes

milestones of development
minerals
motor development
negative reinforcement
neglect
neonatal stage
non-locomotor skills
normative development
paramountcy principle
physical abuse
police protection
policy
positive reinforcement
posture
pre-natal stage
primary reflexes
primary socialisation
procedure
recovery order
referral procedures
resolving conflict
secondary socialisation
senses
separation and loss
sexual abuse
social and economic factors affecting health and development
social learning theory
social smile
supervision order
vitamins
well-balanced diet

Test Yourself

1 What is the difference between growth and development?

2 How are the stages of children's development often divided up?

3 Explain the maturational changes in a child's physical development.

4 How would you summarise the hearing of a newborn baby?

5 How would you summarise the vision of a newborn baby?

6   What is the difference between the terms hypertonic and hypotonic when referring to the physical appearance of a newborn baby?

7   By what age is a good degree of head control usually achieved?

8   At what age are tantrums common?

9   Give an example of how one aspect of development can impact on another.

10 What factors can you name that influence physical development?

11 Name at least three regulations or legislative Acts relevant to health and safety in an Early Years environment.

12 What are the five food groups, and how do they support children's healthy development?

13 Give at least five examples of common emotions, explaining why you consider them to be positive or negative.

14 Give ten factors that contribute to the development of a child's emotional security.

15 What is meant by the term bonding?

16 In what ways do boundaries support the management of behaviour?

17 What is meant by the term 'goodness of fit'?

18 What do the initials ABC stand for in the ABC strategy of behaviour management?

19 What is the role of an Area Child Protection Committee (ACPC), and who is involved?

References and suggested further reading

Bee, H (1992) *The Developing Child* (6th edn), Allyn & Boston

Bruce, T and Meggitt, C (1996) *Childcare and Education*, Hodder & Stoughton

Dare, A and O'Donovan, M (1998) *A Practical Guide to Working with Babies* (2nd edn), Nelson Thornes

(2000) *Good Practice in Child Safety*, Nelson Thornes

(2002) *A Practical Guide to Child Nutrition* (2nd edn), Nelson Thornes

Department of Health (1999) *Working Together to Safeguard the Children*, HMSO

Elliott, M (ed) (1992) *Protecting Children Training Pack*, HMSO

Hobart, C and Frankel, J (1999) *A Practical Guide to Child Observation and Assessment* (2nd edn), Nelson Thornes

Miller, L (1997) *Closely Observed Infants*, Duckworth

Mukherji, P and O'Dea, T (2000) *Understanding Children's Language and Literacy*, Nelson Thornes

Mukherji, P (2001) *Understanding Children's Challenging Behaviour*, Nelson Thornes

Neaum, S and Tallack, J (2000) *Good Practice in Implementing the Pre-School Curriculum* (2nd edn), Nelson Thornes

Sheridan, M (1997) *From Birth to Five Years; Children's Developmental Progress*

(revised edn), Routledge

Walker, C (1998) *Eating Well for the Under-5s in Child Care*,   The Caroline Walker Trust

Websites

www.amazingbaby.com/social.html

www.amazingbaby.com/emotional.html

www.amazingbaby.com/physical.html

www.childline.org.uk

www.baspcan.org.uk

www.sociology.org.uk/p252n2.htm

www.bullying.co.uk

www.kidscape.org.uk

www.parentlineplus.org.uk

www.cwt.co.uk

3 Good practice in child care settings

> **This unit covers:**
>
> - Equal opportunity issues
> - Meeting specific needs in a child care setting
> - Health and safety in child care settings

This unit covers a variety of different aspects of child care, introducing a range of ideas, and highlighting what is meant by good practice. Safety issues are covered, together with **equal opportunities** and a range of genetically inherited conditions. Many of the most common childhood illnesses have also been explained.

Equal opportunity issues

Working within Early Years requires a thorough understanding of what is prejudice and discrimination, and how to show your commitment to diversity within society and within each setting. This means meeting the needs and promoting the value of all children within your care.

The **Children Act 1989** requires local authorities to ensure that daycare provision is staffed appropriately. It states that:

> *'People working with young children should value and respect the different racial origins, religions, cultures and languages in a multi-racial society so that each child is valued as an individual without racial or gender stereotyping. Children from a very young age learn about different races and cultures including religion and languages and will be capable of assigning different values to them. The same applies to gender and making distinctions between male and female roles. It is important that people working with young children are aware of this, so that their practice enables the children to develop positive attitudes to differences of race, culture and language and differences of gender.'*

Children Act 1989, Guidance and Regulations, Volume 2, Section 6.10

Working to the principles of the Children Act ensures that practice in an Early Years setting is consistently good, rather than consistently adequate, and that the children cared for and educated within the setting benefit from this in all areas of their development.

Equality, diversity and rights

These terms can be broadly defined as follows:

- **equality** – the state of being equal;
- **diversity** – the state or quality of being different or varied;
- **rights** – in accordance with accepted standards of moral or legal behaviour, and justice.

Collins Dictionary (1991)

Equality is about what is fair and what is not. It means that an individual's family or cultural background, the way they live, or their past or current state of health should not prevent them from receiving the same opportunities as anyone else in society.

Diversity refers to the range of individual people, each with differing levels of ability, from a variety of cultures and religion, and each with their own experiences, who make up a group or society.

Rights are the entitlements of each individual to receive the same opportunities as others. Many rights are linked to standards of service (such as the Patient's Charter regarding health care) and are protected by legislation (laws).

Legislation

The most relevant charters and Acts of Parliament, which Early Years staff need to understand are:

- Children Act 1989;
- Human Rights Act 1998;
- UN Convention on the Rights of the Child 1989;
- Disability Discrimination Act 2000.

Children Act 1989

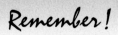**Remember!** Under the Children Act 1989, children with disabilities are defined as 'children in need'.

The principles of the Children Act 1989 include the following points.

- The welfare of the child is paramount (of ultimate importance) and it should be safeguarded and promoted at all times by those people in the position of providing services for a child.
- Children with disabilities are children first with the same rights as all children to services.
- The parents and families of a child are an important element of their lives. This should be recognised, and support given to them to help them fulfil their responsibilities.
- Parents should be valued as partners with local authorities and other agencies working to support their children.
- Children have a right to be consulted and listened to when decisions about them are being made. The views of both children and their parents must be taken into account at all times.
- There should be a co-ordinated approach when offering services to children with disabilities. For example, regarding health, education and social services.

Volume 2 of the Children Act specifically covers daycare, and states that parents have a right to influence the quality of education that their child receives.

The Children Act 1989

Section 22(5)(c) of the Act states that local authorities must give consideration to the religious persuasion, racial origin, cultural and linguistic background of any child within their care. Any provider of care for children can be de-registered if these needs and rights are not properly cared for, as they would not be considered to be a 'fit' person to care for children, under the Act.

Children Act

The Human Rights Act 1998

The Human Rights Act focuses on the individual's right to a life free from torture, loss of liberty, unfair punishment or discrimination. It also refers to respect for private and family life (Article 8), freedom of thought, conscience and religion (Article 9) and the freedom of expression (Article 10). The Act is indirectly linked to the drawing up of no-smacking policies, and is also relevant to the issue of female circumcision (surgery to the genital area of young women in some cultures, illegal in the UK).

The UN Convention on Children's Rights 1989

This is an international agreement on human rights, which has been ratified (formally agreed to) by 191 countries. It consists of fifty-four articles (statements) and its four main principles are:

- non-discrimination – all children have the same rights and are entitled to the same treatment;
- children's best interests – the best interest of the child should be placed as the highest priority when making decisions about their future;
- survival and development of children – children have the right to survive and the right to be able to develop to their full potential;
- rights to participation – the views of children should be taken seriously and they should be able to take part in what is going on around them.

The agreement is important because it brings together in one document all the rights of children, and adults are asked to view children as individuals with all human rights being applied to children everywhere.

Based on a paper by Save the Children (2000)

Examples of articles set out within the UN Convention have been unofficially summarised by authors Flekkoy and Kaufman (1997) as follows:

Article 2   The principle that all rights apply to all children without exception, and the state's obligation to protect children from any form of discrimination. The state must not violate any right, and must take positive action to promote them all.

Article 22   Special protection to be granted to children who are refugees or seeking refugee status, and the state's obligation to co-operate with competent organisations providing such protection and assistance.

Article 23   The right of handicapped children to special care, education and training designed to help them achieve greatest possible self-reliance and to lead a full and active life in society.

Article 30   The right of children of minority communities and indigenous populations to enjoy their own culture and to practise their own religion and language.

All children have the same rights and are entitled to the same treatment

Disability Discrimination Act 2000

This Act is directly relevant to Early Years in that it supports the ethos of the Education Act 1993 of the need to provide all children who have a special need with an appropriate education at a suitable school.

All Early Years settings should have a special educational needs co-ordinator (**SENCO**), who takes overall responsibility for ensuring that the special needs of children are met. In schools this would normally be a member of the teaching staff who liaises with parents and other staff, and keeps records of the special educational needs within the school.

Stereotyping and labelling

Definitions

Role model
A person who is considered to be setting an example to others.

Children learn values and attitudes at a very young age from others who are their **role models**. They look to their role models for guidance, approval and encouragement, and therefore they observe and take on their attitudes and actions. These role models include their families (this is called their primary socialisation) and their friends, both adults and peers, including Early Years staff, teachers and health professionals (this is known as secondary socialisation). This also includes you!

Children baking with an adult

As an Early Years student you will spend time working with a diverse range of children and their carers, and it is important that you understand what is meant by discrimination, stereotyping and prejudice, together with being clear as to what is good practice. It can be helpful to explore how your own views were initially formed, and who or what influenced and shaped them.

Activity 3.1

Activity 2.9 back on page 56 asked you to reflect back on your childhood and who influenced you. Again, reflect here on your childhood and extend your thinking further. Role models almost certainly included parents and teachers, together with nursery or playgroup workers. Who else would you include?

1 In what ways did each of these role models influence you?

2 Were the influences positive or negative, and what made them so?

3 Have you identified any negative influences?

4 How does this make you feel?

Developing personal values is just the first step in working to good practice; putting them into practice is what counts most. Upholding your views is not always easy, and sometimes it can be hard to challenge the practice of others and work in a way that does not compromise your own values. As you gain both confidence and experience in your role you will develop your own strategy for dealing with challenge.

Stereotyping

Images that **stereotype** people can be either positive or negative and are often built up by the influences of other people and the media rather than on personal experience. In stereotyping an individual person we label them as being simply 'part of a group', thus taking away their personal identity. Clearly this can be very unfair.

Activity 3.2

What examples of stereotyping can you think of?

Discrimination and prejudice

To **discriminate** means to give favourable or unfavourable treatment to someone or something because of a specific factor. An example might be if a single mother of five children is never asked to be involved in activities at her children's school because it is assumed she will not have the time or means to do so.

Discrimination can be **institutional**, where the policies or practices of a workplace result in treating certain groups of people differently, or **individual discrimination**, where the **prejudice** (an opinion formed in advance) is the personal bias of one person.

Remember! From Unit 1, Prejudice + Power = Discrimination.

Activity 3.3

Focusing on Early Years settings, consider the following questions:

1 What forms of gender stereotyping or discrimination might you find?

2 What forms of racial or cultural stereotyping or discrimination might you find?

3 What forms of disability stereotyping or discrimination might you find?

The points you have raised in the above activity could most likely be avoided if there is a strong equal opportunities policy in place at the setting. Policies are important because they are drawn up and agreed by the staff of the setting, and copies are usually given to staff, parents, carers and students to read and understand. This helps everyone to work to the same ideas, values and procedures.

Activity 3.4

1 Discuss the following statement with others in your group: 'We do not have racism here. All the children are treated exactly the same'?

2 Think about what this statement might mean for the children.

3 Think about what this statement might mean for you as an Early Years worker.

4 How would you change the statement to make it more positive?

Discriminatory practice

Much discriminatory practice develops through ignorance and a lack of understanding This is sometimes accidental, but often it is conscious. As a professional in the Early Years sector you need to become better informed, so as to avoid discriminating accidentally, and to address any (conscious) personal prejudices you may have. Changing your viewpoint is not an easy thing to do, and you will only achieve this by exploring discrimination further and increasing your understanding of the effects discrimination can have. This in turn will help your values to develop and be consolidated for you further.

Remember ! You cannot enforce your views on anyone, and similarly the views of others cannot be forced upon you.

Definitions

Religion
A person's belief.

Culture
Beliefs, customs and values of people from a similar background.

Custom
Usual practice.

Different religions and cultures

Within different **religions** and cultures there are customs that are linked to diet, dress, worship, actions, gender, birth and death. Some of these are explored in more detail below.

Festivals

There are many different **festivals** and these can provide a wonderful range of learning opportunities for children across all aspects of the education curriculums. Here are some examples.

Jewish festivals

- Tu B'Shevat (February) – celebration of the new year for trees, by planting new trees and trying to eat fruit from Israel.

Hanukkah candles

- Pesach (Passover) – commemorating the Jewish exodus from slavery in Egypt. Matzah is eaten (unleavened bread). Houses are cleaned to ensure that no food containing 'leaven' remains.
- Sukkot (October) – a harvest festival commemorating the forty years Jews spent in the wilderness. A sukkah is a temporary hut for meals and socialising during this time.
- Hanukkah (December) – candles are placed in a 'Hanukkah' candle holder each evening, plus foods are cooked in oil, such as latkes (potato cakes) and doughnuts etc.

Hindu festivals

- Raksha Bandhan (August) – where sisters tie coloured bracelets around their brothers' wrists to symbolise 'protection from evil'.
- Ganesh-chaturthi (August) – a celebration of the birthday of Ganesh. Hindus worship the elephant-headed deity at the beginning of new projects such as exams, moving house etc.
- Navaratri (October) – Navaratri means 'nine nights' (the length of the festival). Food and presents are often given to young girls.
- Diwali (October or November) – lasts for one to five days, the story of Rama and Sita is a popular part of this festival.

Ganesh, the elephant-headed deity

Sikh festivals

- Vaisakhi (the first day of the Indian year) – the Sikh new year during which the five signs of Sikhism (uncut hair, a comb fixed in the hair, a steel bracelet, a short sword and a pair of shorts: known as the five Ks) and the turban are obligatory.

- Diwali (October or November) – this commemorates the release from prison of Guru Hargobind, the last human Guru of Sikhs. It includes wearing new clothes, giving gifts and sweets.

Christian festivals

- Lent – for forty days prior to Easter, a period of giving up something, to mark the forty days that Jesus spent in the wilderness.
- Easter – the celebration of the resurrection of Jesus. Easter eggs are given as a symbol of new life.
- Advent (December) – the first day of the Christian year, four Sundays before Christmas. Four candles are lit in an Advent crown, one on each Sunday.

Muslim festivals

- Eid-ul-Fitr (December) – the end of fasting for Ramadan (lasts three days). Involves family gatherings, new clothes, nice food and gifts.

Chinese festivals

- Yuan Tan (Chinese New Year) – the most important event in the traditional Chinese calendar, which begins on the first day of the lunar calendar each year. Gifts, fireworks and dances such as the lion dance take place at this time.

A Chinese lion dance

Japanese festivals

- Ganjitsu (Japanese New Year) (January) – lasts up to three days. Families get together, decorations are put up, businesses close and people pay their first visit to local shrines.
- Hanamatsuri (April) – Japanese celebration of the birthday of Buddha Shakyamuni. Floral shrines are made, in which images of the infant Buddha are set and bathed.

Activity 3.5

With which cultures would you associate the following items of clothing? If you do not know, carry out research to find the answers:

- sari?
- kimono?
- shalwah and kameez?
- yamulka?
- hijaab?
- turban?

There are many more religions and cultures than those referred to here.

1 Note down the names of others that you already know about.
2 Which other festivals have been explored in your placement?

Diet

Diet is an important aspect of providing appropriately for children's needs. It is essential that the customs of a child's family are upheld within each Early Years setting. There are a number of dietary requirements linked to culture and religion. If there are any concerns or doubts as to the understanding of staff regarding any particular child's diet, parents should always be asked for guidance. The table below sets out a useful 'at-a-glance' guide to what is acceptable and what is forbidden for many of the most commonly found groups of people.

Equipment, activities and visual displays

Every setting should provide a range of toys and books that provide positive images of gender, race and disability, and which avoid stereotyping. Images should be varied, incorporating both men and women, boys and girls all enjoying similar leisure activities, and seen to be involved in tasks both at home as well as at work, school, nursery and so on. A range of cultures should be represented, ensuring that no one culture or gender is seen as always being in more 'powerful' positions than any other – for example, all doctors being portrayed as white and also mostly men, while all nurses are portrayed as women, and often black. Men should not always be the ones digging the garden, nor should women always be the ones washing the dishes or ironing.

Food-related customs

	Jewish	Hindu[1]	Sikh[1]	Muslim	Buddhist	Rastafarian[2]
Eggs	No blood spots	Some	Yes	Yes	Some	Some
Milk/yoghurt	Not with meat	Yes	Yes	Yes	Yes	Some
Cheese	Not with meat	Some	Some	Possibly	Yes	Some
Chicken	Kosher	Some	Some	Halal	No	Some
Mutton/lamb	Kosher	Some	Yes	Halal	No	Some
Beef and beef products	Kosher	No	No	Halal	No	Some
Pork and pork products	No	No	Rarely	No	No	No
Fish	With fins and scales	With fins and scales	Some	Some	Some	Yes
Shellfish	No	Some	Some	Some	No	No
Butter/ghee	Kosher	Some	Some	Some	No	Some
Lard	No	No	No	No	No	No
Cereal foods	Yes	Yes	Yes	Yes	Yes	Yes
Nuts/pulses	Yes	Yes	Yes	Yes	Yes	Yes
Fruits/vegetables	Yes	Yes[3]	Yes	Yes	Yes	Yes
Fasting[4]	Yes	Yes	Yes	Yes	Yes	Yes

from Walker (1998), page 68

'Some' means that some people within a religious group would find these foods acceptable.

1   Strict Hindus and Sikhs will not eat eggs, meat, fish, and some fats.
2   Some Rastafarians are vegan.
3   Jains have restrictions on some vegetable foods. Check with the individuals.
4   Fasting is unlikely to apply to young children.

Tokenism

There is a need to be aware of **tokenism**. This is a pretence at being committed to diversity and equality. Settings with only a tokenist approach may have a few items depicting positive messages in prominent places, but when you explore the resources further, a less overall picture of equality emerges. For example, it may be that the books on the shelf show positive images, whereas many of those in the book box are less positive. Similarly, there may be one or two dressing up clothes relevant to cultures other than Western, but no cooking equipment or tableware that would be familiar to children of cultures other than Western.

Case Study

Sylvia

Sylvia has recently started to work in a nursery class. Through reading stories to the children she has already noticed that there are almost no books with images of people other than white people, and the only book portraying a person with a disability always pictures them on their own, rather than in the main picture. There are two black dolls in the role-play corner, both undressed and in a cupboard, whereas the white dolls are dressed and lying in the prams. There is a wok on the shelf, that doesn't seem to be in use. The children don't ask to play with it, and Sylvia has never seen the staff add it to the play kitchen equipment. A poster on the wall gives a welcome message in a variety of languages, but Sylvia is not convinced that there is a real commitment to promoting equality and cultural diversity within the nursery.

1 What sort of resources would you expect to see, even in a setting with limited finances?

2 Who should Sylvia raise her concerns with?

3 How would you introduce more cultural diversity into the nursery if you were Sylvia?

4 Why are Sylvia's concerns important?

Although having the right resources is important, this does not in itself ensure equality and diversity is being promoted. There is a need for positive language and the correct approach to using the resources and activities provided to ensure that the message of welcome and valuing of diversity is evident to children and their families.

Books and stories

Positive messages within books would include:

- Boys in caring roles, or carrying out household tasks.

- Girls involved in activities or occupations involving strength, or occupations of power and management.

- Minority ethnic groups both depicted in traditional cultural situations and also in occupations of power and management. Illustrations showing mixed cultural activities or the sharing of each other's festivals by a group of children or adults.

- Disabled people carrying out the same tasks as everyone else, and joining in activities alongside able-bodied people.

- Different family groupings; nuclear, extended, step-families, mixed race families to truly represent society.

- Where possible, it is good to have some dual language books. These will help involve parents who speak the languages portrayed and give all children an opportunity to see the written word in their own and an alternative script.

Negative messages within books would include:

- Boys as always physically stronger than girls, in 'macho' roles or positions of power. Girls as cute, pretty and clean, only as carers, in supportive occupations. Minority ethnic groups inappropriately or negatively characterised, depicted in manual occupations, or only in traditional cultural situations.

- Disabled people only as wheel-chair bound, sat to the side of activities, on a different level to others in the illustration.

- Family groupings of the two parents, two point four children image.

The examples of positive and negative images set out for books and stories apply to all resources and activities that involve illustrations.

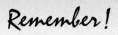

Remember! It is acceptable for there to be range of images, some neutral and some positive, as long as there is an overall emphasis on the positive. It is never acceptable for a setting to continue to include negative images within its resources.

Role play

In the role-play corner issues of gender are mostly found in the use of the resources rather than the resources themselves. The important aspect of gender stereotyping here is to encourage all the children to enjoy all the resources, taking different roles within their play. Culturally, an array of artefacts, clothes and foods from a range of cultures will enhance the learning of all children and positively promote the self-image of children from those cultures.

Activity 3.7

1 Have a look in the role-play area of your current placement setting.

2 What cultures are portrayed by the dolls in your placement? If they are all pink skinned, blonde haired and 'stereotypically English' they are likely to support a racist message of who is important and needs caring for.

There are many resources available that depict a good range of cultures. These include:

• fruit and vegetables from around the world;

• breads and other foods such as pizza;

• cooking utensils;

• tableware, chop sticks, bowls, etc.;

• clothing for dressing up.

Many can be made quite cheaply using materials dyed and printed, and a range of foods can be made from salt dough. Cheap versions of cooking utensils can sometimes be found in markets, or may be donated by parents.

Foods from around the world

Remember! Parents of children from different cultures will usually be pleased to help with improving the resources of the setting. It is always worth asking them for advice. This will be likely to improve the provision of the setting and show that the setting values the culture of the family.

Construction materials

Children often consider construction kits to be boys' toys. This can be due to parents more often buying construction activities for their sons than for their daughters. Encouraging both boys and girls to use construction materials will help erase stereotypical views, but it is important to be aware of who dominates the construction area. Encouraging girls to use construction materials without the 'help' of the boys can sometimes be appropriate. This will ensure that they have opportunities to plan, predict, experiment and achieve on their own. The pictures on the box lids of construction kits often illustrate boys playing rather than girls. This is an aspect that is easy to change by removing the construction activity from its original box and placing it in an alternative container.

Encouraging both boys and girls to use all toys will help erase stereotypical views

Creativity

Creative activities are non-competitive, as you cannot paint your own picture 'wrong'. Opportunities for creative expression involve the use of a range of mediums and a range of utensils, and it is important that brushes or their alternatives are suitable for all children's hands. A child with limited manipulative skills will benefit from chunky brush handles (lightweight wallpaper brushes can be useful), and all children will enjoy the experience of painting with (thoroughly cleaned) roll-on deodorant containers or large sponge rollers.

For children with skin problems such as eczema direct contact with paint and other 'messy' mediums can cause further irritation. Activities such as finger painting under a (supervised) length of clingfilm can keep them involved without risking infection or further discomfort. Using large bubble-wrap as an alternative can add to the sensory experience.

Remember! Strict supervision is needed when using materials such as clingfilm.

The range of festivals celebrated by people of different religions and cultures throughout the year, as described on page 83–86, offer enormous scope for creative activity. Examples include the Hindu Diwali festival of light:

- Diwali cards – a popular design is to use a hand shape and decorate it with the traditional mehndi patterns;
- Rangoli patterns – a decoration laid at the entrance to the home to welcome the goddess of fortune, Lakshi.

Examples of Rangoli patterns

Or you could explore Chinese New Year, the first day of the lunar calendar each year:

- Teng Chieh – the lantern festival denotes the end of the new year celebrations and decorated sheets of paper are cut up and made into lanterns;
- money envelopes (lai see) – it is traditional for children to receive money in red envelopes decorated with gold writing;
- dragons, one of the twelve animals in the Chinese animal years – making a huge dragon can be a super whole group activity, culminating in the 'dance of the dragon'. Activities such as this allow every child to contribute, working together towards a joint goal.

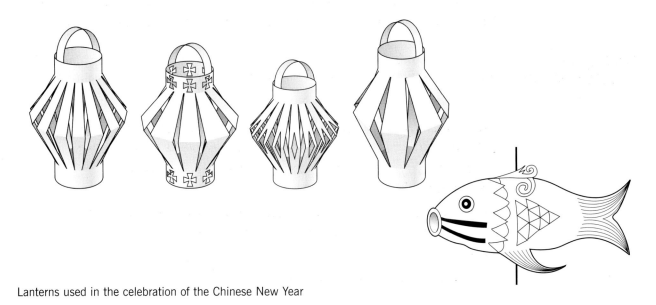

Lanterns used in the celebration of the Chinese New Year

Remember! Providing a range of skin tone colours in both paints and crayons will enable all children to represent themselves and their families accurately in their pictures.

Puzzles

Puzzles can be for table or floor use, and can have both large and small pieces. Again, it is important to consider different levels of manipulative skill. The use of large pieces will help the less able child, as will puzzles with sturdy knobs to lift and place pieces, and issues of positive images apply in the same way as with books and stories.

Remember! Just because a child needs large pieces to meet their physical needs does not necessarily mean that they cannot enjoy a challenging picture. Physical and intellectual needs are not always parallel with each other. Children increase different aspects of their development at different rates.

Music, movement and singing

In this area of the curriculum it is so easy to include diversity. There are a large range of musical instruments available, depicting many cultures, and a large selection of instruments that will accommodate most physical needs. A musical instrument box should not simply hold tambourines, drums and cymbals, as this is so limiting for expression and restricts opportunities to explore the other options available. Dance is an important part of many cultures, and including dance on a regular basis encourages children to explore and communicate through a range of expressions and movements. Combining dance with the use of musical instruments will encourage children to accompany each other, building on their ability to co-operate with others and appreciate each other as equal partners in a joint activity.

Remember! Electronic musical activities, and those involving vibration, are particularly useful for children with severe hearing loss, as they offer multiple sensory experience.

Dance is an important part of many cultures

Libraries

Public libraries loan out tapes and CDs, which are good sources of world music. Children can enjoy a range of songs from around the globe, learning to sing in different languages, placing emphasis on rhythm and dance, while appreciating links to other cultures.

Activity 3.8

Make a list of songs and music from around the world that might be appreciated by children.

Cooking activities

The customs and diets of all children need to be taken into account when planning activities with food, including practical, medical and cultural needs. Examples of medical dietary considerations would include:

- diabetes;
- the condition coeliac;
- cystic fibrosis;
- food allergies, particularly children who are anaphylactic (a potentially life- threatening reaction, which needs immediate medical attention).

Activity 3.9

1 Research the dietary needs of children who have type 1 diabetes (diabetes mellitus).
2 Research the dietary needs of children with the condition coeliac .
3 Research the dietary needs of a child with cystic fibrosis.
4 Draw up a summary of each, and keep it in your file for future reference.

Practical and cultural needs would include:

- children who are vegetarian or vegan;
- children from cultures where certain foods, or combinations of foods, are not allowed (look again at the table on page 87).

Examples of foods linked to religious and cultural festivals that can be made with children include:

- vegetarian foods, such as dahl and chappattis, which can be made with children to celebrate the start of Guru Nanak's travels, as part of the Sikh festival of Baisakhi;

- pancakes are traditionally made on Shrove Tuesday, the day before the start of Lent, the Christian period of forty days leading up to Easter, which Jesus spent in the wilderness;
- coconut barfi (similar to coconut ice) is traditionally offered at the Hindu Raksha Bandhan festival of protection and care between siblings and close friends.

Activity 3.10

Try making gluten-free playdough suitable for use with children who are coeliac. (The recipe can be found in Unit 5.)

 LINKS TO UNIT FIVE, page 204.

Activity 3.11

What other cooking ideas can you come up with?

Persona dolls

A set of dolls have been developed to represent children with a range of disabilities, and children from a variety of cultures. They are called **Persona dolls**, and they are introduced to children by an adult who also introduces the Persona doll's background or their 'special story', which covers their disability, and the situation that brings them to the nursery or classroom, for example as part of a family seeking asylum. This can lead to children discussing and exploring the difficulties that are sometimes faced by others, considering the bias that can be experienced and the hurt that can be felt.

A Persona doll can be provided for any individual need and is an ideal way of encouraging children to accept diversity and pave the way for a new child to settle and integrate easily into the group or class.

Remember! Children need to learn how to value and include others. It is important that you give guidance, and offer suggestions to help their understanding, rather than criticism. The responses and thinking that they learn from home may at times be unacceptable within the setting, and therefore tact is needed in helping parents understand the importance of good (inclusive) practice too.

Raisa

Raisa is Turkish and is new to your school. She is learning English as a second language, and at home and with her friends outside of school she speaks mainly Turkish.

Raisa tries hard in school, and copes very well, but is getting upset by children who laugh at the way she pronounces some of her words.

How could the use of a Persona doll have helped pave the way for easier acceptance of Raisa and her heritage by the other children?

Meeting specific needs in a child care setting

This section of the unit focuses on children with a variety of additional needs, due to differing reasons. It will be helpful to understand a little about genetics, as some of these needs are due to **genetic inheritance**.

Genetic effects on development

Definitions

Genotype
The term genotype is used to describe the complete genetic inheritance of one person.

Phenotype
The term phenotype refers to the visible arrangement of the characteristics that a person has inherited, such as a person's blue eyes, red hair and so on.

Genetic inheritance

The usual number of chromosomes in each of the body's cells is forty-six, with the exception of the sex cells (the sperm and the egg), which have only twenty-three chromosomes each. Male chromosomes are made up of one X and one Y, whereas female chromosomes are made up of two Xs. Conception takes place when the male sperm fertilises the female egg (ovum) and implants itself into the wall of the uterus, using one chromosome from the reproductive cell of each partner. This enables the sex of the conceived child to be determined. Therefore:

$$XY = a\ boy \qquad XX = a\ girl$$

The human body is a complex machine built from its basis of forty-six chromosomes. Each chromosome is made up of thousands of genes and our genetic inheritance is determined by the influences and combination of the genes present in the chromosomes of our parents.

Causes and effects of different conditions

Physical disabilities and learning disorders can occur for a variety of reasons. Some are genetically inherited (caused by the genes of our parents), while some are congenital (they are existing at birth, but are not due to our parents' genes). Both can place limitations on development and require additional support from carers.

Genetically inherited disorders

Genetically inherited disorders can be transferred to an infant in three different ways:

- **autosomal recessive transference**;
- **autosomal dominant transference**;
- **X-linked transference**.

Autosomal recessive disorder can occur when both parents are carriers of the defective recessive gene. There is a 1-in-4 chance of offspring being affected, and a 2-in-4 chance of them being carriers. Autosomal recessive disorders include Batten's disease, cystic fibrosis, phenylketonuria (PKU), sickle-cell anaemia and thalassaemia.

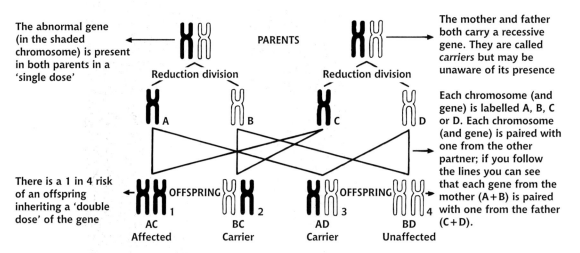

The abnormal gene (in the shaded chromosome) is present in both parents in a 'single dose'

PARENTS

The mother and father both carry a recessive gene. They are called *carriers* but may be unaware of its presence

Reduction division   Reduction division

A   B   C   D

Each chromosome (and gene) is labelled A, B, C or D. Each chromosome (and gene) is paired with one from the other partner; if you follow the lines you can see that each gene from the mother (A + B) is paired with one from the father (C + D).

There is a 1 in 4 risk of an offspring inheriting a 'double dose' of the gene

OFFSPRING 1   2   OFFSPRING 3   4

AC   BC   AD   BD
Affected   Carrier   Carrier   Unaffected

A defective recessive gene

Note: The following descriptions of conditions you may come across during your career are based on *A–Z of Syndromes and Inherited Disorders* (see References and suggested further reading on page 000).

Batten's disease – a summary:

- there are four different types of this condition;
- progressive mental and physical deterioration is seen;
- convulsions are suffered;
- eventual loss of vision is usual;
- life span is usually less than ten years.

Cystic fibrosis – a summary:

- the most commonly found inherited disorder in the UK;
- a sticky mucus is produced in many of the infant's organs;
- obstruction of the bowel is often found soon after birth;

- the lungs and pancreas are particularly affected;
- a high calorie diet is recommended;
- an enzyme supplement is given shortly before each meal to help with the absorption of nutrients;
- lung problems are the most serious aspect;
- physiotherapy (percussion therapy) is needed regularly throughout the day to keep the lungs clear;
- life span is often around twenty years, depending on severity, but this is increasing with improved treatments.

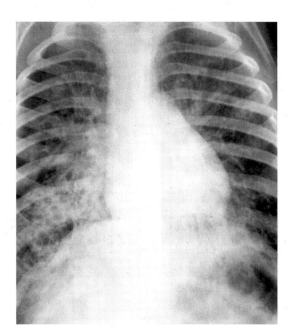

Lungs affected by cystic fibrosis

Phenylketonuria (PKU) – a summary:

- caused by a build-up of the amino acid, phenylalanine;
- a routine test called the Guthrie test carried out on all newborn infants can detect PKU;
- a special diet must be adhered to prevent the following symptoms
  - severe vomiting in the earliest days following birth
  - convulsions occasionally occur
  - skin can be dry and have the appearance of eczema
  - learning disability is moderate to severe;
- life span and intellect is usually normal if the very restricted diet is adhered to for life.

Sickle-cell anaemia – a summary:

- a life-long condition;

- seen in people of Mediterranean countries, African-Caribbean people and in some Asian and Middle Eastern people
- first signs are seen at about 6 months old with swelling of bones on hands and feet;
- it involves an abnormality of the oxygen-carrying substance in red blood cells;
- the shape of the cells becomes changed (sickle shaped) and causes severe pain;
- anaemia is a common and an ongoing problem;
- problems with an enlarged spleen can occur;
- bone infections and enuresis (bed-wetting) are common problems.

Normal and sickle red blood cells

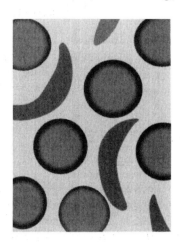

Thalassaemia – a summary:
- a life-long condition;
- two different types of the condition, alpha and beta;
- first signs seen between 3 and 6 months;
- symptoms include anaemia, lack of interest in feeding and vomiting after feeds;
- jaundice is common due to a faster breakdown of the red blood cells;
- enlarged liver and spleen are often a problem;
- diabetes can also occur;
- life expectancy can be shorter in individuals severely affected by the condition.

Autosomal dominant disorder occurs when the carrier is also affected by the disorder themselves. If one parent is an affected carrier there is a 2-in-4 chance of the offspring also being affected. If both parents are affected carriers the incidence rises to a 3-in-4 chance. Autosomal dominant disorders include Huntington's chorea (which does not show symptoms until middle age), Marfan syndrome and osteogenesis imperfecta (brittle bones).

Dominant inheritance

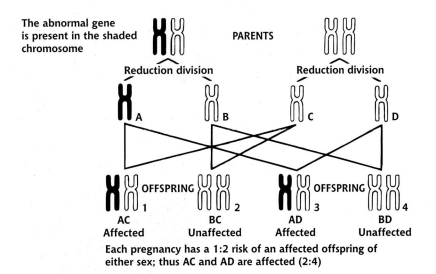

Each pregnancy has a 1:2 risk of an affected offspring of either sex; thus AC and AD are affected (2:4)

Marfan syndrome – a summary:

- children are extremely tall;
- long limbs are in proportion to their tall bodies;
- fingers and toes are often particularly long;
- problems with the spine often occur (scoliosis);
- rounded shoulders can also occur (kyphosis);
- dislocated joints are common as joints can be very weak and flexible;
- in a small number of children joints are particularly stiff (contracted);
- a deformed chest is common;
- poor vision, short sightedness and detached retinas are common;
- problems with the aorta (large artery from the heart) result in a life span reduced to middle age in many sufferers;
- normal intellect is usual, although visual problems may make learning more difficult.

Osteogenesis imperfecta (brittle bones) – a summary:

- small bones are particularly fragile and prone to fracture;
- spinal deformities can occur (scoliosis and kyphosis);
- problems occur with teeth, which are prone to cracking or breaking;
- problems with the small bones of the inner ear can cause hearing problems;
- bruising occurs easily due to fragile blood vessels associated with the condition.

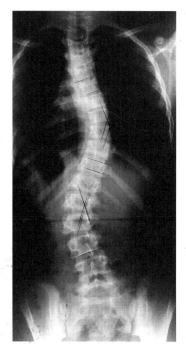

Scoliosis

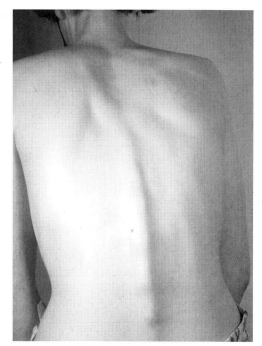

Kyphosis

In the case of **X-linked transference**, the disorders are carried on the X chromosomes of the mother. As the mother has two X chromosomes, the defective X acts in a recessive way in female offspring and a dominant way in males, therefore raising a higher likelihood of male offspring being affected than females. X-linked disorders include Duchenne muscular dystrophy, fragile X syndrome, haemophilia and Lowe's syndrome.

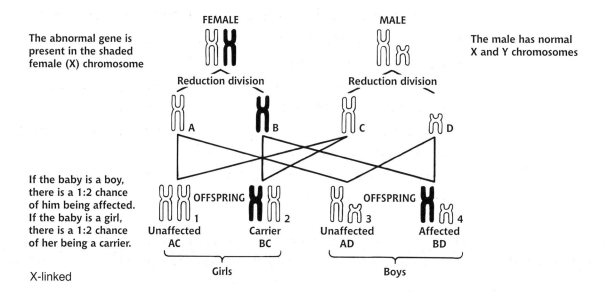

The abnormal gene is present in the shaded female (X) chromosome

FEMALE

MALE

The male has normal X and Y chromosomes

Reduction division

Reduction division

A

B

C

D

If the baby is a boy, there is a 1:2 chance of him being affected. If the baby is a girl, there is a 1:2 chance of her being a carrier.

OFFSPRING

1
Unaffected
AC

2
Carrier
BC

OFFSPRING

3
Unaffected
AD

4
Affected
BD

Girls

Boys

X-linked

Duchenne muscular dystrophy – a summary:

- only boys are affected by the condition;
- first signs are seen at around 18 months old;
- a delay in walking is common;
- falls become increasingly noticeable;
- child will have difficulty in running or climbing due to weakening in the pelvic and leg muscles;
- muscles become increasingly contracted (tight and restrictive);
- this is a progressive condition and boys often need to use a wheelchair by the age of 10 to 12 years;
- chest infections are serious;
- a limited life span usually results from respiratory or heart failure.

Fragile X syndrome – a summary:

- most frequently (and more severely) affects boys;
- girls mostly have a normal level of intelligence;
- boys' intellectual levels can range from severe to just below normal;
- a long, thin face is a usual physical feature;
- large ears and prominent forehead are common in boys;
- life expectancy is normal.

Haemophilia – a summary:

- almost exclusively boys are affected;
- it is a bleeding disorder;
- severe internal bleeding occurs at the slightest knock or injury;
- swelling of joints and bones at the site of injury;
- deformity and pain are common;
- minor surgery (for example dental surgery) can be problematic without special procedures to restrict the blood loss;
- sufferers are particularly susceptible to being infected with hepatitis B, and need to be immunised against it;
- pain killers containing aspirin should not be given as they affect the blood clotting process.

Remember! Aspirin should not be given to any child unless prescribed by a doctor.

Screening in pregnancy

Some conditions can be identified during pregnancy and the process for carrying out these tests is known as **screening**. There are a variety of these antenatal tests that can be carried out. These include the following:

- blood tests;
- ultra-sound scan;
- serum alpha-fetoprotein (SAFP);
- the triple blood test;
- amniocentesis;
- chorionic villus sampling (CVS)

Activity 3.12

Find out about the tests listed above.

1 When are they carried out?
2 How are they carried out?
3 Which groups of women are offered them?
4 What information do the tests provide?

Other commonly found conditions

During a career in Early Years you are likely to work with children with a range of conditions, including some of those summarised above. You are also likely to work with children with:

- Down's syndrome;
- Asperger's syndrome;
- autism;
- cerebral palsy;
- spina bifida.

Down's syndrome – a summary:

- it is an easily identified syndrome at birth;
- children have distinct facial features, which include
  – an upward slant to the eyes
  – an enlarged tongue that often protrudes

    – a shorter than normal neck and slightly smaller head, flattened at the back
    – short, stubby fingers;
- muscle tone is poor; infants with Down's syndrome are very 'floppy';
- physical development is noticeably slower than usual;
- eyesight is often poor;
- congenital heart disease is present in many cases;
- respiratory and ear infections are a common feature, sometimes leading to deafness;
- intellectual development is slow, but can reach the lower levels of normal in some children;
- a life expectancy to around middle age, but occasionally can live to be older.

Children with Down's syndrome are often extremely affectionate

Asperger's syndrome – a summary:
- Asperger's is part of the autistic spectrum;
- the greatest feature of the condition is a lack of interaction with others;
- children tend not to form relationships;
- lack of responses tend to isolate individuals;
- facial expressions tend to be inappropriate;
- body language tends to be stiff;
- communication 'cues' are missed;

- children with Asperger's tend to become obsessed with a specific interest;
- routines can become obsessive and crucial to maintaining normality, with even slight changes causing great distress;
- some individuals have a good level of intellectual ability;
- some individuals are able to live independently and hold down regular employment, but more severely affected individuals need sheltered living facilities.

Autism – a summary:

- this is the most extreme end of the autistic spectrum;
- a child with autism does not seem to need to understand the need to communicate with other people;
- imaginative play is almost non-existent;
- children live in an isolated world;
- delayed speech is common and children play quietly;
- many children with autism also have learning difficulties;
- some children have an above average intellectual ability;
- hand flapping and other repetitive behaviour is common;
- routine is important for security, with great distress shown if routine is changed;
- obsessive interest is shown in minor details of objects, for example, the wheel on a toy car;
- behaviour can be hard to manage, and exhausting for parents and carers;
- a lack of understanding of jokes and humour can lead to comments being taken literally;
- inappropriate social behaviour is common;
- an inability to understand how other people feel is evident in the inappropriate responses often made.

Cerebral palsy – a summary:

- it can occur before birth, due to infection or placenta problems;
- it can occur at birth, following a difficult delivery;
- it can occur immediately after birth, due to head injury or infection;
- the condition is not reversible;
- it does not change in its severity;
- it affects physical movement and limb control;

- speech is often difficult to understand;
- intellectual ability is unaffected;
- physiotherapy and speech therapy are usually offered.

Spina bifida – a summary:

- a failure in the development of the neural tube during pregnancy leads to defects in one or more areas of the vertebrae (the bones in the spine);
- women are advised to increase their intake of folic acid before and during the first months of pregnancy to help prevent neural tube defects occurring;
- minor type (spina bifida occulata) is identified as a dimple or tuft of hair on the lower area of the spine where the vertebrae is not completely joined;
- a slightly more serious version (meningocele) causes a swelling at the lower back allowing spinal tissue to push through a gap in the vertebrae;
- mostly with meningocele the nerves remain undamaged, and therefore disability is minimal;
- the most serious version (myelomeningocele) causes the spinal cord and the meninges (the tissue lining the spinal cord) to push through the gap in the vertebrae;
- with myelomeningocele infection is common due to the membrane breaking;
- also, the individual will be paralysed from the affected part of the vertebrae downwards;
- bowel and bladder problems are common;
- hydrocephalus (water on the brain) is a commonly found additional problem;
- mobility support is needed;
- support in the management of both bowel and bladder is needed;
- varying degrees of learning difficulty are found in individuals with hydrocephalus.

Remember! It is always important to keep clearly in your mind that a child is simply a child. Their specific care needs should not detract from your providing for them as an individual person with the right to enjoy as full a range of activities and experiences as they are able.

Environmental effects on foetal development

Development can be affected even before birth. Examples include the effects of alcohol, smoking and both illegal and (some) prescribed drugs.

A summary of how each of these can affect the unborn child is set out in Unit 8. You may find it useful to refer to that section now.

 LINKS TO UNIT 8, page 334.

Providing appropriate resources for specific needs

Early Years settings caring for children with specific needs need to ensure that they:

- adapt the environment adequately to meet the child's needs;
- provide appropriate resources;
- encourage all children within the setting to become involved with any children with a disability or specific need.

Activity 3.13

How might staff at a setting encourage children to become involved with any children with a disability or specific need?

Adapting the environment

A child with restricted mobility will need a greater area to move about in than children with full mobility. Points to consider include:

- providing plenty of space between activities and tables;
- allowing plenty of space for wheelchairs to turn easily;
- having a table that a child in a wheelchair can use, ensuring integration with others at mealtimes, as well as in play;
- providing suitable seating for a child who needs additional support;
- providing wedges to support a child who needs to lie on their front (prone position);
- providing a mobility stand to support a child who cannot stand unsupported;
- ramps to help independence in using steps into the garden or other areas of the setting;
- lifts (if setting is on more than one floor);
- wide doorways;

- a large toilet to accommodate wheelchairs and walking frames;
- low-level handbasins to encourage independent personal care;
- handrails at child and adult heights where necessary.

To support a child with an autistic spectrum disorder:

- keep the routine as constant as you can;
- try to minimise unnecessary noise and over excitement;
- give opportunities for playing alongside a main group, if group play appears to be overwhelming for them.

To support a child with visual impairment, a constant layout will help them to develop confidence and personal independence. They will also benefit from:

- plenty of natural light;
- plenty of space to move around;
- floors clear of clutter;
- raised edges on surfaces where the enjoyment of activities could become unsatisfactory or floors hazardous, due to objects falling off.

To help visually impaired children identify where they are within the setting or outside, provide:

- textured surfaces at the edge of areas, such as the sand-pit area;
- bright colours or visual clues to help them identify doorways, steps and so on.

'Come on Andy – join in!'

Play equipment and toys – examples

For children with physical difficulties:

- ball pools stimulate the whole body;
- large beanbags offer supported movement;

- soft play areas offer opportunities to explore, reducing risk of injury;
- trikes and other ride-ons with straps for feet;
- trikes with a trailer, to take a friend;
- pushalong toys with additional weighting to aid balance;
- large balancing ball, to lie on and roll.

Activity 3.14

What other examples of toys for children with physical difficulties can you find out about?

For children with sensory loss:

- safety mirrors offering concave and convex reflections;
- sensory balls, quoits etc. made from textured rubbers and plastics;
- Braille blocks, with textured letters and numbers;
- resources offering sound, such as rainmakers, music boxes etc.;
- resources offering visual experiences, such as bubble tubes, wind horses, mobiles;
- resources made from natural materials to help children explore taste, texture etc.

Activity 3.15

What other examples of toys for children with sensory loss can you find out about?

Health and safety in child care settings

Any setting wishing to care for young children must register with the local authority. The exceptions to this are settings such as toddler groups where the parent or carer remains with the child throughout. Criteria for gaining registration is quite extensive and involves agreeing to work to a range of regulations, Acts, guidelines and care standards. These cover the setting up of the provision, and the maintenance of all **health and safety** practice. The regulations are overseen by statutory authorities such as Social Services Inspection and Registration Units (joined with OFSTED from September 2001), Environmental Health Officers, Local Education Authorities and the Health and Safety Executive. They include:

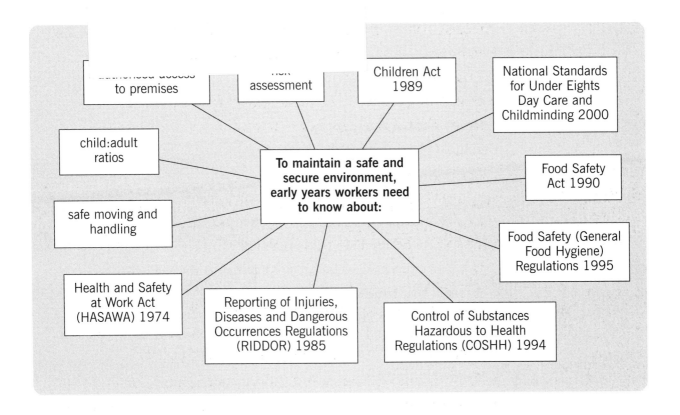

The details of registration criteria are found in the 'Guidance to the National Standards (2000) For Under Eights Care'. There are five versions of these guidelines covering the five main categories of Early Years care. They are:

- full daycare;
- sessional daycare;
- childminding;
- creches;
- out of school care.

Activity 3.16

Copies of the above National Standards Guidance should be in your college library, and will usually be available at your placement too.

1 Arrange to have access to a copy.

2 Compare the similarities and differences between different settings if you can.

3 Why do you think National Standards are so important?

Fire safety

Fire safety is covered within the National Standards. Regarding fire safety in daycare settings (including childminders' homes), the main issues are:

- accessibility of the register;
- suitable places for smoke alarms;
- means of escape from the building;
- the type of heating and any fire/heating guards used;
- the safety of all electrical appliances;
- the storage of any flammable materials;
- means of preventing unsupervised access to the kitchen;
- ensuring that fire exits remain unobstructed;
- responsibility for checking fire exits regularly.

The National Standards also cover health and safety issues such as:

- **adult:child** ratios;
- minimum space requirements;
- maximum numbers of places in a setting;
- toilets and handbasins.

Adult:child ratios

Standard recommended staff:child ratios for the under fives in day care and education settings

Type of setting/Age range	Ratio	Comments
Under 5 years' full day care *0 to 2 years* *2 to 3 years* *3 to 5 years*	1:3 1:4 1:8	Because of management and administration duties, managers or officers-in-charge should not be included in these ratios where more than 20 children are being cared for
Nursery schools and nursery classes	2:20 (minimum)	One adult should be a qualified teacher and one a qualified nursery assistant
Reception classes in primary schools		Where 4-year-olds are attending Reception classes in primary schools, the staffing levels should be determined by the schools and local education authorities

Childminding		All these ratios include the childminder's
Under 5 years	1:3	own children and apply to nannies
5 to 7 years	1:6	employed by more than two sets of parents
Under 8 (no more than three	1:6	to look after their children
being under 5) years		

Day care services for school age		A higher ratio may be necessary if
children		children with special needs are being cared
Where 5- and 7-year-olds are	1:8	for. A lower ratio may be appropriate
cared for on a daily or		for some short sessional facilities not
sessional basis (i.e. care at		lasting the full day
the end of the school day		
and full care in school holidays)		
Where facilities are used by		Providers should ensure that there are
children aged over 8 years		sufficient staff in total to maintain the
as well as under 8 years		1:8 ratio for the under eights.

reproduced by kind permission of The Stationery Office, from The Children Act 1989,
Guidance and Regulations Volume 2, Seventh Impression, 1998

If children with special needs are included in the setting, a higher ratio of staff to children may be necessary, depending on the specific needs of the child or children.

Minimum space requirements

Age of child	Square feet	Square metres
0–2 years	37.7	3.5
2 years	26.9	2.5
3–7 years	24.8	2.3

Maximum numbers of places

No setting is allowed to place more than twenty-six children in one room except for special occasions, such as a Christmas party or a concert. This is regardless of the size of the room. A separate room is always needed for babies and toddlers, adjacent to changing and food preparation facilities.

Toilets and handbasins

Hot and cold running water should always be available.

- Water temperatures in children's handbasins should not exceed 39°C (102°F).
- There should be a minimum of one toilet and one handbasin for every ten children in the setting.
- Staff should have separate toilet and handwashing facilities.

Health and safety at work

Relevant legislation that ensures a healthy and safe environment includes:

- Food Safety Act 1990;
- Food Safety (General Food Hygiene) Regulations 1995;
- Control of Substances Hazardous to Health Regulations (COSHH) 1994;
- Reporting of Injuries, Diseases and Dangerous Occurrences Regulations (RIDDOR) 1985;
- Health and Safety at Work Act (HASAWA) 1974.

The Food Safety Act 1990 and the Food Safety (General Food Hygiene) Regulations 1995

This legislation includes guidelines on both **personal** and general **kitchen hygiene**. It can be summarised as follows:

Personal hygiene
This involves:

- regular hand washing throughout the day;
- washing hands before all food preparation;
- washing hands after any activity with the potential for bacteria
  - nappy changing
  - using the toilet
  - coughing
  - sneezing
  - nose blowing;
- use of antibacterial soaps;
- nails kept clean and short;
- cuts and sores covered;
- use of disposable gloves.

Also:

- hair should be kept tied back to reduce the risk of infestation, cross-infection and general untidiness;
- clean clothing and overalls should be worn at all times, changing as necessary for food preparation and cooking activities;
- covering nose and mouth when coughing and sneezing should be automatic, and needs to be encouraged in children too.

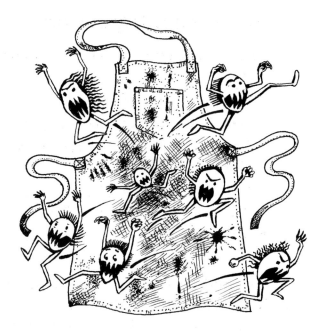

Kitchen hygiene

This involves:

- keeping surfaces cleaned and free from bacteria;
- ensuring all surfaces used are unblemished and not chipped;
- using separate boards for cooked or uncooked foods;
- using separate knives for cooked and uncooked foods;
- keeping floors cleaned thoroughly;
- washing up as dirty utensils occur, to eliminate additional bacteria growth (where possible use a dishwasher as this is the most effective method);
- all waste being wrapped securely and bins emptied regularly;
- regular cleaning and defrosting of refrigerators and freezers;
- ensuring the temperature of a refrigerator is kept at 4–5°C (39–41°F);
- storing cooked foods at the top of the refrigerator, raw foods below;
- minimal handling of all foods;
- keeping food well covered;
- ensuring use-by dates are adhered to;
- any reheated food being served piping hot;
- not keeping food warm for more than a few minutes.

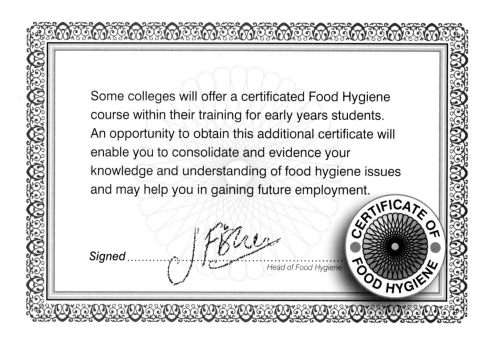

Some colleges will offer a certificated Food Hygiene course within their training for early years students. An opportunity to obtain this additional certificate will enable you to consolidate and evidence your knowledge and understanding of food hygiene issues and may help you in gaining future employment.

Signed .... Head of Food Hygiene

CERTIFICATE OF FOOD HYGIENE

COSHH Regulations: Control of Substances Hazardous to Health Regulations 1994

Health problems such as the irritation of the skin, asthma or similar conditions can occur due to the presence of certain chemicals in some substances. There are a range of symbols drawn up by COSHH that have been devised to warn people in advance of potential hazards. Most of these substances will not be present in Early Years settings, however, bleach and some other cleaning products can cause irritation and respiratory reactions.

In schools chemicals may be used within the context of design technology or art. Although many products are now 'safe', potentially harmful substances include some marbelling inks and spirits for cleaning, and some spray paints and glues. These would usually only be handled by adults, but children may be present during their use. A risk assessment should be carried out by all settings and any potentially hazardous products identified. Relevant information on the storage, use and treatment following spills should be noted.

Remember! Cleaning products should not *at any time* be left where they can be reached by children. Always read the instructions for the use and dilution of any product, and the importance of ventilation when using them.

Activity 3.17

1   Research a range of symbols that warn of potential hazards.

2   Make a note of what products they were found on.

3   Ask permission to look around your current work placement to identify how many potentially 'hazardous' substances there are.

4   Were they all stored appropriately?

5   Were they all recorded on the register following the settings risk assessment?

RIDDOR: Reporting of Injuries, Diseases and Dangerous Occurrences Regulations 1985

These regulations:

- require the reporting of all deaths that occur;
- require the reporting of any injuries that result in a child, a parent or a visitor being taken to hospital from the setting;
- require a telephone report to the local authority.

Reporting also applies to the death or serious injury of a member of staff. If a member of staff is injured (but not seriously) or becomes ill due to their work the local authority should be informed in writing. There is a special form for written reports.

All settings should have an accident book in which they report *all* accidents and incidents, both large and small.

All settings should have an accident book

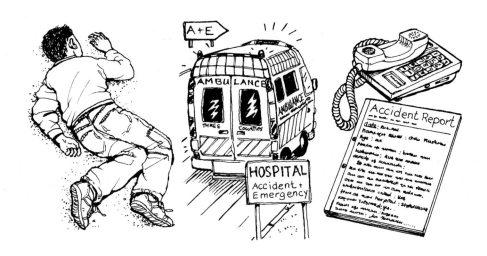

HASAWA: Health and Safety at Work Act 1974

This Act protects employees and anyone else who could be affected by the procedures of a setting. It requires settings to have a safety policy and to assess, and reduce accordingly, the risk of accident or injury.

There should be a written health and safety policy and a named person with responsibility for health and safety in any setting that employs more than five people.

Local authorities can (under the Children Act 1989) ask Early Years settings to produce health and safety policies, irrespective of how many people are employed by the setting.

Activity 3.18

1 Why do you think it is good practice to have a health and safety policy?

2 Who benefits from a health and safety policy?

3 If you have not done so already, ask to read the health and safety policy next time you are in a placement and make a note of all areas of safety and health that it covers.

4 How does it compare with your own ideas? What else would you include in a health and safety policy?

Remember! The policy should be available for parents to read if they so wish. All staff and students should be asked to read the health and safety policy.

Health and safety during outdoor activities

When providing outdoor play space it is important that suitable play surfaces are used. Concrete, gravel and similar surfaces are not suitable because they do not absorb the impact if a child falls, often resulting in serious injury. A more suitable surface for general play is grass, but during dry summer months this will also become hard and unyielding.

It is particularly important that any surface under and around climbing or play equipment from which a child may fall a distance of 60 cm (2 ft) or more should be able to absorb some of the impact of the fall, reducing the risk of serious injury. Impact-absorbing playground surfaces include:

- loose-fill substances such as tree bark or sand (at least 30 cm/1 ft deep);
- 'wet pour' rubber, which sets to form a spongy surface;
- thick rubber tiles.

All surfaces should meet the safety standard BSEN 1177. They should be kept in good condition, with any damage repaired. Sand or tree bark should be raked regularly to remove any debris or animal excrement.

All surfaces should meet the safety standard BSEN 1177

Outings

The destination of any outing with young children should be suitable for the age group, ensuring that there is no open water that will seriously restrict children's freedom. Adult to child ratios need to be higher than when indoors:

Age of child	Adult:child ratio
0–2 years	1:1
2–5 years	1:2
5–8 years	1:5

The adult in charge of an outing should ensure that:

- an accurate register is with them at all times;
- the register is checked regularly throughout the day;
- written parental consent has been given;
- all adults understand their role and responsibilities;
- adults know which children they are responsible for;
- a small emergency first aid kit is readily available;
- arrangements for calling for emergency services are made;
- identification badges for children have *only* the name of their school, nursery or pre-school on it, not the children's own names.

Activity 3.19

1 Why is it important not to have a child's name on their identification badge?

2 Why are adult:child ratios higher when on outings?

3 Why are parental consent forms important?

Case Study

Fatima

Fatima is planning to take her nursery and after school club to the zoo for their summer outing. There will be twenty children between the ages of 2 and 5 years, and ten children between the ages of 5 and 8 years.

They will be going on a coach, and taking lunch with them.

1 How many adults will Fatima need to accompany her on the trip?

2 What will she need to arrange in advance?

3 What will she need to take with her on the day?

Provision of food and drink in any setting

All food preparation must adhere to the guidelines of the Food Safety Act 1990 and The Food Safety (General Food Hygiene) Regulations 1995. Unit 2 offers a discussion of nutrition and meeting dietary needs. You may find it helpful to refer back to that section.

LINKS TO UNIT 2, page 45.

Toileting

Every effort should be made to encourage children to develop independence in the bathroom. They also have a right to privacy, within sensible boundaries of supervision.

Potties should be safely and hygienically stored, and cleaned thoroughly after each use.

Each setting should have a policy regarding:

- who is allowed to change babies' nappies;
- who is allowed to supervise in the bathroom;
- the wearing of disposable gloves;

- the safe disposal of nappies, baby wipes etc.;
- the safe disposal of cleaning materials;
- the sending home of soiled clothing.

Cleaning of the environment

This includes both the setting itself and the equipment and furnishings within it:

- **cleaning of the environment** should take place at the end of each session, or day;
- cleaning should also take place as necessary throughout the day;
- carpeted floor surfaces should be easily cleaned with a vacuum cleaner;
- washable non-slip surfaces should be cleansed with a mop (disinfected daily);
- suitable anti-bacterial products should be used regularly to cleanse all surfaces;
- toys and activities should be cleaned with anti-bacterial products regularly;
- the cleansing of surfaces is particularly important before any food preparation, cooking activities or before snacktime;
- there is usually a rota of staff to ensure that the setting is kept clean and hygienic at all times.

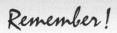 *Remember!* Staff should not be carrying out cleaning duties while still responsible for supervising children.

Cleaning of consumable materials

For example:

- sand should be sieved daily to remove any 'bits', and cleansed regularly;
- any sand that has been spilt on the floor should be sieved and cleansed before returning to the sand tray or else discarded;
- outdoor sand-pits should be kept securely covered when not in use to prevent fouling by animals, and rubbish and garden debris gathering;
- water should be replenished daily, and water trays cleaned and disinfected regularly;

- pets should be kept scrupulously clean, following normal petcare routines;
- dough should be renewed regularly and stored in a refrigerator;
- dough should be discarded and replaced following any infectious illness in the setting to avoid repeated cross-infection.

All pets should be kept scrupulously clean

Health and safety during everyday activities

As you read through Unit 5, you will find references to health and safety issues as appropriate to individual activities. Some general points regarding health and safety are set out below.

Ensuring that the physical environment of an Early Years setting is safe and secure includes giving consideration to:

- the layout of the setting;
- the space available;
- the furniture and fixtures and their positioning;
- the mobility of the children, taking into account any specific physical needs;
- the safety of all toys, activities and equipment;

It also includes the heating, lighting, ventilation and ease of cleaning of the equipment and the setting itself.

The layout of the setting needs to allow sufficient space for:

- children to play in groups;

- children to use the floor;
- differentiated use of the rooms for quiet activities, messy activities, active play etc.;
- displaying children's creativity, both two-dimensional and three-dimensional;
- storing equipment and activities, allowing access to some items by the children;
- moving safely between activities;
- safe evacuation of the building in an emergency;
- rearranging activities and equipment without undue disruption to the setting;
- staff to oversee activities in general while involved in other areas of the room.

Furniture and fixtures

- All cupboards, shelving and any other permanent storage must be securely held in place, and any doors should close firmly and remain closed when not in use.
- Access to storage should not interrupt play, or be hazardous to children playing.

Storage should be easy to access and clearly labelled

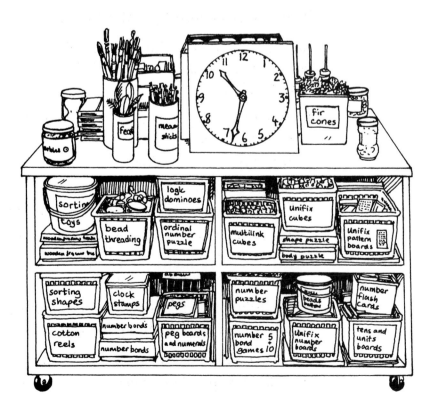

- Mobile storage needs to be stacked carefully, avoiding overloading or the risk of items falling.
- Furniture should be child sized.
- Ideally, tables that can combine to extend or alter shape should be used.
- Furniture should be sturdy, and be kept in good condition.
- Wooden chairs should be checked regularly for splinters and plastic moulded chairs examined for any cracks.
- All surfaces used by the children should be hygienic and in good condition.

Mobility of children

- The layout of a setting needs to take into account the mobility needs of the children it caters for.
- Baby rooms will need a significant area of floor space to encourage mobility and floor play with staff.
- Children with a physical need may require larger spaces between activity areas to accommodate a wheelchair, walking frame or support from an adult.
- In a setting caring for a child who is blind or severely visually challenged, a familiar layout will allow them a degree of autonomy and independence.

Safety of toys, activities and equipment

- All equipment used in Early Years settings should be made to a recognised safety standard. The chart below shows an up-to-date range of safety marks.

Heating

- Room temperatures must be between 18–20°C (65–68°F).
- A wall thermometer should be on display and checked regularly.
- Whenever possible, radiators should be controlled by thermostats.
- Fire guards or heater guards should be fitted where necessary.

Lighting

- Natural light is important to avoid headaches and eye strain.
- Lighting must be adequate for safe working practice.
- Accidents are more likely to occur in poorly lit settings.

Safety marks

Mark	Name	Meaning
	BSI Kitemark	Indicates a product has met a British safety standard and has been independently tested
	Lion Mark	Indicates adherence to the British Toy and Hobby Association Code of Practice and ensures a product is safe and conforms to all relevant safety information
	Age Warning	Indicates: 'Warning – do not give the toy to children less than 3 years, nor allow them to play with it Details of the hazard, e.g. small parts, will be near the symbol or with the instructions
	BEAB Mark of the British Electrotechnical Approvals Board	Indicates that electrical appliances carrying this mark meet a national safety standard
	BSI Safety Mark on gas appliances, light fittings and power tools	Indicates the product has been made and tested to a specific safety standard in accordance with the British Standards Institute
	Safety Mark on upholstered furniture	Indicates upholstery materials and fillings have passed the furniture cigarette and match tests – a lighted cigarette or match applied to the material will not cause the article to burst into flames
	Low Flammability labels	Children's pyjamas, bathrobes made from 100% Terry towelling and clothes for babies up to 3 months old must carry a label showing whether or not the garment has passed the Low Flammability Test. Either of these two labels is acceptable. Always look for these labels when choosing such garments.
	Keep Away From Fire label	Indicates the garment is not slow burning and has probably not passed the Low Flammability Test. Great care must be taken anywhere near a fire or flame

Ventilation

- Children and staff work best within a well-ventilated environment.
- Good ventilation lessens opportunities for cross-infection.
- Ventilation points need to be kept well cleaned, as they can easily attract dirt and a build-up of bacteria.

Potential hazards in Early Years settings

There are many **potential hazards** for young children, as they do not understand fear, or recognise danger in the earliest years when they are most vulnerable. As they get older, they often have a false idea of their own capabilities, with interest and daring exceeding physical strength, judgement and ability.

Activity 3.20

Choose one of the following options:

1 With a partner, draw a large outline of a house with a garden.
2 With a partner, draw a large outline of a nursery or classroom setting.
3 With a partner, draw a large outline of a children's playground.

   a) Draw (or indicate in writing) a range of the usual items you would find in your chosen setting.

   b) What potential hazards can you identify?

   c) How could the settings be made safer?

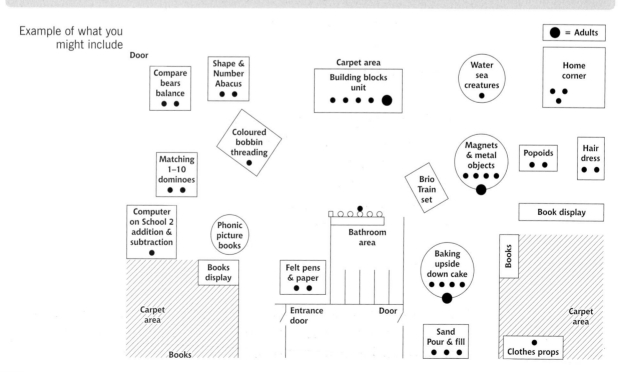

Example of what you might include

126

Basic first aid procedures

Knowledge of first aid is essential in Early Years settings, as the initial actions following an accident or incident can have a significant impact on the eventual outcome. First aid is about limiting the effects of an accident or incident and taking action to aid the recovery of the person concerned. Every Early Years setting is required to have at least one person on duty in the setting at all times who is qualified in emergency first aid procedures. All staff should know who these individuals are and where they can be found. Each first aider needs to be regularly updated and assessed externally, renewing their qualification every three years to ensure that they remain up to date with current thinking, and that they can still remember and carry out **basic first aid procedures**. Knowledge of what a first aid box should contain and how its contents should be monitored is also important.

Individuals working as nannies and childminders should produce a first aid box for themselves and take on the responsibility for arranging to update their first aid qualification at appropriate intervals.

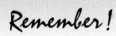 **Remember !** Most people will (thankfully) never have to use the majority of the techniques they learned during their first aid training, but none of us knows when we might have to, so we need to be prepared.

As an Early Years worker you will need to know how to cope with many differing situations, including how to:
- check for signs and symptoms;
- prioritise treatment;
- deal with an unconscious casualty;
- use the ABC procedure;
- deal with allergies and anaphylaxis;
- treat minor and major injuries
  - treat cuts and grazes
  - treat burns and scalds
  - treat fractures and sprains
  - deal with poisoning
  - deal with breathing difficulties
  - deal with foreign bodies
  - treat seizures.

Each of these situations will be covered during your first aid training. Written instruction can also be found in first aid manuals. The illustrations below should also be a useful source of reference.

First aid manuals

First aid manuals are produced by recognised bodies such as the Red Cross and St John Ambulance. If you are taking a first aid course as part of your BTec First in Early Years programme, your college will let you know which you will need to acquire. It is important that you always refer to the most up-to-date edition, as procedures change from time to time, based on new understanding.

Remember! A first aid manual, as with all other written first aid instructions, should never be used as an alternative to attending a recognised training course in first aid.

Administering first aid

The table below sets out the appropriate first aid treatment for a range of accidents and incidents that may occur in an Early Years setting. You should familiarise yourself with each of these.

Injury	Signs	Action
Sprain	Child cannot put weight on the affected ankle May limp or hop Complains of pain	Remove the shoe and sock Raise and support the foot to reduce any swelling Apply a cold compress against it, wrap with cotton wool padding and crêpe bandage. Rest, ice, compression, elevation (RICE) Keep the ankle elevated Call the doctor if the foot may be broken or take to the accident and emergency department at the local hospital
Fracture	Signs depend upon the site of the fracture: • pain • swelling • loss of use of a limb or inability to walk or stand • tenderness increased with movement	Call for the establishment's first-aider to administer first aid depending on the site of the injury Contact the parents Take the child to the accident and emergency department if a fracture is suspected

Injury	Signs	Action
Swelling	May occur after a fall or knock when the injured area expands Compare the affected limb (arm or leg) with the other limb when a swelling will be apparent	Reduce swelling by holding a cold compress against it for 30 minutes Rest Ice Compression Elevation – raise and support the injured part
Splinter	Sharp pain in the hand Limping if in the foot Close inspection will reveal the site, and a small piece of the splinter may protrude through the skin	Wash the area with warm water and soap Use a pair of clean tweezers to remove the splinter Encourage a little bleeding by squeezing the area Inform parents if the splinter cannot be removed
Bruise	Purple-blue coloured areas on the skin – darker on black skin. They fade to yellow before disappearing 10–14 days later Common sites on children are forehead, elbow, knees, shins	Cold compress to prevent further bleeding underneath the skin Bruising in unusual and unexpected areas should be investigated e.g. armpits, back, abdomen, buttocks, inside the thighs, etc
Cuts and grazes	Bleeding	Sit the child down Wash the injured area with water and clean cotton wool or gauze – wipe away from the open wound Apply direct pressure if bleeding will not stop Remove any dirt and gravel carefully Cover the area with a gauze dressing
Poisoning	Child has swallowed poisonous berries or leaves, alcohol, drugs, chemicals or bleach Find out exactly what has been swallowed and how much Keep containers, berries or leaves to show to the doctor	Comfort and reassure DO NOT TRY TO MAKE THE CHILD VOMIT DO NOT GIVE THE CHILD ANYTHING TO DRINK Call the doctor or an accident and emergency (A & E) department Contact the parents. Put the child in recovery position if they are unconscious

Injury	Signs	Action
Bites	Irritation and pain at the site Puncture teeth marks in the skin after an animal bite	Rinse the wound under running water for 5 minutes Wash the area with soap and water Cover the wound with a dry dressing Check that the child is immunised against tetanus
Stings	Sudden cry when the sting occurs May see sting sticking out at the tip of a swollen area Itching Irritation and pain at the site	Carers should remain calm as this will reassure a frightened child Sting may be removed carefully if possible, avoiding pressure on the poison sac Wasp sting – apply dilute vinegar Bee sting – apply bicarbonate of soda Apply cold compress followed by calamine Observe for signs of an allergic reaction
Burns and scalds	Pain Inflamed skin Blistering	Put affected area under cold, running water for 10–15 minutes to cool it. This will also help to reduce pain. Remove clothing when the area has been cooled (remove tight clothes before the area begins to swell) Cover with a clean, soft, non-fluffy cloth, cling film is adequate. These will keep the area cool and prevent infection Take to the A & E department if the burn is larger than a 10 pence piece

Cooling a burn

1 Cool the burn with cold water for at least 10 minutes

2 Remove cooled clothing that is not sticking to the burn
Continue to cool the burn

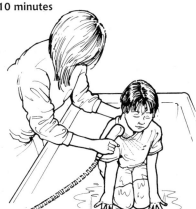
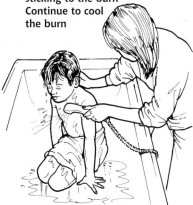

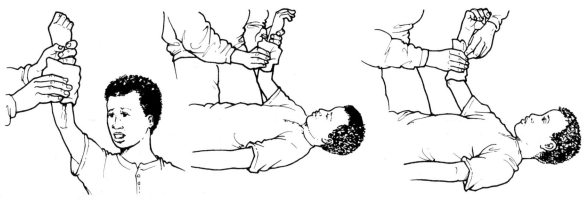

1 Apply pressure to the wound and raise the injured part

2 Lay the child down, while continuing to apply pressure and keep the injured part raised

3 Keeping the injured part raised cover the wound with a firm, sterile dressing and a bandage

Dealing with bleeding

Dealing with a nose bleed

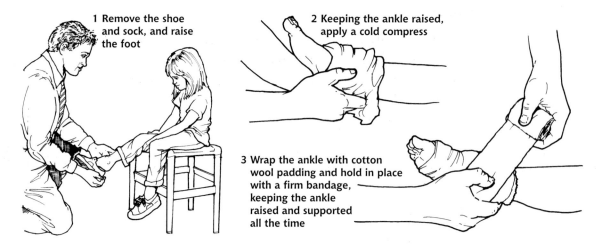

1 Remove the shoe and sock, and raise the foot

2 Keeping the ankle raised, apply a cold compress

3 Wrap the ankle with cotton wool padding and hold in place with a firm bandage, keeping the ankle raised and supported all the time

Dealing with a sprained ankle

Dealing with an emergency

As children's bodies are still developing, it is not always appropriate to use the same techniques for emergency first aid as you would use on an adult as you may injure the child further. In some cases, techniques designed for adults can be extremely dangerous to a young child. For example, tilting the head of a young infant back too far may actually occlude (block) the airway, rather than open it. Similarly, if too much pressure is placed on the soft tissue under the jaw when opening the airway, this may in fact block it.

The following section offers an easily accessible overview of emergency procedures for babies and young children.

Remember ! These procedures should be carried out by a qualified first aider. You will learn the techniques during your first aid training course.

Stage 1

- Review the situation, assessing as far as is possible what has happened.
- Decide what are your immediate priorities.
- Stay calm.
- Consider if there is anyone else who could help you.
- Professional help should be sought unless only a minor injury has occurred (if on your own *shout for help*).
- Whenever possible, any other children present should be reassured and led away.

Stage 2

- Remove any dangers. You will be of little use to the casualty if you become injured yourself. Ask yourself:
  - Is it safe to proceed with first aid? For example:
  - Is the fire out?
  - Is the electricity turned off?

> *Remember !* You should not be putting yourself in unnecessary danger too.

Stage 3

- Assess the casualty for any response. It must be remembered that with very young children, inability to speak will not automatically mean they are unconscious. They may still be in the pre-verbal stage of their development. Consider:
  - Is the child moving?
  - Have they opened their eyes?
  - Have they given a verbal response, a cry, moan or any other vocalisation?
  - If no response is obtained it is likely that they are unconscious.
  - You will need to begin the ABC procedure.

The ABC of resuscitation

> *Remember !* These procedures should only be carried out by a qualified first aider.

A stands for the AIRWAY

The airway needs to be kept clear. If it becomes blocked and the child stops breathing they will soon become unconscious. This will eventually lead to the heart slowing down and stopping due to the lack of oxygen.

Remove any obvious obstructions from the child's mouth, but be aware that a 'blind-sweep' with your finger may block the child's airway further! Ask yourself:

- Is the chest rising and falling?
- Is the tongue well forward?
- Can you hear breathing sounds when your ear is close to the mouth?
- Can you feel the breath on your cheek?
- If not, you will need to open the airway for the child.

To open the airway in a baby:

- place the baby on their back, tilting their head back slightly;
- use one finger under the chin to move it forwards (imagine they are sniffing a flower, and position them accordingly);
- look, listen and feel again for breathing;
- if there is no change you will need to try artificial ventilation (B in the ABC).

Opening a baby's airway

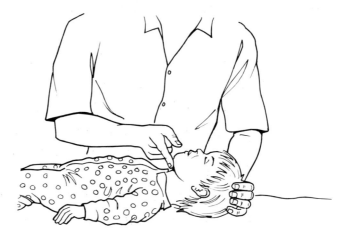

To open the airway in an older child:

- place the child on their back;
- place two fingers under the chin;
- place a hand on the forehead and tilt the head backwards, again ensuring not to tip it too far;
- look, listen and feel again for breathing;
- if there is no change you will need to try artificial ventilation (B in the ABC).

Opening a child's airway

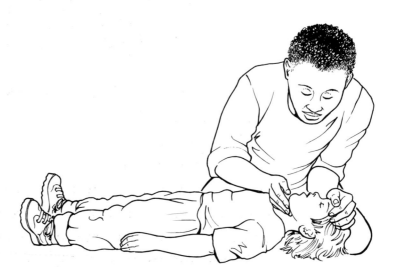

B stands for BREATHING

Have a look at the casualty's tummy. Can you see the child moving? If breathing has stopped, you may need to do this for them. Whenever possible, send someone to call for an ambulance. If you are on your own, perform the following procedure for 1 minute and then go and call an ambulance yourself. If the casualty is a young baby, you may be able to take them with you and continue the breathing procedure for them.

Remember! These procedures should only be carried out by a qualified first aider.

To carry out artificial ventilation for a baby:

- open the airway as in A;
- place your lips around the mouth and nose of the baby;
- give five 'rescue' breaths (breaths that are hard enough to make the chest move as though the casualty had taken a deep breath for themselves);
- continue to blow, very gently, at a rate of twenty breaths per minute;
- after each breath, remove your mouth and watch for the chest to fall as the air expires;
- if, after five rescue breaths, you have not been able to establish effective breathing, re-check their mouth and head position and try again.

Artificial ventilation for a baby

To carry out artificial ventilation for an older child:

- open the airway as in A;
- pinch their nostrils together;
- place your lips firmly over the child's mouth;
- as with a baby, give five rescue breaths, then...
- blow gently into the mouth at a rate of twenty breaths per minute;
- again, as with a baby, remove your mouth after each breath and watch the chest fall as the air expires.

Artificial ventilation for a child

Note: The updated UK Resuscitation Council guidelines state that only professionally trained health workers should check the pulse during resuscitation attempts.

C stands for CIRCULATION

The circulation is the beating of the heart, which keeps the blood flowing through the body. The most usual signs of circulation are breathing, coughing or movement. If you cannot see signs of circulation, you will need to start the procedure known as chest compression.

Remember! These procedures should only be carried out by a qualified first aider.

Chest compression for a baby:

- place the tips of your fingers one finger's width below the baby's nipple line;
- press down sharply to between one-third and one-half of the depth of the chest;
- give five compressions per one breath, 100 compressions per minute if working alone.

Chest compression for a baby

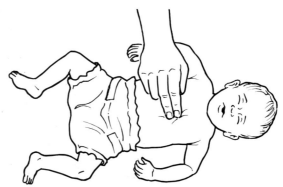

Press on lower breastbone with two fingers

Chest compression for a child:

- use the heel of your hand rather than your fingers;
- press down sharply to between one-third and one-half of the depth of the chest;
- work in cycles of fifteen compressions per two breaths, 100 compressions per minute if working alone.

Chest compression for a child

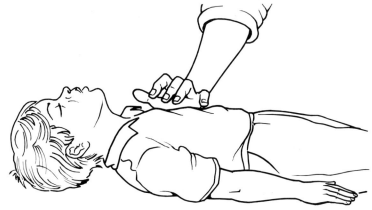

Press on breastbone with heel of hand

Remembering the ABC will enable you to carry out procedures in the right order. The procedure needs to be continued until either the child begins to recover or professional help arrives.

Remember ! It can be dangerous to continue with chest compressions once the casualty has started to recover.

The recovery position

Once a child has begun to breathe for themselves they need to be placed in the recovery position.

The recovery position for a baby

Hold the baby in your arms with their head tilted downwards to help keep the airway open.

The recovery position for a baby

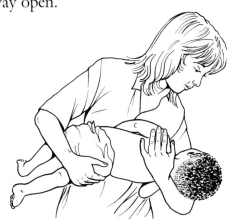

The recovery position for a child

1 Ensure that the airway is open.

2 Bend the arm nearest to you at a right angle. Bring the child's furthest arm across the chest and cushion their cheek with the back of their hand.

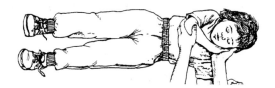

3 Roll the child towards you. Keep the child's hand pressed against their cheek. Bend the outside knee, grasp them under the thigh and, keeping the near leg straight, pull them towards you.

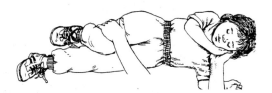

4 Bend the child's top leg at a right angle to the body to keep them on their side and to prevent them from rolling on to their front. Tilt the head back to ensure the airway remains open. Check their head is still cushioned by their hand.

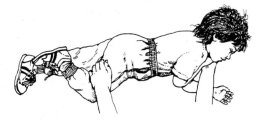

Once a child has been made comfortable in the recovery position they should be closely monitored, and reassured as necessary until professional help arrives.

First aid boxes

Every Early Years setting needs to have a **first aid box**. It is a legal requirement of all employers, under the Health and Safety (First Aid) Regulations of 1981. The container should be both airtight and waterproof and it should be easily recognised – the most usual design is green with a white cross. The box should always include a guidance sheet on emergency first aid. Every setting will have different requirements according to the numbers and needs of its children and staff. The first aid box should be checked regularly and kept in good order by a specified person.

Local policy

In some local authorities there are recommendations not to use certain items, such as plasters and lotions, because of the risk of allergy in some children. Each setting needs to ensure that its first aid box is drawn up in accordance with local policy.

Parental consent forms

Written parental consent is needed regarding emergency treatment for each child. Some parents have cultural or religious beliefs, which will mean they withhold permission for some forms of treatment.

Contents of a first aid box

An employer with ten or more staff is required by law to include the following in its first aid box:

Some of the contents of a first aid box

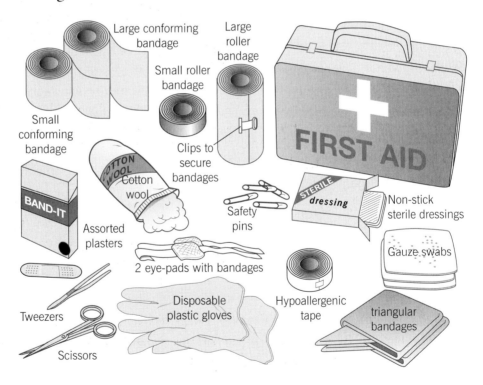

Individually wrapped sterile adhesive dressings (various sizes)	20
Sterile pads	2
Triangular bandages (ideally these should be sterile)	4
Safety pins	6
Individually wrapped unmedicated wound dressings 12×12 cm	6
18×18 cm	2
A pair of disposable gloves	1
First aid guidance leaflet	1

Additional items

An Early Years setting will also need to include additional items such as:

- scissors (kept only for first aid use);
- tweezers;
- several pairs of disposable gloves;
- non-allergic tape;
- non-allergic plasters (if used);
- bandages in various sizes;
- sterile gauze;
- a digital thermometer (never a glass or mercury thermometer);
- a checking sheet for the contents.

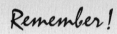

Remember! A specified person (or persons) should be responsible for checking and replenishing the first aid box regularly, and after every use. A checklist of the minimum requirements should be kept in the box. A form should be kept in the box, and be signed and dated after every check and each time the box has been cleaned. All staff should be aware of parents' wishes in the event of emergency treatment for their child.

Other types of emergency

Accidents are only one type of emergency that Early Years workers need to know how to react to. Others include:

- fire;
- suspected or actual gas leaks;
- flooding;
- bomb scares.

A checklist for emergencies

- Each setting should have a clear procedure for evacuating the building.
- All staff should know who and what they are responsible for on evacuation.
- All staff should know where they are to congregate following the evacuation.
- An agreed procedure for ensuring that the emergency services have been called must be established.

- The manager of the setting is likely to take charge, but consideration should be given to what happens if it is the manager who has had the accident!
- Students should not be given responsibility for evacuating children from the setting.
- As a student you should be fully aware of what the emergency procedure involves and where you should go.
- All adults should remain calm and help to reassure the children.
- Emergency exits should be signposted with appropriate symbols.
- Emergency exits should be kept clear at all times.
- Emergency exits should be unlocked (though childproof) and be easily opened from inside.
- Clear instructions for emergency evacuation procedures should be displayed at all times.
- All staff, students and parents should familiarise themselves with the instructions. Where more than one language is spoken in the setting, copies of the procedure should be translated accordingly.

Examples of emergency exit signs

Recognising common childhood illnesses

There are many **common childhood illnesses**. Most last only a short period of time, but can be very unpleasant during the process. Others, such as **meningitis**, are far more serious. Long-term consequences can result from some conditions and the severity of conditions such as measles, particularly in children who have not been immunised, should never be underestimated. In being able to identify some of the common conditions you will be able to help prevent cross-infection of the condition by notifying parents and carers, and arranging to exclude the affected child from the setting.

For additional information on the following conditions, together with a range of other health issues, you may find it helpful to refer to the publication *Child Health. Care of the Child in Health and Illness* (see References and further reading on page 000).

Common childhood illnesses include:

- chickenpox;
- rubella;
- measles;
- mumps;
- hand, foot and mouth;
- coughs and colds;
- gastro-intestinal problems.

Remember! A serious condition that all Early Years workers should know about is meningitis.

Chickenpox	What is chickenpox?	• Chickenpox is an itchy and highly contagious condition, which is spread by droplet infection (tiny droplets of moisture from the nose or mouth of another person). • It causes spots that blister, weep and subsequently crust over.
	What causes chickenpox?	• It is a viral infection called herpes zoster. • The same virus can cause shingles in adults who have previously had chickenpox, if exposed to the virus a second time.
	Recognising chickenpox	• Spots appear in groups, initially on the torso and then more 'groups' of spots appear anywhere on the body over several days. • The spots turn into fluid-filled blisters, which weep and then dry after about 3 days. • As the spots appear in successive groups, they will also dry up in successive groups.

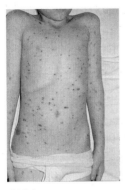

Chickenpox

Initial actions		• Comfort and reassurance are needed. • If initial spots appear in a daycare setting, parents need to be contacted. • Paracetamol is usually given to reduce the discomfort. • Antihistamines can be useful in reducing the irritation. • Calamine (or similar) lotion can be applied to the spots to soothe them. • Using bicarbonate of soda in a cool bath can also help reduce the itching.
Ongoing care		• Paracetamol is usually given as needed, for example to reduce a raised temperature. • Use of calamine and bicarbonate of soda over a few days. • Ensure the child has plenty of fluids and is kept comfortable. • Cut finger-nails short to avoid scratching. • In young babies cotton mittens can be useful.
Possible complications		• Some children have internal spots: nostrils, throat, vagina, anus. • Secondary infections can occur through scratching. • Encephalitis: inflammation of the brain is rare but serious. • Pneumonia: inflammation of the lungs is also rare but serious.
Immunisation?		• None available at present, but a vaccine is currently being developed. • It is important that pregnant women and children and adults with a reduced immunity due to conditions such as leukaemia or HIV are not exposed to the chicken-pox virus.
Incubation period and potential to infect others?		• The incubation period for chicken-pox can be up to 21 days. • Children are infectious for about 3 days prior to the first spots appearing. • They remain infectious until all the scabs have dried over.

Rubella (German measles)	*What is rubella?*	• Rubella is usually only a mild condition in children. • It involves a high temperature and an all-over rash.
	What causes rubella?	• Rubella is passed as a virus through droplet infection.
	Recognising rubella	• The appearance of the rash is usually preceded by a raised temperature. • The all-over pale rash, which usually starts on the face, does not itch. • Glands are often swollen behind the ears and in the neck.
	Initial actions	• Paracetamol to reduce the temperature. • Drinking plenty of fluids should be encouraged.
	Ongoing care	• Avoid contact with women who are or could be pregnant as contact during the first 12 weeks can affect the foetus. • No other special care is needed, and children usually recover quickly.

	Possible complications	• In children and adults there are unlikely to be complications.
		• To an infected foetus, complications can include:
		  – loss of hearing or vision
		  – impaired hearing or vision
		  – heart deformities
		  – learning difficulties.

	Immunisation?	• Rubella vaccine is given as part of the MMR triple vaccine at aged 15 months and 4 years.
	Incubation period and potential to infect others?	• The incubation period for rubella is 14–21 days. • Children are infectious from about 7 days prior to the rash appearing and until 4–5 days afterwards.
Measles	*What is measles?*	• Measles is a highly contagious virus with a distinctive rash. • It can be a very serious condition.
	What causes measles?	• The virus is passed through droplet infection.

Recognising measles	• Children usually appear unwell for 3–4 days before the rash appears. • Runny nose and general cold symptoms are common. • The rash is dense, blotchy and red, usually starting on the neck and face before spreading down over the whole body. • White spots form inside the mouth, on the cheeks (Koplik's spots). • Eyes become sore and an avoidance of bright lights is common.
Initial actions	• Paracetamol should be given to reduce the raised temperature. • Plenty of fluids should be encouraged. • Children would only be visited by a GP in exceptional circumstances, but in most health authorities will usually be seen by a health visitor to confirm diagnosis, and referred to the GP if necessary. • Children will normally be most comfortable resting with curtains closed to reduce the light.
Ongoing care	• Paracetamol as necessary. • Continued high fluid intake.
Possible complications	• Eye infections may need antibiotics. • Ear infections may need antibiotics. • Hearing needs to be checked within a few weeks of illness if ears were affected. • Inflammation of the brain can occur (encephalitis).
Immunisation?	• Measles vaccine is given as part of the MMR triple vaccine at age 18 months and 4 years.
Incubation period and potential to infect others?	• The incubation period for measles is 8–14 days. • Children are infectious from the day before the symptoms appear until 4–5 days afterwards.

Mumps	*What is mumps?*	• Mumps is an inflammation of the salivary glands. • These are found in front of and below the ears. • It can be a very painful condition.
	What causes mumps and how is it spread?	• It is caused by a virus and is spread by droplet infection.
	Recognising mumps	• Initially children feel unwell for 2 or 3 days before the swelling occurs. • Swelling and tenderness occurs on either or both sides of the face. • A raised temperature is usual. • Earache is common. • Eating and drinking can cause pain due to restricted movement of the jaw.
	Initial actions	• Paracetamol to reduce the temperature. • Drinking plenty of fluids should be encouraged (using a straw might be helpful).
	Ongoing care	• Timing paracetamol to be given shortly before meals will help pain when eating. • Easy-to-eat foods should be offered such as soup, jelly or stewed fruits.
	Possible complications	• Hearing loss or even deafness. • Meningitis – inflammation of the meninges. • Orchitis – inflammation of the testes (unusual in young children).
	Immunisation?	• Mumps vaccine is given as part of the MMR triple vaccine at 15 months and 4 years. • Having the condition provides the body with natural immunity
	Incubation period and potential to infect others?	• The incubation period for mumps is 14 to 21 days. • Children continue to be infectious for several days after the symptoms have appeared.

Hand, foot and mouth disease	What is hand, foot and mouth?	• This is a mild, but highly infectious condition, which is common in children of pre-school age. • It is in no way connected to foot and mouth disease found in cattle and other hoofed animals.
	What causes hand, foot and mouth?	• It is a viral condition spread by droplet infection. • The virus is called coxsackie.
	Recognising it	• A child's temperature may be raised slightly. • Very small blisters are often found inside the cheeks, which may ulcerate. • Blistery spots with a red surrounding edge appear about 2 days after the mouth blisters on hands and fingers, and tops of feet.
	Initial actions	• Paracetamol to reduce the raised temperature. • Plenty of fluids: avoid anything that might irritate the sore mouth. • Foods suitable for a slightly sore mouth should be offered.
	Ongoing care	• Prolonged mouth blisters may require an appointment with the GP.
	Possible complications	• No real complications noted.
	Immunisation?	• There is no immunisation available for hand, foot and mouth disease.
	Incubation period and potential to infect others?	• There is no known incubation period.

Case Study

Russell

Russell is six and is in the Year 2 class at your placement. He was not his usual bright and cheerful self this morning and did not run around at playtime as he usually would. Russel is now running a raised temperature and has a pale rash on his face. He says his ears hurt and his neck feels lumpy.

1 What do you think might be wrong with Russell?

2 How should he be cared for?

3 Might there be any long-term health problems linked to Russell's illness?

4 If yes, what might they be?

Coughs and colds	What are coughs and colds?	• Coughs and colds can vary from the very mild to quite severe. • They can be highly contagious.
	What causes coughs and colds?	• Coughs and colds are caused by viral infections. • They are passed through droplet infection. • Coughs can also be part of another condition, such as bronchitis or pneumonia.
  Coughs and colds are caused by viral infections	Recognising them	• Colds usually start with a raised temperature and runny nose and eyes. • Accompanying coughs can be dry and ticklish, or deep and chesty.
	Initial actions	• Paracetamol to reduce the raised temperature. • Plenty of fluids should be offered.
	Ongoing care	• Continued paracetamol as necessary.
	Possible complications	• Ear infections may require antibiotics. • Chest infections may require antibiotics.
	Immunisation?	• There is no immunisation for the common cold.
	Incubation period and potential to infect others?	• Each cold virus is unique and so there is no known incubation period.
Gastro-enteritis	What is gastro-enteritis (vomiting and diarrhoea)?	• Gastro-enteritis is the most common irritant of the stomach and intestinal lining.
	What causes gastro-enteritis?	• It is caused by bacteria and viruses. • It can be passed in food due to poor hygiene during food handling. • It can be passed by direct or indirect contact.

Recognising it	• Children appear unwell, lethargic and miserable before the onset of the main symptoms, which include: — vomiting — diarrhoea — raised temperature — loss of appetite.
Initial actions	• Only clear fluids (cooled boiled water) should be given for 24 hours. • Re-hydration drinks may be used for children over the age of 1 year, particularly if symptoms are severe.
Ongoing care	• Breast-fed babies should continue to breast feed as usual. • If there is no improvement after 24 hours, medical advice should be sought, particularly in very young children. • Continue with clear fluids, together with 'ice-pops' to give the child some sugar. • Light foods should be offered when appetite returns. • Diet drinks are not considered to be suitable for children.
Possible complications	• Dehydration can easily occur in very young children and babies. • If children cease to pass urine frequently medical advice should be sought. • Intravenous fluids may need to be given in severe cases.
Immunisation?	• There is no immunisation available.
Incubation period and potential to infect others?	• Strict hygiene is needed to try and minimise the spread of infection. • Gastro-enteritis often 'sweeps' through families, nurseries and schools.

Meningitis

What is meningitis?

- Meningitis is an inflammation of the protective covering of the brain and spinal cord. This is known as the meninges.

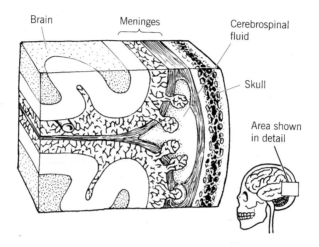

Brain   Meninges   Cerebrospinal fluid

Skull

Area shown in detail

The meninges cover the brain and spine

What causes meningitis and how is it spread?

- Meningitis can be caused by different organisms, and can be either viral or bacterial.
- Bacterial meningitis is always the more serious type.

Recognising meningitis

- Symptoms for both viral and bacterial meningitis are similar in the early stages.
- In babies:
  - high temperature
  - drowsy and irritable
  - vomiting
  - crying and restless
  - fontanelles may bulge in a very young baby due to pressure inside the skull
- In children:
  - headache
  - vomiting
  - averting eyes from the light (photophobia)
  - a stiff neck (the muscles become rigid making it difficult for the neck to be moved forward towards the chin).
- Particularly important:
  - in bacterial meningitis the symptoms will rapidly increase and the child will quickly become very ill
  - septicaemia may develop (infection of the blood)
  - the septicaemia rash looks like bruising appearing

	– the septicaemia rash is flat with dark, purple or pink spots – the septicaemia rash does not fade or disappear when pressed (try this with a glass) – the development of the septicaemia rash is an extreme emergency.
Initial actions	• Always call an ambulance if meningitis is suspected or take child to hospital yourself if this is quicker. • Keep child in a darkened room until emergency services arrive. • Reassure the child as best you can and try to reduce their temperature.
Ongoing care	• Intravenous antibiotics will be given by doctor or hospital staff. • A lumbar puncture (cerebrospinal fluid taken from the spinal canal through a fine hollow needle) is carried out to check that the condition is meningitis, and to identify the correct type of the condition.
Possible complications	• There are not usually any complications with viral meningitis. Bacterial meningitis can cause deafness, brain damage, epilepsy and, in some cases, death.
Immunisation?	• Vaccinations are only available against bacterial forms of meningitis. • Haemophilus influenzae type b (Hib) and meningitis C is given to infants as part of the infant screening programme. • Meningitis C vaccine is offered to teenagers and young adults who have not benefited from the introduction of the infant screening programme.
Incubation period and potential to infect others?	• The incubation for meningitis can vary between 2 and 10 days. • At times local communities are screened for signs of meningitis following an outbreak. This usually involves throat swabs and prophylactic antibiotics (used as a preventive measure). On occasions schools, pre-schools etc. may close temporarily to avoid further risk of infection.

The immunisation programme

Age	Immunisation	Method
2 months	HiB and meningitis C Diphtheria, whooping cough and tetanus Polio	1 injection 1 injection By mouth
3 months	HiB and meningitis C Diphtheria, whooping cough and tetanus Polio	1 injection 1 injection By mouth
4 months	HiB and meningitis C Diphtheria, whooping cough and tetanus Polio	1 injection 1 injection By mouth
12–15 months	Measles, mumps and rubella (MMR)	1 injection
3–5 years: pre-school booster MMR booster	Diphtheria and tetanus Polio Measles, mumps and rubella	1 injection By mouth 1 injection
11–14 years	BCG (Bacillus Calmette-Guerin) vaccine to protect against TB (tuberculosis). All chidren are Heaf-tested first to check their immunity.	1 injection
15–18 years: leaving school booster	Diphtheria and tetanus Polio	1 injection By mouth

Key terms

You should now understand the following key words and phrases. If you do not, read through the chapter again and review them.

ABC of resuscitation
adapting the environment to meet a
   child's needs
adult:child ratios
autosomal dominant transference
autosomal recessive transference
basic first aid procedures

Children Act 1989
cleaning the environment
common childhood illnesses
contents of a first aid box
culture
custom
Disability Discrimination Act

discrimination	Persona dolls
diversity	personal hygiene
equal opportunities	positive and negative messages
equality	potential hazards
festival	prejudice
fire safety	religion
genetic inheritance	rights
genetically inherited disorders	role model
health and safety	screening
Human Rights Act	SENCO
kitchen hygiene	stereotyping
meningitis	tokenism
National Standards for Under Eights Day Care and Childminding	UN Convention on the Rights of the Child
parent consent forms	x-linked transference

Test Yourself

1 What do the words equality, diversity and rights mean?

2 What is the UN Convention on the Rights of the Child 1989?

3 What is a SENCO, and what is their role in Early Years settings?

4 If you add power to prejudice, what is the likely outcome?

5 Which religion celebrates the festivals Tu B'Shevat and Sukkot?

6 Which religion celebrates the festivals Navaratri and Diwali?

7 Name three food customs, each from a different culture.

8 What is tokenism?

9 What is a Persona doll?

10 What do the terms genotype and phenotype mean?

11 Give at least three examples of genetically inherited disorders.

12 What is the more common name for the condition osteogenesis imperfecta?

13 What screening tests during pregnancy can you name?

14 What is the 'autistic spectrum'?

15 What causes foetal alcohol syndrome, and how does it affect children?

16 What five categories of care are covered by the National Standards (2000) for Under Eights Care?

17 What range should room temperatures be between in Early Years settings ?

18 What do the initials ABC stand for when administering emergency first aid?

19 With which common childhood illness do you associate Koplik's spots?

20 With bacterial meningitis, what does the dark purplish rash indicate and how can it be recognised from other rashes?

References and suggested further reading

Dare, A and O'Donovan, M (1997) *Good Practice in Caring for Young Children with Special Needs*, Nelson Thornes

— (2000) *Good Practice in Child Safety*, Nelson Thornes DfEE (2001) *Special Educational Needs. Code of Practice*

Gilbert, P (2000) *A–Z of Syndromes and Inherited Disorders* (3rd edn), Nelson Thornes

Keene, A (1999) *Child Health. Care of the Child in Health and Illness*, Nelson Thornes

Malik, H (2002) *A Practical Guide to Equal Opportunities* (2nd edn), Nelson Thornes

Nursery World (1999) *All About Celebrations: Activity Book*, TES

Pre-School Learning Alliance (1996) *Equal Chances: Eliminating Discrimination and Ensuring Equality in Pre-schools* (revised edn), PLA

Sadek, E and Sadek, J (1996) *Good Practice in Nursery Management*, Nelson Thornes

The Caroline Walker Trust (1998) *Eating Well For Under-5s in Child Care*

Websites

www.cwt.org.uk

www.hse.gov.uk

www.toy-tia.org

www.babycentre.co.uk

www.specialneeds.co.uk

www.downsed.org

www.medinfo.co.uk

www.netdoctor.co.uk

Intellectual and communication skills

This unit covers:

- Sensory and intellectual development
- Language and communication skills development
- Activities to promote development
- The role of the Early Years worker

As well as physical growth and development, which can be observed and measured quite easily, children develop their knowledge and understanding too. This is often referred to as intellectual (or **cognitive**) development. The development of knowledge and understanding is closely linked with the development of language and communication skills, and it involves the senses too.

Sensory and intellectual development

Sensory development

Definitions

Perception
Feedback of information through the senses.

At birth, the infant's nervous system is incomplete and understanding their level of **sensory** awareness is not easy. It has been established by researchers that an infant's system for vision is not initially strong, but that it develops considerably in the first few months, whereas an infant's hearing is quite well developed right from birth. The main areas of sensory development studied are vision, hearing and **perception**.

Vision

From birth infants turn to look at sources of light. They show an interest in the human face, and researchers (particularly Robert Fantz in the 1950s) have repeatedly shown that the human face receives a greater response than other similar options, for example, a 'head' with facial features muddled up.

An illustration of Fantz's faces

Within a few days of birth babies can demonstrate both spontaneous and imitative facial expressions, and the eyes of the newborn infant can at times be seen to move in the direction of sounds. These early visual interactions (eye contacts) between the infant and their carer strengthens the process of bonding and therefore enhances their emotional security.

A newborn infant making eye contact

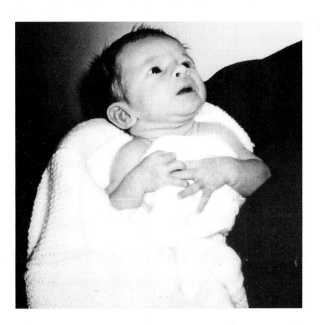

Stages of visual development

Birth	• Infant turns to the source of light. • Imitative facial expressions are seen, for example, poking out the tongue. • The human face gains the greatest level of an infant's attention. • An infant's eyes do not at first move co-operatively.
1 month	• Infant turns to light source. • Staring at face of an adult carer is usual. • The eyes are now usually working in co-operation. • Vision is held by a bright mobile or similar object. • The infant can visually track their mother's face briefly.

3 months	• The eyes move in co-operation. • A defensive blink has been present for some time. • The infant follows the movement of main carer. • A more sustained visual tracking of face or similar. • Infant may now be demonstrating visual awareness of their own hands.
6 months	• Infant is visually very alert. • Infants appear visually insatiable (their eyes fix on anything and everything). • Their eyes and head move to track objects of interest.
12 months	• Hand–eye co-ordination is seen as small objects are picked up using pincer grasp (index finger and thumb). • The infant's eyes follow the correct direction of fallen or dropped objects.

(Based on Sheridan, M (1991) *From Birth to Five Years; Children's Developmental Progress*, NFER Nelson)

A checklist for visual development

Concerns regarding vision would include:

- lack of eye contact with main carer;

- no social smile by six weeks;

- lack of visual tracking of carer's face or bright mobile by two months;

- lack of visual response to breast or bottle feed;

- lack of co-operative eye movement after three months;

- lack of signs that infant reaches out for toys in response to visual stimulus;

- lack of mobility or directed attention by twelve months.

Hearing

At birth, the hearing of infants is acute (sharp), as their **auditory perception** (sense of hearing) is not yet cluttered by the sounds of everyday living. They can often be seen responding to sound by blinking and through startled movements (the startle reflex). Newborn infants respond to the sound of their mother or main carer. They also show signs of auditory awareness by turning towards other sounds. Many infants are settled by calming or familiar music, often first heard within the safety of the womb.

Stages of auditory development

Birth	• Startle reactions to sound is normal. • Blinking is common in response to ongoing gentle sounds. • The infant turns to sounds, including their mother's voice.
1 month	• Infant is still startled by sudden noises. • They stiffen in alarm, extending their limbs. • They usually turn to sound of a familiar voice. • Also usually calmed by the sound of a familiar voice.
3 months	• The infant turns head or eyes towards the source of sounds. • They often appear to search for location of sounds. • They listen to musical mobiles and similar sounds.
6 months	• They now show considerable interest in familiar sounds. • Infant turns to locate even very gentle sounds. • Now vocalises deliberately, listening to self. • Infant vocalises to get attention, listens and then vocalises again. • Infant can usually imitate sounds in response to carers.
12 months	• Now responds to own name. • Infant's behaviour indicates hearing, by appropriate response to carers.

(Based on Sheridan, M (1991) *From Birth to Five Years; Children's Developmental Progress*, NFER Nelson)

A checklist for auditory development

Concerns regarding hearing would include:

• lack of response to sudden or loud noises in first few months;

• lack of response to familiar sounds, either by listening or by being calmed;

• no tracking of gentle sounds by nine months;

• no indication of turning to the sound of familiar voice;

• limited changes in vocalising from about six months;

• no obvious response to carers' simple instructions at a year.

From one year onwards the development of speech is the greatest indication of how well a child hears, although health problems such as 'glue ear' or repeated ear infections can have an effect on hearing.

Infant perception in general

Perception is the feedback of information via the body's senses. These senses help in the understanding of all that is happening both to us and around us. Visual perception (sight) and auditory perception (hearing) are two early indicators (both physical and perceptual) that development is progressing as expected. Vision and hearing link directly with language and cognition (understanding), and are both assessed specifically at regular intervals during infancy and early childhood.

Babies are startled by sudden noises or sudden movements. They also respond to familiar textures, for example their mother's skin. Again this is sensory feedback – the experience of touch and movement (kinaesthesia).

Case Study

Kos

Kos is six months old, and his parents are concerned that he doesn't seem to respond to his environment in the way his older brother did at a similar age.

Kos smiles a lot and visually tracks people, and also toys if shown them first. He makes very little noise apart from crying when his needs are not being met, mostly making cooing sounds.

1 Do you think Kos's parents are right to be concerned?

2 If yes, what would concern you about Kos's progress?

3 How would you expect Kos to be responding at this stage?

Milestones of intellectual development

The chart below details the milestones of intellectual development.

Birth to 1 year	• The infant's main source of learning is to explore orally (with their mouth) throughout most of the first year. Jean Piaget (a psychologist) called this the sensory motor stage. • By about 4 months, recognition of an approaching feed is demonstrated by excited actions and squeals. • By 9–10 months the infant achieves what Piaget called object permanence. They know that an object exists even if it has been covered up. For example, they pull a cover off a teddy they have seen hidden to 'find' it again. • The understanding of simple instructions or statements begins from about 9 months, and this is clearly evident by 1 year old, for example, 'Wave bye bye to Daddy'.

The infant's main source of learning is to explore orally

1 to 2 years

- Toddlers of this age are very curious, and they investigate everything they can.
- They are interested in all that happens around them.
- A precise pincer grasp (index finger and thumb) is seen now.
- They enjoy putting objects into containers.
- They take toys to their mouth less often now.
- They enjoy activities that need fitting together, for example, simple construction or a 'build up' clown.
- They will place an object on another – a two-object tower.

2 to 3 years

A busy toddler

- From two years they rarely take toys to mouth.
- Brief imitation is seen of everyday activities, for example, the feeding of a doll.
- They are usually content to play alone.
- Simple role play is demonstrated.
- They can build 6–8 objects into a tower.
- They can follow simple instructions, for example, 'Fetch your shoes please'.
- They can succeed with simple jigsaw puzzles.
- Vertical and horizontal lines are drawn.

3 to 5 years

- Children of this age can usually draw a person with the main details.
- Role play is frequent and detailed by 5 years of age.
- Floorplay is very complex; cars, trainsets, farms and so on.
- Understanding of time, linked to routine is emerging, for example they begin to understand that they will be picked up from pre-school after the singing has finished.

From five years onwards

From around age five onwards co-operative play becomes very involved, with considerable role play requiring accuracy and detail. Much time is taken in planning who will take on which role, and who will do what. Children increasingly develop skills to add up, subtract, put in order, read and write. The basis of all these skills has been built through the activities supported by the foundation stage curriculum. Examples of this are set out in Unit 5. You may find it helpful to refer to that section now.

LINKS TO UNIT 5, page 204.

Language and communication skills development

As human beings the main way in which we communicate with one another is through language. It involves our facial expressions, the tone of our voice, body posture and our expression of meaning through the use of words or symbols.

Language development is:

- rule governed – grammatical rules are present in each language (syntax);
- structured – the sound system that makes up the speech sounds (phonology);
- symbolic – words have meaning, building into phrases and so on (semantics);
- generative – it is the basis of the sharing of knowledge (pragmatics).

Prerequisites for language

Language development is affected by other areas of our development too. For example, socially and intellectually an understanding of the need to interact with others as a means of communication is vital, as are the physical abilities of vision, hearing and speech. Without these, it can be difficult for language to develop normally. Children learn the basis of their culture through communication, observing how others act and interact. Through this they develop an understanding of themselves and how they fit within their peer and social groups (this is known as 'goodness of fit'). This process is described in socialisation theory.

Psychologists believe that language plays an important part in all aspects of human development, with some theorists arguing that language is the basis of learning. An important debate has involved many people asking the questions:

'Is language dependent on thought?' or 'Is thought dependent on language?'

Activity 4.1

There are clearly very close links between the two areas of learning, namely language and thought. What do you think about them? Do you think understanding is needed in order for language to fully develop? Or do you think that language enables understanding to develop? Discuss your thoughts with others in your group.

Theories of language

There are a number of different theories about how language develops. They are summarised briefly below.

Association theory

Association theory is about the child gradually building their language by associating words with what they see, for example, learning that a tree is a tree, a dog is a dog and so on. This works well up to a point, but does not take into account all aspects of language, for example those words used to describe feelings or emotions.

Behaviourist theory

Behaviourist theory is about a child's language development being shaped by the responses given to them by the adults in their lives (positive reinforcement), encouraging the child to repeat a specific sound over and over again. For example, a child who repeatedly makes the sound 'Dadada' will be likely to have the sound positively reinforced by their mother if she says 'Yes, Dada will be home soon', whereas, if the same child makes the sound 'Nununu' it may well go unresponded to by the mother, as it has no specific meaning within the English language. Those sounds will eventually be lost to the child. This theory is based on the social learning theory.

Biological theory

The biological theory, also known as the language acquisition device, states that infants are born with an inbuilt programme for language. Noam Chomsky, the theorist behind it, called it the infants' language acquisition device (LAD). He considered that children absorb the language they hear, decode it and develop an understanding of its rules and grammatical structures.

Maturational theory

Maturational theory states that as long as children are exposed to language, they will simply pick it up as their development progresses in other ways too, as they develop and mature.

Interactionist theory

Interactionist theory is about children's language reflecting what they have experienced and what they understand. Many of the most respected theorists agreed with this theory, including Jean Piaget, Lev Vygotsky and Jerome Bruner.

Other research

Research has shown that children born to deaf parents (but who can themselves hear) are able to learn words from the radio, television, videos and so on, but they need to be actively involved in conversation with other people in order to develop their understanding and use of grammar. For some children an introduction to speech therapy sees a sudden improvement in their language structure, which soon brings them up to the expected level of language development for their age.

Stages of language development

As with every aspect of development, children develop language at differing rates within what is considered to be the normal range. This process of **language development** can be divided into ten basic **stages**. They are as follows:

1 non-verbal communication/expression;
2 speech-like noises;
3 controlling sounds, using mouth and tongue;
4 imitating sounds;
5 first words;
6 development of vocabulary (fifty words is usual at two years);
7 putting words together to form simple phrases and sentences;
8 use of grammar;
9 use of meaning;
10 using language to develop other skills, for example, early literacy.

Chart of language development

Age	Understanding	No. of words	Type of words	Average length of sentence
3 mths	Soothed by sound	0	Cooing and gurgling	0
6 mths	Responds to voice tones	0	Babble	0
1 year	Knows own name and a few others	1	Noun (naming word)	1 word
18 mths	Understands simple commands	6–20	Nouns +	1 word

Age	Understanding	No. of words	Type of words	Average length of sentence
2 yrs	Understands much more than they can say	50+	Verbs and pronouns (action + name)	1–2-word phrases
2½	Enjoys simple and familiar stories	200+	Pronouns I, me, you Questions What and Where	2–3 word phrases
3	Carries out complex commands	500–1000	Plurals Verbs in present tense Questions Who	3–4 word phrases
4	Listens to long stories	1000–1500	Verbs in past tense Questions Why, Where, How	4–5 word sentences
5	Developing the ability to reason	1500–2000	Complex sentences with adult forms of grammar	

Activity 4.2

During your placement experience, make a note of the differences in speech, questioning and grammar of children at different ages and stages.

The development of speech sounds in the English language

Speech sounds are made up of consonants and vowels. The approximate sequential development of consonants in the English language is as follows:

At age 2 years	m, n, p, b, t, d, w
At 2½ years	k, g, ng (as in sing), h
2½–3 years	f, s, l, y
3½–4 years	v, z, ch, j, sh
4½ years onwards	th (as in thin), th (as in the), r

Double consonants such as sp, tr and fl and also the sounds r and th, can develop as late as 6½ years in some children.

Consonants

Consonants are 'closed' sounds. This means that for a consonant sound to be produced, there is an obstruction to the airflow, by parts of the mouth coming into contact with each other, or almost contacting.

Try saying the word 'book'. To pronounce the 'b' in book, the lips need to come into contact. Now try the word 'sand'. To pronounce the 's' in sand, the tip of the tongue touches the ridge just behind the top front teeth. These are examples of how the obstructions are made.

Vowels

The basic vowel sounds are a-e-i-o-u , but there are other vowel sounds too. These include the double sounds such as 'ee', 'oo' and so on. Vowels are 'open' sounds. There is no obstruction to the airflow during pronunciation and each sound differs according to the position of the mouth.

- If the lips are spread widely, the sound 'ee' is produced.
- If the lips are rounded the sound 'oo' is produced.
- Vowels can be long sounds as in the word 'more'.
- They can also be short sounds as in the word 'pack'.
- There are simple vowels such as: 'o' as in pot, 'u' as in put, 'a' as in pat. They are simple because once the mouth is set in position it does not need to alter in order to produce the sound.
- There are also more complex vowel sounds such as: 'oy' as in the word boy and 'ow' as in the word cow. With these sounds, there is the need for a change in mouth and/or tongue position for the full sound to be made.
- All vowels in English involve the vibration of the vocal chords.

Syllables and words

Speech sounds combine together to form syllables. A syllable is made up of a combination of consonants (c) and at least one vowel (v). There can be up to three consonants before a vowel and up to four consonants after a vowel in the English language.

Examples of syllables:

be	= cv	(1 consonant and 1 vowel)
and	= vcc	(1 vowel and 2 consonants) and so on ...
plot	= ccvc	
strip	= cccvc	
tempts	= cvcccc	

The more consonants in a syllable, the harder it will be for a child to pronounce.

Words

Syllables, in turn, combine together to form words. Some words will have just one syllable, for example 'cat', 'dog' and 'hen'. These are called monosyllabic words. All other words have more than one syllable and are known as polysyllabic words. Even in adulthood, some people have difficulty in pronouncing some polysyllabic words. Common mispronunciations include:

- laboratory (often mispronounced 'labroratrory');
- certificates (often mispronounced 'cerstificates').

Activity 4.3

1 What words do you find difficult, or stumble over, on occasions?

2 What words have you noticed other adults having difficulty with?

3 How complex are the syllable combinations of these words?

Case Study | *Daisy*

Daisy plays contentedly alone, and often is seen briefly imitating everyday activities in her play, for example, having a cup of tea, or combing her doll's hair. She responds to simple instructions such as 'Please fetch your coat Daisy'. She only rarely takes toys to her mouth now.

1 How old do you think Daisy is likely to be?

2 What else would you expect to see regarding Daisy's development?

3 How well developed would you expect Daisy's language to be?

Language as a means of communication

Language is essential for us to communicate our needs, to express our feelings and to extend our experiences beyond our own environment by interacting with other people. These interactions enable us to develop

Language is essential to human beings

our understanding further and to learn new skills. Spoken language is our most important means of communication and it is strengthened by facial expression, tone of voice and body language.

Remember! Being a good communicator is one of the most important aspects of working in the field of Early Years.

Language disorders and delayed speech

Concerns regarding language development would include the following:

- lack of non-verbal communication with parents and carers in early weeks;
- significant feeding difficulties (speech therapists can often be involved at this early stage);
- lack of vocalisation from three months onwards;
- no babbling from eight to nine months onwards;
- lack of verbal responses to play;
- vocalisation completely out of line with the development norms.

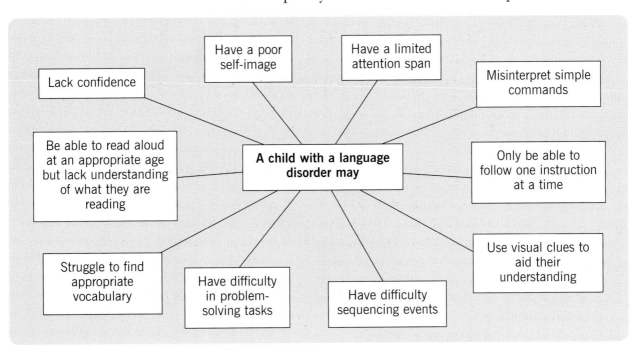

When expressing themselves, a child with a language disorder may:

- have difficulty in finding appropriate words;
- use words in a confused order;
- have difficulty in giving explanations;

- use confused grammar;
- miss out grammatical word endings;
- use confused sounds within individual words.

From reading the above points you will appreciate that language disorder can affect other aspects of learning and development for a child too. Additional factors that can affect language include medical problems such as glue ear. This is a condition of the middle ear in which a sticky mucus is formed that is unable to drain away through the eustachian tubes in the normal way. If it becomes severe and is left untreated it can lead to permanent hearing loss.

A cleft lip and palate is another medical and physical problem that can affect speech. A child born with one or both of these physical conditions will automatically be referred to a speech therapist, to ensure that the most appropriate feeding positions are established right from birth.

A cleft lip and palate can cause difficulties with speech

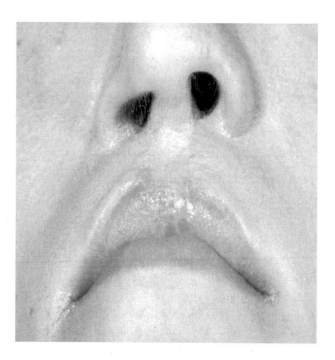

Language delay

As with language disorder, any significant delay in language developing along the expected norms would be monitored, and a referral made to a speech therapist as appropriate. There are environmental, medical, social, cultural and genetic factors that can impact on language development. A range of these has been set out in the spidergram below.

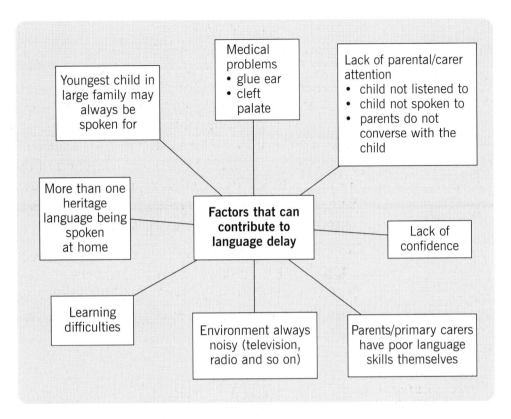

Many children have phases of unclear speech but they do not all need to be seen by a speech therapist. Many temporary disorders are due to the child hastening to say something and stumbling over it in their eagerness and excitement. This common occurrence is known as **dysfluency**.

Dysfluency

Hesitation occurs as a child tries to express themselves. The dysfluency is often associated with the child attempting to use a more complex language structure. Speech therapists refer to this as 'Normal developmental dysfluency' as it does not usually need professional intervention.

Normal developmental dysfluency

When conversing with a dysfluent child it is important to give them time and attention to make the effect of the dysfluency as minimal as possible.

A dysfluency checklist

Do   speak steadily and clearly yourself.

Do   give the dysfluent child your full attention.

Do   avoid interrupting the child whenever possible.

Do   focus on 'what' they are saying and try to ignore the dysfluency.

Do not ask the child to repeat it, or to start again.

Do not tell the child to 'take a deep breath' before they speak.

Do not tell the child to 'slow down'.

Do not ask the child to 'think it through' before they speak.

Do not allow discussion of their dysfluency in their presence.

If, however a child's dysfluency continues for more than a short period of time, or if the parents or the child appear to be worried by the dysfluency, then a referral will usually be made. The British Stammering Association has drawn up the following guidelines in order to help with decision-making regarding referrals. A referral is made if the child has dysfluent speech and one or more of the following factors are present:

- a family history of stammering or speech or language problems;
- the child is finding learning to talk difficult in any way;
- the child shows signs of frustration or is upset by their speaking;
- the child is struggling when talking;
- the child is in a dual language situation and is stammering in the family's first language;
- there is parental concern or uneasiness;
- the child's general behaviour is causing concern.

(Adapted from Mukherji, P and O'Dea, T (2000)
Understanding Children's Language and Literacy, Nelson Thornes)

Remember ! At times language disorders can be a sign indicating an autistic spectrum disorder.

 LINKS TO UNIT 3 pages 105–106 for information on Asperger's syndrome and autism.

Elision

The term elision refers to the times when children regularly miss out part of a speech sound altogether. It is a common occurrence, particularly with the second consonant of a cluster of two. For example, the 'st' in the word postman would become pos'man, and the 'pt' in the word slept would become slep'.

In young children this is part of the maturational development of speech patterns. In older children and adults it is usually more likely to be due to habit!

Activity 4.4

Television can have both a positive and a negative influence on communication and learning in young children.

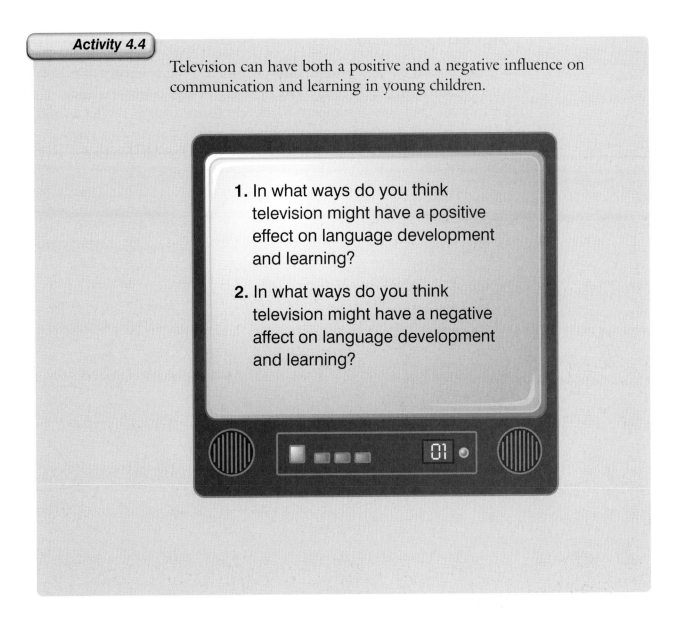

1. In what ways do you think television might have a positive effect on language development and learning?

2. In what ways do you think television might have a negative affect on language development and learning?

Self-expression

Children need opportunities to express themselves through a range of different situations. This is known as **self-expression** and includes speech and conversation, art, music and role play. A child who has not as yet gained the words they need to make themselves understood fully, for whatever reason, will benefit from experiencing a variety of these alternatives. This will include children for whom English is not the first language, for children with limited hearing, and for those in the younger age groups. The use of body language, hand movements and facial expressions will be important too.

Signed language

Signing is used by deaf people, those whose hearing is impaired, people with certain forms of disability and by many people communicating with them. There are a number of different forms of sign language, and each is a language in its own right. Each language has its own rules regarding grammar and how the words are put together. Signing involves facial, hand and body movements. Examples include:

- sign language;
- Makaton;
- bliss symbols;
- cued speech;
- Braille;
- PECS (Pictorial Exchange Communication System).

The standard manual alphabet: each of the letters is represented by different hand positions

- Bliss symbols: 'A universal language of pictographic symbols, which is used by people with reading and writing disabilities.'

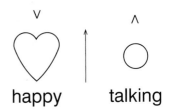

happy   talking

Bliss symbols: each child using this system has their own chart of the symbols they wish to use

- Makaton: 'A basic signing system using signs borrowed from British sign language, used by people who have severe learning difficulties.

Makaton signs: a system used by many children and adults who have communication difficulties

boy
Brush right index pointing left across chin

rabbit
Palm forward 'N' hands, held at either side of head, bend several times to indicate ears

fish
Right flat hand waggles forward like a fish swimming

bird
Index finger and thumb open and close in front of mouth like a beak

- Braille: 'A touch-based reading and writing system used by people who are blind.'

Braille is a system of letters made from raised dots

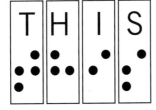 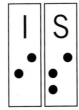 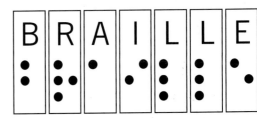

Cued speech: 'A system of eight handshapes made in four locations near the face to assist children (or adults) who are deaf, in lip-reading.'

Picture Exchange Communication System (PECS)

This system initially involves pictures of specific interest to the child, for example, preferred foods, toys and activities. The child is encouraged to select a picture and hand it to the adult to indicate their request. Each picture is backed with a velcro fastening and can be placed on to a 'picture exchange board'.

As the child's ability to communicate using this system develops, the adult introduces pictures to assist in the building up of sentence structures, and the child selects pictures from a board, locates the adult and hands the pictures or requests to the adult.

Case Study

Declan

Declan is five years old and has just started to attend the reception class of Hollybank primary school. He lives with his parents, who are both deaf, and can sign competently. Declan speaks very little, as his world has tended to be very quiet up until now, only attending a pre-school for two mornings each week.

1 How might Declan benefit from being in school full-time?

2 How important will it be for staff to encourage Declan to continue his signing as he develops his speech?

3 What creative activities do you consider will be of particular benefit to Declan?

English as a second language

Children for whom English is not their first language need to be provided with opportunities for communication that value their bilingualism and help them to build on their developing English skills. As with babies and toddlers in every language, understanding is usually more advanced than speech, therefore children who are learning English as a second or additional language will be able to understand questions and follow instructions before they are able to converse confidently with others.

To help a child learn English alongside their **heritage language** it is important that they have opportunities to:

- learn within context, for example, being shown a cup when asked if they would like a drink;
- be involved with activities that have meaning for them;
- have conversations with people that are supported by gesture and expression, to increase their opportunities for understanding;
- listen to the spoken word, through conversation, taped stories, songs and similar;
- have respect shown for their heritage language;
- have praise and pleasure shown to them for their efforts and their achievements;
- see language, both English and their heritage language, written down in a variety of contexts, for example, in books, on labels, posters and letters.

Remember ! Giving instructions to children in bite-size pieces enables them to absorb the information more easily. This applies to all children, not only those learning English as a second language.

Activity 4.5

Language is necessary for learning as well as for communicating.

1 How many ways can you think of in which language is used to enhance learning?

2 How many forms of language have you used during the past week?

3 Think about the activities available to the children in your placement. How do staff incorporate language opportunities into each activity?

Activities to promote development

To understand the role of play in development you first need to understand the sequence in which the play stages develop. Initially children learn through observing what others are doing, gradually moving towards imitating and then co-operating with them. They are usually set out under the following headings:

- solitary play;
- parallel play;
- associative play;
- co-operative play.

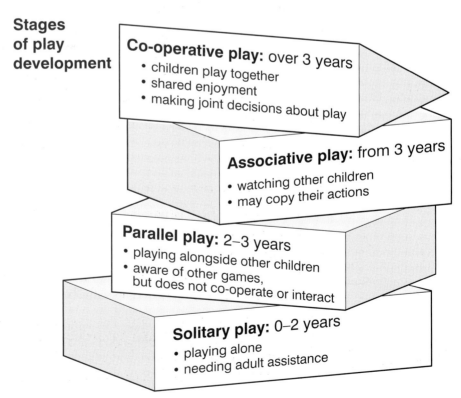

Stages of play development

Co-operative play: over 3 years
- children play together
- shared enjoyment
- making joint decisions about play

Associative play: from 3 years
- watching other children
- may copy their actions

Parallel play: 2–3 years
- playing alongside other children
- aware of other games, but does not co-operate or interact

Solitary play: 0–2 years
- playing alone
- needing adult assistance

Social play stages

As you can see from the building blocks above, socialisation develops stage by stage, and a child's play moves from the solitary actions of the toddler absorbed in their own world through to the complexity of games involving rules seen in the infant school playground. This ability to co-operate with others also moves through stages, which are dependent on both the age and stage of development of the individual child, and the opportunities and experiences that have been made available to them.

Solitary play

The first stage of play is referred to as solitary play. The child plays contentedly alone, still needing the reassurance of the adult. This play is typical up to aged two years. It is frequently imitative, demonstrating a basic understanding of the actions of others within a child's social world. An example of solitary imitative play would be the child pretending to brush the hair of a doll or teddy, usually very briefly.

Solitary play

Parallel play

The next stage in play is parallel play in which a child finds enjoyment playing alongside, but not with, another child. The children do not necessarily even acknowledge that each other exists, and make no reference to what the other is doing. This is true parallel play, one child playing parallel to the other. It usually begins to emerge between two and three years of age.

Parallel play

Associative play (looking on play)

At this stage in social play the child begins to watch the actions of others, enjoying their play from a distance. They are not as yet ready to play with others, but will learn a great deal from their observations. This stage of play is typically seen between three and four years of age.

Associative play

Joining in play (simple co-operative play)

By four years old most children will be ready to play co-operatively with others. This simple co-operative play begins in an uncomplicated manner, involving the shared enjoyment of a similar activity. A good example of this would be a group of children all dressing dolls together. There are no rules and no restrictions. It is simply a pleasurable play experience, with others.

Simple co-operative play

Co-operative play (complex co-operative play)

This last and most developed stage in the process of children's play involves them interacting as a group. This can involve the physical co-operation (shown in the illustration below) needed to complete a joint task, or play that includes complex rules, involving the taking on of agreed (though 'evolving as they go') rules.

Complex
co-operative play

It is important to remember that social development and play are affected by various experiences and this includes the effects of stereotyping.

Children learn about social behaviour from watching and imitating other people. They are particularly influenced by the adults whom they admire and look up to. As an adult working with young children you are a role model for them, and therefore you should be aware of how your actions, attitudes and words can affect them.

Remember! Messages can be portrayed by actions, words, attitudes and non-verbal behaviour. Messages can be both positive and negative.

You may find it useful to re-read the section on social learning theory in Unit 2 now.

 LINKS TO UNIT 2, page 38.

Case Study

Water play
Ephraim is two years four months old, and Thalia is two years three months. Anna is three years old and Adrianna is three years and three months. You have been asked to set up a water play activity suitable for them all.

1   What would you include in the way of resources?

2   Would you expect any of the children to interact during their play? If yes, who? If not, why not?

3   What are the most likely stages of play to be seen demonstrated by these children?

Activity 4.6

Using the table below as a guide, construct a chart showing the range of typical activities enjoyed by children across the different play stages, and tick those activities you feel support development in each of the skill areas. Here are some activities you may use. Add any others that you feel are appropriate.

	Locomotor skills	Non-locomotor skills	Manipulative skills	Hand/eye co-ordination	Memory	Concentration	Sensory development	Communication	Sharing/competition	Problem-solving
construction										
dressing up										
water play										
sand play										
circle time										
junk modelling										
dance and movement										
puzzles										
listening to music										
books and stories										
dough										
role play										
pencil use										
threading reels and buttons										
puppets										

Remember! Your knowledge and understanding of play will develop with experience. You may find it useful to return to this activity again at a later date.

Activity 4.7

Children learn best if they are able to incorporate their own ideas and interests too.

1 Why do you think this might be the case?

2 How does being able to contribute affect your own involvement in an idea or situation?

3 In what ways could you involve children in choosing the focus of an activity?

4 What areas of the children's development do you consider you would be supporting in this way?

Adult expectations of children

Every adult has certain expectations of children. This will vary from person to person and can be influenced by generation, experience and culture.

Activity 4.8

Think about the differences in the expectations of a range of people you know. This might include your parents or grandparents, or other people of their generation. Also consider your own expectations of children.

1 What differences have you identified regarding behaviour?

2 What differences have you identified regarding social politeness and manners?

3 How do the expected levels of respect for elders vary?

4 What about the levels of expected independence in children?

5 What other differences can you identify?

Adult involvement

There are three main theories regarding **adult involvement** and how it can affect children's learning. They are known as:

- the transmission model;
- the laissez-faire model;
- the social constructivist model.

Transmission model

- The **transmission model** refers to adults who control the learning process for the child.
- The adult decides what learning will take place by being directly involved with the child's activity.
- The child has fewer opportunities to put forward their own ideas.
- The adult's dominance means that children's ideas often go unheeded.
- Children cease to be actively involved.

This can result in children who are less likely to readily try out new experiences.

Laissez-faire model

- The **laissez-faire model** refers to adults who 'leave the children to get on with it'.
- The adult does not get actively involved with the children's activities, not wanting to 'interfere' with the children's learning.
- There are lots of opportunities for children to make choices and explore their own ideas.
- The lack of adult involvement can mean that children are unable to extend their learning as far as they could have done.

This can result in children not being able to reach their full potential.

Social constructivist model:

- The **social constructivist model** refers to the way that children are encouraged to learn by being involved with the environment around them.
- Children are encouraged to interact with all they see.
- The emphasis is on learning through practical experience.

This usually results in children who learn at a pace suited to their stage of development. An important theory introduced by the theorist Lev Vygotsky suggests that a child can be helped to a higher level of understanding by an adult who is able to support their learning sensitively. This does not mean forcing new skills upon a child, but that by observing when a child seems ready to move forward in their thinking, they can be encouraged to try something different, or more complex, helping them to understand it.

This often results in children achieving a new level of understanding.

For example, a child who was unable to get her construction model to stand was helped by an adult to try adding a larger block to the base, therefore achieving stability for the model. At a later date, the same child was being observed once again, and she was seen constructing a stable model in the same way as before, demonstrating that her understanding had moved forward to the new level.

Play can move
understanding forward
to new levels

Case Study

Dawn

Dawn has set up a creative activity in which she is supervising four children.

You notice that Dawn is directing the children as to where they should stick the various pieces of material, and has an example for them to copy. She is correcting them if they position the pieces in the 'wrong' place.

1   What model of adult involvement is Dawn following?

2   How might Dawn's approach affect the activity for the children?

3   What approach would you have taken if you were Dawn?

The learning value of activities

Sometimes it is easy to see **the learning value of activities** and toys, for example, a pushalong dog clearly helps the development of balance and walking in toddlers. Sometimes, however, the learning value is less obvious. The following pages set out a range of popular activities, noting the support they give to different aspects of children's development. The activities are set out under the following headings:

- social development;
- emotional development;
- physical development;
- intellectual development;
- language development.

Activity 4.9 on page 197 gives you an opportunity to explore your understanding of how the Early Learning Goals, which form the foundation stage curriculum link into these developmental areas.

Construction play

Social development
- developing confidence in selecting resources
- sharing resources with others
- negotiating exchanges of resources
- asking for resources and responding to requests
- building, using own ideas from observations of their own environment

Emotional development
- showing satisfaction with own achievements
- showing frustration and disappointment if their intentions fail

Physical development

- handling the resources with increasing confidence and skill
- manipulative skills development with smaller construction pieces
- precision and increased ability to place pieces carefully
- large motor skills development when using large boxes, tables, chairs and so on
- use of senses to explore the shape and texture of the various construction pieces, for example, Stickle bricks, Duplo, Popoids

Intellectual development

- increased ability to understand how pieces fit together
- development of planning and intention skills
- increased understanding of stability and strength
- increased understanding of weight and height
- increased understanding of the differences between various resources
- increased ability to select and group pieces together by size, shape, colour etc.
- helps develop sustained concentration

Language development

- development of new words and terminology, for example, build, construct, stability, planning
- describing plans and intentions
- discussing ideas and what they are doing

Sand play

Social development
- playing alongside or with other children
- development of the ability to interact with others
- imitating the actions of others
- passing and exchanging tools and resources
- sharing tools and resources

Emotional development
- sand can be a soothing experience
- sand can be a very satisfying experience
- it is a safe, non-fail activity – you cannot play with sand 'wrong'
- development of confidence in interacting with others

Physical development
- handling the sand, experiencing the feel and textures of both the sand itself and the various tools that may be provided (sensory experiences)
- manipulative development – the skills needed to use both dry and wet sand
- increasing control over body movements

Intellectual development
- understanding about the properties of sand
- dry sand pours
- wet sand moulds etc.
- learning that adding water can alter the sand and the type of play
- increased understanding of absorbency
- increased understanding of the effects various sand 'tools' can have
- helps develop sustained concentration

Language development
- development of new words and terminology, for example, sift, sieve, pour, trickle, mould, pat, shape etc.
- increased ability to express ideas and plans

Water play

Social development
- playing alongside and then with others
- selecting tools and resources to use
- sharing and passing tools to others
- swapping and negotiating for tools
- asking for tools and resources and responding to requests

Emotional development
- water can be a soothing experience
- water allows a sense of achievement
- it is a non-fail activity – you cannot play with water 'wrong'
- displaying expressions of pleasure and excitement at new and favourite activities

Physical development
- increased manipulative skills
- increased control over body movements
- handling the water, noting the feel, texture etc.
- physically tipping, pouring from one container to another

Intellectual development
- increased understanding of what water can do
- investigating and trying out ideas
- increased understanding of full up and empty
- increased understanding of volume and capacity
- increased understanding of floating and sinking
- helps develop sustained concentration

Language development
- development of new words and terminology, for example, float, sink, pour, swish, splash, empty, full, more, less, greater than, less than, heavier, lighter

Dough play

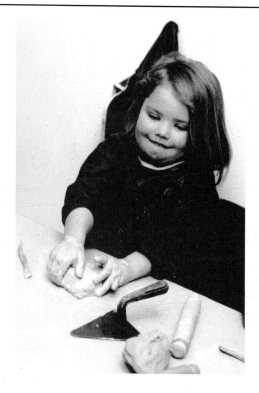

Social development
- alongside or with others
- developing confidence in their own ability to interact with others
- sharing the dough
- asking for resources or tools and responding to requests
- passing tools to others

Emotional development
- dough is a very satisfying medium to use
- it is a non-fail activity – you cannot play with dough 'wrong'
- actions can be repeated and developed – you can make, squash and remake

Physical development
- handling the dough – experiencing the feel and texture
- manipulative skills development – rolling, prodding, poking, pulling, pushing, moulding
- increased control over body movements

- developing an increased control of the tools – knives, cutters, forks, rolling pins, graters etc.

Intellectual development
- increased understanding of what tools are appropriate for which actions
- selecting tools for intended actions
- developing planning skills to make intended 'end results'
- helps develop sustained concentration

Language development
- new words and terminology to describe the various actions, for example, rolling, pressing down, forming a ball
- describing texture and how each action feels
- increased ability to explain ideas and make suggestions

Role play, including dressing up

Physical development

- large motor skills development as they dress and undress themselves
- manipulative development skills as they manoeuvre buttons, zips etc. with increased control and dexterity
- precision and dexterity is seen as children lay the table, set out the items for a shop etc.

Intellectual development

- demonstrating understanding of different people's roles
- demonstrating understanding of cooking processes – cakes go in the oven, pans go on the hob etc.
- demonstrating understanding of shopping processes – asking for items, paying for them, taking them home
- selecting appropriate resources for different roles
- using one object to pretend it is something else (symbolic play)
- opportunities for matching, grouping and pairing – cups to saucers, knives to forks etc.
- demonstrating knowledge of various situations – hospitals, cafes etc.
- responding to ideas and situations

Social development

- imitation of others – being mummy, making dinner, brushing a doll's hair, going shopping etc.
- linking up with the games of others
- co-operative play, planning who will be who, and what each will do
- demonstrating understanding of social greeting and politeness – hello, please, thank you etc.

Emotional development

- increased confidence in interacting with others
- a sense of release and understanding through acting out situations that may concern, confuse or worry them, for example, a new baby at home, mummy crying, going into hospital
- development of understanding how other people might feel
- role play offers opportunities for children to move in and out of reality, as their needs arise

Language development

- opportunities for conversation
- opportunities to express ideas from their own imagination
- using language to organise and make suggestions
- interacting with others
- development of new vocabulary as new 'game situations' arise
- writing skills develop as they make shopping lists, menus for the cafe etc.

Activities involving paint

Social development
- opportunities to make choices – choosing colours, paper sizes etc.
- sharing ideas with others
- using their observations as a basis for their pictures etc.

Emotional development
- paint is satisfying and non-competitive – you can't paint your own picture 'wrong'
- opportunities to show pleasure and excitement at new and favourite activities
- development of confidence in joining in the 'messiest' activities

Physical development
- manipulative skills development when using pens, brushes, rollers etc.
- increased control of body movements
- handling paint textures – runny paint, thick paint etc.
- handling and using the various alternative 'tools', for example, sponges, print blocks, straws, rollers etc.
- learning how to fold paper and card for printing and making cards etc.

Intellectual development
- developing the ability and confidence to make choices
- mixing colours to make additional colours
- choosing colours, showing understanding to illustrate specific things, for example, blue for the sky, green for the grass
- experimenting with new ideas and activities – printing etc.
- developing and identifying patterns in colours, shapes etc.
- using paint to demonstrate what they have observed

Language development
- using language to describe colours, textures etc.
- using language to describe ideas and intentions
- discussion of what they have painted or created

Junk modelling

Social development
- developing confidence in selecting materials
- observing others and learning from them
- sharing and negotiation skills regarding resources

Emotional development
- satisfaction when model is complete
- pride when showing models, or having them admired
- learning to deal with frustration if model falls apart
- learning to deal with disappointment if not enough of a certain size box etc.

Physical development
- manipulative development skills
- increased control of body movements
- increased ability to hold items in place while constructing
- development of use of staplers, fasteners, tape etc.
- handling a range of materials — texture, feel etc., for example, glue is sticky, Sellotape is tacky
- increased understanding of safety issues, such as the safe use of scissors.

Intellectual development
- increased understanding of how things hold together
- making choices regarding which junk items to use
- planning from their own imaginations, for example rockets, space ships
- planning from observations of their environment, for example making a vacuum cleaner
- increasing their understanding of stability and instability
- increasing their understanding of strength
- developing understanding of the need to negotiate regarding the space to build and the items required to build something specific
- helps develop sustained concentration

Language development
- new words and terminology regarding shape, size, materials
- asking for items and resources
- using language to describe their model
- using language to describe their plans and intentions
- discussion of the size, shape, colour and use of their models.

Books and stories

Social development

- often a shared experience
- can be one-to-one or in a group
- helps children learn about their social world (families, holidays, everyday situations)
- helps extend understanding of situations that may cause concern (new baby, moving house, having a tantrum, illness)
- helps develop observation skills
- often offers opportunities to join in with actions – to be part of a group

Emotional development

- a range of emotions can be explored (having a new baby, having tantrums, worries about moving house, going into hospital etc.)
- the repetition of familiar stories and the repeated sequences in many books is comforting to most children
- books and stories offer opportunities to express emotions, for example, laughter, mock 'fear' etc.

Physical development

- manipulative skills development through handling books appropriately – turning pages, holding books the right way up, holding books still while looking at them
- hand/eye co-ordination skills in following the text even before they can read
- there are often opportunities for actions alongside stories

Intellectual development

- developing an understanding of how books 'work' – from top to bottom and left to right (in English)
- understanding that books can be both for pleasure and a source of information
- children learn a great deal about their own environment through the stories they hear and the books they look at
- a child's understanding is consolidated by the repetition of familiar stories

Language development

- development of new words and terminology:
  - about new objects, new situations, other cultures
  - through joining in with repetition
  - through describing what will happen next
  - through suggesting what might happen next

Musical instruments

Social development
- this is often a joint activity with others
- children learn to play co-operatively
- development of understanding how to respond to instructions and guidance regarding when to start and when to stop
- taking turns to play

Emotional development
- there can be an emotional release through music
- gentle sounds can soothe a distressed child
- bold sounds can liven up a sad or unusually quiet child
- children learn to enjoy and value the sounds and instruments of their own culture
- children learn to enjoy and value the sounds and instruments of other cultures
- understanding of the need to consider other people can be learnt through taking turns to listen to each other play

Physical development
- manipulative skills development through the use of instruments
- large motor skills development through the opportunities to balance, dance and march to music (locomotion)

- developing the ability to move rhythmically
- linking music to dance and movement
- learning about the different feel of various instruments, for example, cymbals – metal, drums – skins, maracas – wooden, shakers – gourds (a hollowed-out fruit)

Intellectual development
- increased knowledge of the origins of instruments and music
- increased knowledge of the different types of sounds that can be made
- sequencing and patterning within music
- linking music to dance and movement
- understanding the changes in pitch, tempo etc.
- helps develop sustained concentration

Language development
- increased vocabulary, for example,
  - sound names
  - instrument names
  - rhythmic words: slow, slow, fast, fast, slow
  - development of voice pitch and how it can be changed to match different instruments
  - increased listening skills

Puzzles

Social development
- with younger children this is often a shared activity with an adult
- floor puzzles are usually enjoyed in pairs or small groups
- pictures often depict objects of situations from children's own environment and experience

Emotional development
- confidence increases alongside skill development
- satisfaction is experienced when puzzles are completed
- learning to deal with frustration if puzzle becomes difficult to achieve

Physical development
- manipulative skills development
- increased ability to handle small pieces
- increased ability regarding hand/eye co-ordination

Intellectual development
- developing understanding of how to match pieces to gaps, identifying shape, size etc.
- learning through trial and error in the earliest stages
- demonstrating understanding of processes by matching pieces to accompanying pictures
- helps develop sustained concentration
- eventual development of memory regarding the completed picture, helping the child visualise what they are trying to achieve

Language development
- using language to talk about the picture
- using language to talk about shapes, size and how to position pieces
- new words, for example, place, hold, edges, twist, turn, flat, turn over etc.

Stacking toys and posting boxes

Social development
- initially this would be a shared activity with an adult or older sibling
- children learn to build jointly with another person
- knocking down the tower would be another joint fun action
- working together, the adult will help the child (perhaps hand over hand) to guide them to success in posting a shape in a post box or shape sorter
- opportunities for child to select which piece to post, or which piece to stack next

Emotional development
- satisfaction and pleasure is seen when successful
- pleasure and excitement is seen in knocking down the tower
- increased confidence is developed in line with increased physical (manipulative) skills

Physical development
- manipulative skills development – handling with increasing control
- precision and positioning skills
- hand/eye co-ordination
- exploration of shapes with both hands and mouths

Intellectual development
- learning to stack by size (beakers and rings)
- learning to enclose by size (beakers, 'Russian doll' style objects)
- matching shapes to correct shape holes
- learning by trial and error
- counting opportunities as stacking and sorting objects occurs
- learning about colours as each colour is stated for them by the adult

Language development
- shape names are introduced by the adult
- colour names introduced by the adult
- counting
- introducing vocabulary, such as biggest, smallest, bigger than etc.

Threading reels and buttons

Social development
- often playing alongside or with others
- making decisions and selecting resources
- asking for resources and responding to requests
- sharing and swapping resources

Emotional development
- this is a calm, satisfying activity
- a sense of pleasure is seen in achievement
- children enjoy being able to make their own choices

Physical development
- manipulative skills development
- hand/eye co-ordination
- increased control over body movements
- handling the threading of objects with increased ability and precision

Intellectual development
- developing the ability to sequence by shape, size and colour
- developing the ability to group by shape, size, colours etc.
- learning to plan and have intentions
- learning to add on and count
- learning to take one away
- helps develop sustained concentration

Language development
- development of words and terminology:
  - colour names
  - shape names
  - counting
  - using language to ask for and negotiate
  - using language to talk about length, purpose etc.

Linking activities to the Early Learning Goals

To ensure you understand the **Early Learning Goals**, refer to Unit 5, where each area of learning is set out clearly. You may find it helpful to read through them before you carry out the following activity.

LINKS TO UNIT 5, pages 231 to 244.

Activity 4.9

1 Using the Early Learning Goals for each of the six areas of learning, copy the table on the following page and identify how each of the activities set out on the previous pages support each early learning goal. The activity sheet below provides an example of how you could set this out.

2 Compare your answers with others in your group.

3 Discuss how well have each of you done.

Musical instruments

Personal, social and emotional development • select and use activities and resources independently	*Knowledge and understanding of the world* • begin to know about their own culture and beliefs and those of other people
Communication, language and literacy • explore and experiment with sounds, words and textures	*Physical development* • move with control and confidence
Mathematical development • talk about, recognise and recreate simple patterns	*Creative development* • recognise and explore how sounds can be changed, sing simple songs from memory, recognise repeated sounds and sound patterns and match movements to music

Personal, social and emotional development	Knowledge and understanding of the world
Communication, language and literacy	Physical development
Mathematical development	Creative development

Activities for children with specific needs

All children within a setting, whatever their specific need, must be considered when planning activities. Part of the planning process includes identifying how different levels of need can be incorporated. At times this will simply mean providing a greater level of support through increased adult involvement. At other times it will mean exploring the resources you are planning to use more thoroughly and providing more appropriate resources where necessary.

Examples might include:

- providing paint brushes with chunkier handles for a child with reduced manipulative skills
- providing puzzles with larger knobs on to aid lifting and replacing of pieces, again to aid manipulation
- ensuring that balls and hoops are of a bright colour to help children with visual impairment follow them more easily
- ensuring there is sufficient space at a table to accommodate a child in a wheelchair or using a standing frame
- providing opportunities for a child who may be overwhelmed by group activities to play near to the main group, by providing a mini sand tray, small bowl of water etc.

Activity 4.10

What other examples of resources to support specific needs can you think of?

The role of the Early Years worker

As an Early Years worker you will need to demonstrate a calm, reassuring manner in order to ensure that parents feel confident in leaving their child in your care. They will expect you to use common sense, to be aware of health and safety issues, and to show interest in their child. Unit 7 focuses specifically on the role of Early Years staff in working in partnership with parents, and issues are discussed there in greater detail, but it can be broadly summarised now by saying that the following aspects of your work all contribute to the building of good relationships and providing safe, stimulating care for the children.

Involving parents wherever possible
– parents should be made to feel welcome within the setting and encouraged to be as involved with the setting as they are able to be. This will include discussions with their child's key worker or the setting's supervisor, as well as being involved with fundraising and social events. The amount of involvement will vary according to circumstances and each parent should be valued for whatever level of involvement they are able to contribute

A calm, reassuring manner
– to help parents feel confident that you can care for their child appropriately

Consulting and communicating with parents
– parents should be included in any decisions made regarding a child, and their advice and opinion should be both sought and valued

Being a good listener
– at times parents may have concerns about their child and need to talk them over with another person who knows their child well

Meeting individual needs
– identifying and providing for the specific needs of each child to enable them to be fully involved in the setting and what it provides

Being able to give praise and encouragement
– it is important that effort is acknowledged as well as achievement

The role of an Early Years worker involves:

Promoting equal opportunities
– issues of equality regarding gender, culture and disability need to be fully understood, together with an understanding of how personality can also be an important consideration (the opportunities for a shy child as well as those of the more outgoing child)

Use of observation skills
– to identify any potential problems regarding a child, or any specific aspect of their care that needs to be altered in any way

Being aware of security needs
– issues such as who is allowed to collect a child from the setting and what to do about strangers arriving at the setting need to be fully understood

Being a good teamworker
– to be aware of the need to work with others and not in isolation, to ensure that your actions complement the actions of others in the team, rather than hinder or contradict

Upholding health and safety
– all general health and safety rules should be adhered to at all times with all staff ensuring that they understand the procedures for the setting and the rationale (thinking) behind them

Providing appropriate care plans
– the individual needs of children must be taken into account when planning for their daily and longer term care

Upholding confidentiality
– the importance of working within a 'needs to know' basis regarding confidentiality is vital in maintaining the privacy of children and families with whom you work

Key terms

You should now understand the following key words and phrases. If you do not, read through the chapter again and review them.

adult involvement
associative play
auditory perception
cognitive
co-operative play
dysfluency
early learning goals
heritage language
laissez-faire model
language delay
language development
language disorder
learning value of activities

parallel play
perception
pre-requisites for language
self-expression
sensory
signed language
social constructivist model
solitary play
stages of language development
stages of play development
theories of language
transmission model
visual development

Test Yourself

1 What are the three main areas of sensory development?

2 List at least four indicators that would raise concern regarding an infant's vision.

3 List at least four indicators that would raise concern regarding an infant's hearing.

4 What does the term 'perception' mean?

5 What pre-requisites for language can you think of?

6 How many theories of language development can you think of, and what are they?

7 What are the ten main stages of language development?

8 How many words, on average, can a two-year-old toddler say?

9 What are the main differences between vowels and consonants in speech?

10 Give at least four concerns that may indicate delayed speech.

11 What is meant by the term 'normal developmental dysfluency'?

12 How many forms of signed language can you think of?

13 Give at least five important points to remember when supporting a child to learn English as a second language.

14 What are the main stages of play development?

15 Thinking about the foundation stage curriculum, list at least ten activities that can support personal, social and emotional development.

16 Thinking about the foundation stage curriculum, list at least ten activities that can support communication, language and literacy.

17 Thinking about the foundation stage curriculum, list at least ten activities that can support mathematical development.

18 Thinking about the foundation stage curriculum, list at least ten activities that can support knowledge and understanding of the world.

19 Thinking about the foundation stage curriculum, list at least ten activities that can support physical development.

20 Thinking about the foundation stage curriculum, list at least ten activities that can support creative development.

References and suggested further reading

Bruce, T and Meggitt, C (1996) *Childcare and Education*, Hodder & Stoughton

Dare, A and O'Donovan, M (1997) *Good Practice in Caring for Children with Special Needs*, Nelson Thornes

Green, S (2002) *BTEC National Early Years*, Nelson Thornes

Hobart, C and Frankel, J (1999) *A Practical Guide to Activities for Young Children* (2nd edn), Nelson Thornes

Mukherji, P and O'Dea, T (2000) *Understanding Children's Language and Literacy*, Nelson Thornes

Qualification and Curriculum Authority (QCA) (2000) *Early Learning Goals*, DfEE

Sheridan, M (1997) *From Birth to Five Years; Children's Developmental Progress* (revised edn), Routledge

Tassoni, P and Hucker, K (2000) *Planning Play and the Early Years*, Heinemann

Series

Stepping Stones series by Nelson Thornes. Titles include:
At Home and Far Away
Gardens
Ourselves

Toys
Creatures Great and Small
Food

Journals and magazines

Examples include:
Nursery World
Nursery Education
Nursery Projects
Child Education

Websites

www.deafchild.org

www.pampers.com

5 Children's activities and play

Adults as well as children play. There is little difference between an adult trying out a new electrical appliance and a child exploring a new toy. Both are finding out what it does, determining what each part means and how to make or programme it to produce the required response. Think about the last time you used a new music system or something similar. The pleasures are much the same and the actions (exploration and investigation) are mixed with reward and the further development of understanding.

Play is important to a child's development.

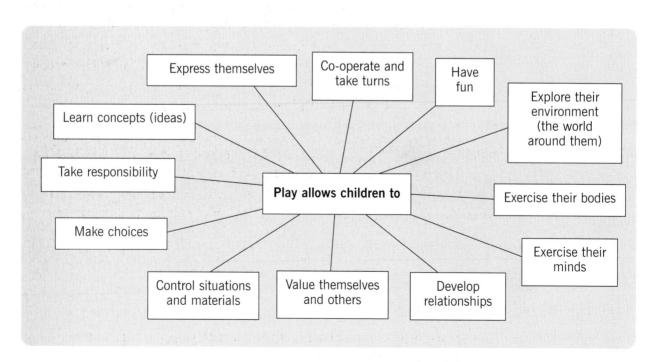

Express themselves

Co-operate and take turns

Have fun

Explore their environment (the world around them)

Learn concepts (ideas)

Take responsibility

Play allows children to

Exercise their bodies

Make choices

Exercise their minds

Control situations and materials

Value themselves and others

Develop relationships

Play helps children develop holistically (as a whole person). This means that it helps them develop:

- socially – building relationships with others;
- intellectually – learning more about the world they live in;
- morally – understanding right and wrong, fair and unfair, good and bad;
- physically – building on their physical skills, to achieve new ones and enhance those they already have;
- linguistically – through opportunities to talk, question and discuss;
- emotionally – helping them feel independent and secure;
- spiritually – encouraging a sense of wonder and enquiry in children, and also an understanding of cultural beliefs.

Planning activities to promote development

As you prepare activities for children there are a number of specific points that need to be taken into consideration. You need to remember that each child is an individual with their own needs and unique stage of development. They have different concentration spans, and individual preferences. Therefore, working with a group of children means that you need to consider the stage of development of all the children, not just the stage of development of the majority, and plan the activity to support each of their needs. Having decided upon the main aim of your planned activity, you will need to think about how you will cater for children who will need help and guidance to fully cope with it, and also decide how you will extend the scope of the activity to meet the needs of children who are more able and therefore require more complex tasks. This is known as **meeting differentiation of need.**

Remember! Planning sometimes needs to support one or more specific areas of the curriculum. This applies to both the foundation stage curriculum and the national curriculum, depending on the age range you are working with. Look at pages 230–231 and 244–245 for further details of both curricula.

Preparation

When planning an activity it is **important that you prepare** for it fully. You will need to think about:

- the people who need to be consulted (for example, the class teacher or room supervisor);
- the design of play activities;
- the outcomes to be achieved (will you need to try to meet an early learning goal, or stepping stone and so on?);
- how the activity fits into the planned Early Years curriculum for the children;
- cultural differences and how you can ensure these are met;
- equal opportunities and whether your activity will offer them;
- how much time you have for planning;
- how much time the activity will take;
- how much space you will need for the activity, taking into account the numbers of children and the environment in which you will carry it out (room, hall, garden and so on);
- what equipment and resources you will need;
- your role as either an adult helper or as leader of the activity, and what difference this makes;
- what level of supervision will be required;
- any safety precautions you will need to take;
- any practical problems likely to arise and how to avoid them or put them right;
- how to provide opportunities for children to learn new skills and ideas;
- how to adapt the ideas for younger children, or those with particular needs.

You will also need to produce:

- a written plan to show how the activity will be carried out;
- a checklist showing the sequence of actions and proposed timings;
- confirmation regarding how you intend to record achievement of the planned outcome;
- a way of evaluating the activity.

From the lists above you can see that planning play activities for an Early Years setting does not simply mean getting out the toys or materials. It can be quite time consuming, and takes a great deal of advance thinking and preparation. It should be remembered that the best Early Years provisions are built on forward planning and teamwork.

The exploration of practical activities

This section of the unit is about what might be included in the activities you provide. It notes many of the options that are possible through the use of each activity, and a range of activities are set out below with a list of ideas under each activity heading. It needs to be understood that this is not an exhaustive list. There are many more activities that could be included. You will be able to build up a list of ideas as your career develops.

The practical aspects of health and safety, and positive environment are discussed in Unit 3, along with sensory activities. You may find it helpful to refer to this unit as you plan your activities.

LINKS TO UNIT 3, pages 76–153.

Other useful links can be found in Unit 4, which covers examples of how activities support development, and in Unit 6, where activities to stimulate babies are discussed.

LINKS TO UNIT 4, pages 154–203.

LINKS TO UNIT 6, pages 293–300.

Creative activities

Creative activities can be divided into the following groups:

Painting: this would include –
• colour mixing
• using brushes • using rollers
• using combs • marbelling
• blowing through straws
• drawing, crayoning, using chalks and charcoal

Collage (sticking):
• using a multitude of 'bits and pieces', all of them safe for the age of the children using them

Printing:
• using hands and feet
• using blocks, templates, cotton reels, pastry cutters etc.
• using string, making butterfly prints

Junk modelling:
• with a range of 'fastenings', including glues, Sellotape, staples and crocodile fastenings (early design and technology)

Glueing and sticking:
• using clear glue, Sellotape, sticky paper

> *Remember!* With the younger age groups small parts need to be removed or used under strict supervision.

Adults should support and encourage creative activity such as collage

Creativity includes:

- adult-led activities;
- children being encouraged to use free expression;
- the skill of using scissors;
- mark-making implements (drawing, colouring etc.);
- a range of creative resources.

Music and language

The area of music and language activities incorporates:

- conversation, description and the general use of language;
- musical instruments from around the world;
- songs and rhymes;
- rhythm and dance;
- music and movement;
- listening to music;
- making music;
- background music.

All these activities should involve the use of world music.

Remember ! Babies enjoy music too, but be aware of instruments with edges that may hurt them.

Books and stories

Included under this heading would be:

- group story times
- one to one story times
- the use of big books
- drama and stories involving participation by the children
- using props, such as puppets
- reading with children

- children having daily access to books by being able to choose a book freely
- children enjoying books on their own, preferably in a cosy corner or quiet area
- both adults and children using books as a source of information, as well as pleasure

Construction activities

Construction can be either on a large scale or small scale. It can involve household equipment and furniture or it can be a bought commercial product. A combination of each of these is best.

Examples would include:
- large scale – chairs, tables, the clothes horse;
- small scale – construction kits such as Duplo, Lego, Mobilo, Stickle bricks, wooden blocks of different shapes and sizes.

Remember ! Babies can choke on small parts and should not have access to small piece construction kits. Guidelines for suitable ages are usually given on packages and in advertising catalogues.

Role play

Role play offers opportunities for so many aspects of everyday life. Children can become familiar people who have a link to them already, for example, the doctor or a postal worker, or 'types' of people they have seen in real life, in books or on television, for example, lorry drivers, pilots, train drivers. Role-play corners can be made into different types of settings, and ideal examples would include a shop, a post office, a railway station or a hospital.

A role play setting

Opportunities to develop understanding through role play are almost endless. To take one example, regarding language and literacy, opportunities are vast, with children having opportunities for writing letters, making train tickets, producing signs and price tags, setting out menus and taking lunch orders. They can set out bills, write cheques and so on, each activity reinforcing and developing their understanding of the world in which they live and the role of language and literacy within it.

Similarly, understanding early mathematics is developed as children match cups to saucers, group similar items together and count how many of any item is needed.

Resources for role play include:

- dressing-up clothes for both boys and girls to enable them to be men and women, in a variety of domestic and employed roles, and reflecting a range of cultures;

- domestic (household) equipment to support learning about a range of cultures and to show particular value of the cultures reflected in the children attending the setting;
- a range of dolls and teddies, with prams, cots, baby baths and baby equipment to help children identify with, and act out domestic and care routines familiar to them will also be beneficial to the children's development.

Remember! Dressing up clothes need to be washed regularly and hats should also be regularly cleaned, especially if there have been any cases of headlice in the setting.

Activity 5.1

1 Think what you could provide for a home corner setting.
2 Note the sorts of scenes you are likely to see being played out.
3 List the opportunities for each of the six areas of learning during this type of play.

Remember! The six areas of learning are personal, social and emotional development; communication, language and literacy; mathematics; knowledge and understanding of the world; physical development; creative development.

Cooking

Cooking is an excellent activity for young children. It is both fun and a good learning opportunity. It is important that any dietary or cultural need is taken into account, and any doubts should be checked with parents or carers. Suggestions for cooking with children include:

- suitable healthy snack ideas;
- making reference to different cooking methods – baking, mixing, rolling, pan cooking;
- foods for different ages, understanding their suitability for toddlers and older children;

- foods popular with specific cultural groups;
- links to festivals and special occasions;
- personal preferences of children.

Ideal foods to prepare and cook include:

- bread, chappattis, pitta bread and pizza bases;
- cakes, buns and biscuits;
- sweets;
- pancakes;
- simple vegetable soups;
- fruit salads;
- sandwiches.

Activity 5.2

Plan a suitable cooking activity of your own choice for a group of young children. Start by making a recipe card for the activity. It will need to include:

How to make a recipe card

1. Title of the recipe e.g. Butterfly cakes, vegetable soup.
2. Whenever possible, add a picture. This helps to make the activity more realistic for the children as they can see what they are aiming to achieve.
3. State what equipment will be needed.
4. State what ingredients will be needed.
5. Set the process and measurements out clearly, stage by stage. Although the children are unlikely to be able to read these, adding an illustration of kitchen scales etc. will help them understand.
6. Explain how long it needs to cook (if at all).
7. Give suggestions for decorations, icing and so on.
8. If the recipe links to a particular festival or celebration, make sure that it is clearly stated, showing how it links and why it is relevant to the festival or celebration.

Gluten-free playdough

What you will need:

I cup of rice flour
I cup of corn flour
I cup of salt

4 teaspoons of Cream of Tartar
2 cups of water
2 tablespoons of vegetable oil
Food colouring

What to do:

1. Place all the ingredients in a saucepan. ▷
2. Stir well whilst cooking over a gentle heat. ▷
3. Continue to stir as the mixture changes from runny to firm.
4. Remove from the cooker and turn out onto a board.
5. Knead well to ensure a smooth texture throughout. ▷
6. When cool, place in a plastic container.
7. This dough should keep well if stored in a refrigerator when not in use.

Remember:

It is not appropriate to add textures such as oats to gluten-free playdough.

An alternative idea could be to make a bird cake. This not only gives a nice weighing and mixing activity; it teaches children that other creatures also need care and a nutritious diet.

Remember! Cross-infection can be prevented by teaching children the importance of handwashing and not putting hands to their faces while cooking or preparing food. Also, use of ovens and cooker hobs must remain the role of the adult – children are safest if kept out of the kitchen completely.

Outdoors play

The physical fitness levels of young children is of increasing concern to health professionals, and the additional opportunities for physical activity that can be planned for out of doors can contribute to helping children develop a healthy attitude to being outside and in the fresh air.

Many of the activities that take place indoors could be taken out into the garden too. The outdoor environment should ideally be seen as an extension of the indoor play area. However, this section includes activities that are mostly planned for outside.

Equipment for locomotor skills, running, climbing, cycling and so on, such as:
- climbing frames
- a slide
- trampet
- bikes
- trikes
- ride-ons
- see-saws

Equipment for non-locomotor skills, throwing, catching and so on, such as:
- balls
- beanbags
- quoits
- skittles

Equipment for fine motor skills, hand and finger manipulation, such as:
- water tray
- sand tray or sand-pit
- gardening

Action games such as:
- Simon says
- Farmer's in the den
- There was a princess long ago

'Ground' games using chalk, such as:
- hopscotch

Spontaneous games using:
- tents
- dens
- table ends

Remember! Sand-pits need covering when not in use. Water needs replenishing daily. Strict handwashing must take place after gardening.

Natural (and malleable) play

So many of our children's toys and equipment today are made of plastic and other man-made materials. It is therefore important that children have the opportunity to experience **natural materials** whenever possible. Play materials that come under this heading include:

Sand
- Wet and dry, with and without other textures (e.g. shells).
- On its own or with tools such as rakes, diggers, buckets, sieves and sand wheels.

Water
- Plain, coloured, bubbly, warm, cold.
- On its own or with objects to develop various scientific and mathematical concepts, such as floating and sinking, absorbency and measurement of quantity.

Sand is a valuable, natural asset to play

Clay

- On its own.
- Or with tools for cutting, rolling, prodding and shaping.
- Dough is also malleable but it is not a natural material.

Wood and woodworking

- Under careful supervision.
- Using 'proper' child-sized tools.

It is important that 'real' rather than 'toy' tools are used

It is **important that real tools are used** rather than toy tools, as this helps to develop children's understanding of and respect for the use of real tools.

Remember! Although real tools are always the preferred option, there will be a need for continuous supervision to teach children how to use them safely, and to respect what each tool can do.

Gardening

- Including digging, planting, watering and weeding.
- Involving flowers and plants from seedlings or bulbs.
- Vegetables and salad items to pick and enjoy for lunch or snacktime.
- Plants in soil beds, pots or jars.
- Fast-growing plants such as sunflowers, beansprouts and cress.

Remember! Ensure that all plants are safe for children to handle, avoiding sharp thorns, poisonous berries etc.

Small world play

Any toys that are a scaled-down version of real life are referred to as **small world play**. This includes activities such as:

- dolls' houses
- farms and farm animals
- zoos and zoo animals
- a car mat and vehicles
- a garage
- train sets.

As children develop they will often combine small world activities and play quite complex games for extended lengths of time.

Activity 5.3

1 Why do you think small world play is enjoyed so much by young children?

2 Choose a small world activity from the above list and try to explain its value to another student.

Information and communication technology (ICT)

Information and
computer technology

Technology will be of increasing importance to the young children you work with as they move through school and into the adult world. Many will have used a computer at home already. There are a range of computer programs that re suitable to use with young children in early years settings. Examples include programmes that support the development of:

• number skills

• letter sounds

• general knowledge and creativity

Programmable toys are also available which enable children to set up actions and make decisions, developing both their interest and their skills in handling technology.

Structured activities

Many resources have a specific structure to them. This means that they need a specific action in order for them to be used as they are intended. Examples include:

• play tray puzzles (with knobs to lift each piece out);

• jigsaw puzzles;

• floor and table puzzles;

• threading activities such as cotton reels or large buttons;

• sewing cards, binker (woven cloth rattan for learning to sew) and other easy to puncture materials such as felt;

• shape sorters and posting boxes;

• peg boards;

• bead frames;

• pattern boards, using nails and elastic bands.

Activity 5.4

1 Why do you think structured materials are important?
2 How do structured materials support social and emotional development?
3 How do structured materials support intellectual development?
4 How do structured materials help physical development?

Remember! Small parts such as pegs and beads are not suitable to be given to younger age groups.

Paired and small group play

Activities that involve co-operation help children learn to share, to take turns, to have patience and to lose graciously.

Examples of such activities include:

- picture lotto;
- dominoes;
- memory pairs;
- noughts and crosses;
- box games such as snakes and ladders.

Remember! Floor and outdoor versions are also available for some of these activities. This adds another dimension to the play, as they are usually larger boards, with much larger pieces.

Interest tables

A lovely way to support learning is to provide an **interest table** that focuses specifically on one topic or a general area of learning. Interest tables extend both learning and imagination. They are usually linked into the current theme or topic that is being covered within the setting. It is usual to encourage children to bring items for the interest table, providing an excellent potential link with their home and family. Having a variety of objects 'on loan' from children's homes is also an important way to encourage respect for the belongings of others.

Outdoor version of indoor games add another dimension to play

Good examples of topics for an interest table include:

- Seasons;
- Ourselves;
- Transport;
- Seaside.

What other topics have you seen?

Each interest table should include:

- a variety of objects to raise interest, curiosity and the desire to explore and investigate;
- objects to stimulate the senses of sight, touch and smell;
- on occasion auditory stimulation (hearing) may also be possible;
- taste would not usually be included, but could be introduced through a linked activity to the interest table, for example, by

making mince pies linked to a Christmas theme, or coconut barfi linked to a theme about the Hindu festival of care and protection (Raksha Bandhan);

- reference books, and familiar and new stories can be displayed;
- labels are useful to help children start to link the written word to the names of objects;
- if working with older age groups, simple questions might be appropriate and add to the children's development, by encouraging discussion and further thinking.

An interest table

Activity 5.5

Select a topic of your choice and plan an interest table.

1 What will you be aiming for the children to learn?

2 What items will you include?

3 What books could you add to the table, linked to your topic?

4 How might your interest table be linked to other activities within the setting?

Remember! Be sure that no items are included that could be hazardous for a child to explore unsupervised.

Improvised games

Although it is important to plan ahead and to form a basic structure to the children's day, at times it can be just as valuable to encourage children simply to play with each other. Some children do this spontaneously, but others may need suggestions to help them get started. Examples of improvised play include:

- playing chase;
- hide and seek;
- hopscotch;
- What's the time Mr Wolf?;
- May I cross the river please?;
- hand clapping games.

What other examples of improvised play have you seen?

Each of these games helps give children a sense of belonging, of being part of something. This helps to boost self-esteem and develops social interaction skills.

Outings with children

Most children love going on an outing

Going on an outing is an exciting experience for most children, and for many it will be the first time they have been somewhere special without their parent or main carer. **Outings with children** need careful planning and this is covered in detail on pages 119–20 of this unit.

Suitable outings for children of a variety of ages could include:

- the zoo;
- a country farm or a city farm;
- a country park;
- going on a listening walk (specifically getting everyone to focus on what can be heard);
- a walk to look at the local environment – buildings such as houses, churches or shops, or aspects of nature such as trees, wild flowers, wildlife and mini-beasts;
- a hands-on science or technology centre, where many new ideas can be tried out;
- an interactive museum, specially designed for young children.

Remember ! Although an outing can be exciting, some children may feel quite apprehensive about it, particularly if it is an unknown experience for them. They may need a great deal of reassurance initially. Also, strict supervision is needed when taking children outside of the setting.

You may find it useful to refer back to Unit 3 for more guidelines on organising outings.

LINKS TO UNIT 3, page 119.

Carrying out planned activities

When preparing activities for young children there is a need to take into account a number of factors. The overall aim of the activity needs to be clear, but you must also consider:

- the environment in which the activity will take place;
- what facilities the activity will require, for example, will you need floor space, a table surface, access to handwashing facilities;
- the numbers of children who will be enjoying the activity at any one time;
- the amount of **supervision** that will be necessary;
- whether you have sufficient resources for the activity (enough for everyone to have a turn);
- how long the activity will last;
- health and safety issues relevant to the activity;

- how much help individual children will be likely to need;
- the impact the activity could have on the rest of the setting, for example, will it create a great deal of noise, excessive mess or a high level of excitement?

Case Study

Beth

Beth is a student preparing an activity that will be assessed as part of her course assignment. Beth has decided to prepare a creative activity involving printing. She intends to use halved potatoes with shapes cut into their surfaces.

1 Ideally, where should the activity take place?

2 What facilities and resources will the printing activity require?

3 How many children will it be practical to join in the activity at any one time?

4 How much supervision will be necessary?

5 How could Beth decide on the amount of resources she should prepare?

6 How long do you think the activity would last?

7 What health and safety issues would be relevant to this activity?

8 How much help would individual children be likely to need?

9 What level of impact would the activity be likely to have on the rest of the setting?

10 What different sorts of printing activities can you think of?

Beth has decided to prepare a creative activity using printing

Case Study

Monica

Monica is a student preparing an activity that will be assessed as part of her course assignment. Monica has decided to prepare an outdoor activity involving the planting of bulbs. She intends the children to dig an area of soil, clear away any snails etc. that they see, and then plant and water the bulbs.

1 Ideally, where and when should the activity take place?

2 What facilities and resources will the planting activity require?

3 How many children will it be practical to join in the activity at any one time?

4 How much supervision will be necessary?

5 How could Monica decide on the amount of resources she should prepare?

6 How long do you think the activity would last?

7 What health and safety issues would be relevant to this activity?

8 How much help would individual children be likely to need?

9 What level of impact would the activity be likely to have on the rest of the setting?

10 What different sorts of planting activity can you think of?

Monica has decided to prepare an outdoor activity using planting

Setting up and using play equipment – general points to remember

Point 1: The equipment or play materials provided must be appropriate for the ages of the children who are going to be using them. Guidance is usually given by manufacturers, and should be referred to if in any doubt. For example, small parts are not suitable for toddlers and babies.

Point 2: Safety surfaces are necessary underneath any equipment from which a child may fall a distance of 60 cm (2 ft) or more. (See Unit 3 for details of the types of surfaces that can be used.) This applies to all large equipment, for example a climbing frame or a slide.

 LINKS TO UNIT 3, page 119.

Point 3: Equipment should be placed on surfaces that are suitable for the way they will be mostly used. For example, play tunnels are best placed on grass or smooth concrete rather than gravel or stones, as children will be crawling on their knees as they play. Similarly, drawing and colouring materials are best placed on a table as this allows children to hold the paper securely and gives them a smooth surface to rest on.

Point 4: The layout of the setting needs to ensure that there is sufficient space for children to move about the room freely and safely.

Point 5: Staff should be able to supervise the children easily, without unnecessary barriers to their vision. Consideration should be given to the position of cupboards, bookshelves and so on.

Point 6: Furniture and fixtures must be securely in place, locked if appropriate, kept in good condition, and any storage facilities should be safely stacked and never be overloaded.

Point 7: When providing construction materials it is important that there is either sufficient of the material for each child to have a worthwhile experience while playing, or to limit the numbers of children using the activity at any one time. If children find that they are unable to build what they wish to build with a resource, due to lack of sufficient pieces, they are likely to lose interest in the activity altogether and therefore lose out on a potential learning opportunity in the long term.

Point 8: When providing children with resources for model making, building or small world toys, such as farms and car mats, it is important that their play will not be continuously interrupted by other children walking across their activity, or from a draught caused by an opening door, knocking over their models or animals. This type of disturbance will lower the enjoyment experienced by the child and possibly lead to frustration and dissatisfaction with the activity itself.

Point 9: Many activities can be provided both indoors and outdoors. It can be nice for the children to 'ring the changes' regarding where certain activities are placed, and it is good to encourage children to go out into the fresh air. However, it is important to provide shade for children on sunny days and they should not be exposed to the sun when it is at its highest in the sky. It is also unsuitable for children to play out on very foggy, damp days.

Point 10: All equipment needs to be kept in good condition and cleaned regularly and appropriately with an anti-bacterial cleaning product.

Point 11: Equipment should be safety marked whenever possible.

Point 12: Plants and animals offer an important learning experience for young children. They do, however, need to be carefully considered before incorporating within the setting. Animals should be avoided if there is a child with a severe allergy. Staff need to be prepared to carry out pet care routines, keeping the pets scrupulously clean. Pets and plants can be a useful way to help children learn about caring for the needs of others. They can learn about the similarities and difference between humans, animals and plants in their needs for food, water and sunlight.

Remember ! Plants should be non-poisonous, without thorns or berries.

In Unit 3 you will find a more in-depth discussion of issues such as setting out a room, accommodating children with a specific need, and safety and health issues. You might wish to refer back to that section now.

LINKS TO UNIT 3, pages 108–126.

Avoiding stereotyping and discrimination

- Check that books, posters, puzzles etc. show positive images of men, women, boys, girls, people with varying disabilities and people from varying cultures.

- Read books yourself before you read them to a child or group of children to ensure that no negative messages are given.

- Provide a range of resources in the role-play corner to positively reflect a range of cultures and to enable children of either gender to be whoever they wish to be. This applies to clothing, utensils and any pretend foods.

- Ensure that all children are encouraged to use all equipment and resources in the setting.

- Introduce a range of festivals and celebrations to children, widening their knowledge of the world around them.

- Answer children's questions honestly and sensitively. There is nothing wrong with them being inquisitive about the differences they notice. It only becomes a problem if they begin to place different values on those differences.

- Challenge prejudice or racism if you come across it.

Case Study | *Jermaine*

Jermaine is building a wall with the 'life-size' plastic bricks. Carmen wants to join in the activity too. She picks up some bricks and starts to add them to the wall. You hear Jermaine tell her, 'No Carmen, you're a girl, you can't do building. Girls can't be builders'.

1 What will you say to Jermaine?

2 What will you say to Carmen?

3 What else should you do?

Case Study | *Akram*

Akram is playing at the dough table with Morris and Teigan. Vijay sits down to play, but Akram tells him he musn't, because 'you're a Sikh and my parents say I musn't play with Sikhs'.

1 What will you say to Akram?

2 What will you say to Vijay?

3 What else should you do?

Giving children appropriate support

Deciding on how you can best give children **appropriate support** in their learning will depend on:

- their age;
- their stage of development;
- the activity they are involved in;
- the aims of the activity.

Depending on the age of the children you are working with and their levels of ability, you will need to provide some or all of the following:

- clear explanations;
- initial guidance as a prompt to get them started;
- gradually decreasing levels of guidance;
- continuous guidance, prompting them throughout the activity;
- physical support, perhaps help with cutting or in how to hold a pencil;
- language support, offering explanations and naming objects for them;
- close supervision, particularly of younger children;
- gradually decreasing levels of supervision, as children become more competent;
- generalised supervision, particularly when children are carrying out activities that are familiar to them.

Evaluating activities

Evaluating activities is important as it enables you to reflect on how well you have targeted, planned and carried out the activity, thinking about how well the children have achieved your intended aim for them. Also, you can think about how successful your judgements were regarding resources, supervision, health and safety issues. It also gives you the opportunity to reflect on what changes you would make next time to improve the activity.

Activity 5.6

Using the headings opposite, evaluate an activity that you have planned and carried out by yourself.

Activity

Did you target the activity appropriately?

What worked best?

What problems (if any) occurred?

Did the activity meet the intended aims?

Were resources sufficient?

Was supervision appropriate?

Were there any health and safety issues?

What would you change another time?

The foundation stage curriculum

The DfEE's **foundation stage curriculum** is used as a guideline for learning for children from three years until they begin to follow the national curriculum key stage 1. This will normally be introduced during Year 1 or 2 of primary school. The principles of the foundation stage are supporting, fostering, promoting and developing children's:

- *personal, social and emotional well-being:* in particular by supporting the transition to and between settings, promoting an inclusive ethos and providing opportunities for each child to become a valued member of that group and community so that a strong self-image and self-esteem are promoted;

- *positive attitudes and dispositions towards their learning:* in particular an enthusiasm for knowledge and learning and a confidence in their ability to be successful learners;

- *social skills:* in particular by providing opportunities that enable them to learn how to co-operate and work harmoniously alongside and with each other and to listen to each other;

- *attention skills and persistence:* in particular the capacity to concentrate on their own play or on group tasks;

- *language and communication:* with opportunities for all children to talk and communicate in a widening range of situations, to respond to adults and to each other, to practise and extend the range of vocabulary and communication skills they use and to listen carefully;

- *reading and writing:* with opportunities for all children to explore, enjoy, learn about and use words and text in a broad range of context and to experience a rich variety of books;

- *mathematics:* with opportunities for all children to develop their understanding of number, measurement, pattern, shape and space by providing a broad range of contexts in which they can explore, enjoy, learn, practise and talk about them;

- *knowledge and understanding of the world:* with opportunities for all children to solve problems, make decisions, experiment, predict, plan and question in a variety of contexts, and to explore and find out about their environment and people and places that have significance in their lives;

- *physical development:* with opportunities for all children to develop and practise their fine and gross motor skills and to increase their understanding of how the body works and what they need to do to be healthy and safe;

- *creative development:* with opportunities for all children to explore and share thoughts, ideas and feelings through a variety of art, design and technology, music, movement, dance and imaginative and role-play activities.

Based on DfEE (2000), pages 8–9

Providing learning opportunities across the foundation stage

The following material has been taken from the DfEE publication 'Curriculum guidance for the foundation stage'.

The Early Learning Goals for each of the six areas are listed, followed by an additional extract from each, giving examples of how to support learning across part of each area of the six aspects of the foundation stage. College libraries or resource centres would usually stock copies of the full document. You will find it useful to refer to it at some point.

Early Learning Goals for personal, social and emotional development

By the end of the foundation stage, most children will:

- continue to be interested, excited and motivated to learn;
- be confident to try new activities, initiate ideas and speak in a familiar group;
- maintain attention, concentrate and sit quietly when appropriate;
- have a developing awareness of their own needs, views and feelings and be sensitive to the needs, views and feelings of others;
- have a developing respect for their own cultures and beliefs and those of other people;
- respond to significant experiences, showing a range of feelings when appropriate;
- form good relationships with adults and peers;
- work as part of a group or class, taking turns and sharing fairly, understanding that there need to be agreed values and codes of behaviour for groups of people, including adults and children, to work together harmoniously;
- understand what is right, what is wrong, and why;
- dress and undress independently and manage their own personal hygiene;
- select and use activities and resources independently;
- consider the consequences of their words and actions for themselves and others;

- understand that people have different needs, views, cultures and beliefs, which need to be treated with respect;
- understand that they can expect others to treat their needs, views, cultures and beliefs with respect.

In order to foster these goals, children need opportunities to work both alone and in groups of different sizes. They need to develop independence and be able to both lead and follow.

Early Learning Goals for making relationships

Stepping stones	Examples of what children do	What does the practitioner need to do?
Feel safe and secure and demonstrate a sense of trust Seek out others to share experiences Relate and make attachments to members of their group	Ahmed has brought a favourite toy he received for his birthday to show to his group at snack time. He entrusts it to the practitioner to look after. Terry tells his friend during role play in a travel agent's how frightened he felt during a heavy storm when he was on holiday in a tent. Abigail shows Henry, a new child, the sandpit. She pats the side for him to sit next to her. She hands him a spade and he copies her as she digs. She regularly looks at his face.	■ Respond promptly and with genuine interest to children's shared discoveries, information and news ■ Provide stability in staffing and in grouping of the children ■ Have consistent and appropriate expectations of all children, that take account of their development and culture ■ Establish routines with predictable sequences of events ■ Provide time, space and materials for children to collaborate with one another in different ways, for example building construction, solving problems, sharing confidences ■ Provide a role play area resourced with materials reflecting their family lives and communities
Demonstrate flexibility and adapt their behaviour to different events, social situations and changes in routine	The children are frustrated by the fact that they cannot play outdoors because the big mower is in use, but they understand why it would be dangerous.	■ Demonstrate a positive attitude to change ■ Recognise and exploit opportunities for children to praise and demonstrate flexibility in response to change ■ Prepare children for changes that may occur in the routine

Value and contribute to own well-being and self-control	Jeff and Oliver have disagreed in the past, but Jeff asks Oliver to help him build a marble run because the practitioner has told him Oliver had built one before	■ Give children practice in resolving social conflict ■ Provide activities that involve turn-taking and sharing ■ Support children in linking with others with openness and self-confidence, for example to seek help
Form good relationships with adults and peers Work as part of a group or class, taking turns and sharing fairly, understanding that there need to be agreed values and codes of behaviour for groups of people, including adults and children, to work together harmoniously	Children from the pre-school came to visit the reception class they were to join after Christmas. The reception children showed them round the classroom and talked about what they were doing that day. Gina opened the door and ran outside. Peter fetched her back and explained, 'We can only go outside when an adult has opened the door, so we know there's someone to make sure we're safe.' The children were very excited when the local city farm brought a lamb to visit them. They all wanted to hold the bottle to feed the lamb, but waited quietly until it was their turn.	■ Ensure that children and adults make opportunities to listen to each other and explain their actions ■ Involve children in agreeing codes of behaviour and taking responsibility for their implementation

DfEE (2000), pages 36–37

Early Learning Goals for communication, language and literacy

The objectives set out in the 'National literacy strategy: Framework for teaching for the reception year' are in line with these goals. By the end of the foundation stage, most children will be able to:

- enjoy listening to and using spoken and written language, and readily turn to it in their play and learning;
- explore and experiment with sounds, words and texts;
- listen with enjoyment and respond to stories, songs and other music, rhymes and poems and make up their own stories, songs, rhymes and poems;

- use language to organise, sequence and clarify thinking, ideas, feelings and events;
- sustain attentive listening, responding to what they have heard by relevant comments, questions or actions;
- interact with others, negotiating plans and activities and taking turns in conversation;
- extend vocabulary, exploring the meanings and sounds of new words;
- retell narratives in the correct sequence, drawing on the language patterns of stories;
- speak clearly and audibly with confidence and control, and show awareness of the listener, for example by their use of conventions such as greetings, 'please' and 'thank you';
- hear and say initial and final sounds in words, and short vowel sounds within words;
- link sounds to letters, naming and sounding the letters of the alphabet;
- read a range of familiar and common words and simple sentences independently;
- know that print carries meaning and, in English, is read from left to right and top to bottom;
- show an understanding of the elements of stories, such as main character, sequence of events, and openings, and how information can be found in non-fiction texts to answer questions about where, who, why and how;
- attempt writing for various purposes, using features of different forms such as lists, stories and instructions;
- write their own names and other things such as labels and captions and begin to form simple sentences, sometimes using punctuation;
- use their phonic knowledge to write simple regular words and make phonetically plausible attempts at more complex words;
- use a pencil and hold it effectively to form recognisable letters, most of which are correctly formed.

Early Learning Goals for language and communication

Stepping stones	Examples of what children do	What does the practitioner need to do?
Use familiar words, often in isolation, to identify what they do and do not want Use vocabulary focused on objects and people who are of particular importance to them	Ming, playing in the home corner, exclaimed, 'My doll!' when another child tried to pick it up. Every time she heard it fly overhead, Janice rushed to the window and shouted, 'Helicopter, helicopter?'	■ Take part in children's play, modelling appropriate vocabulary ■ Introduce new words in the context of activities ■ Engage children's interest in words from stories, poems and songs ■ Recognise the special additional needs of children with sensory or communication difficulties, making use of their preferred means of communication, such as signing
Build up vocabulary that reflects the breadth of their experiences Begin to experiment with language describing possession	'One day I got up, and one day I said, "come on ... be quick," to my mum, and one day I went out to play in the snow,' said Natalie.	■ Extend children's language, and model the correct use of words ■ Show interest when children use words well to communicate and describe their experiences
Extend vocabulary, especially by grouping and naming Use vocabulary and forms of speech that are increasingly influenced by experience of books	In talking about his visit to his grandad, Aaron said, 'Once upon a time, I went ...'	■ Encourage children to sort, group and sequence in their play – use words such as *last, first, next, before, after, all, most, some, each, every* ■ Encourage language play, for example through stories like 'Goldilocks' and action songs that require intonation
Extend their vocabulary, exploring the meanings and sounds of new words	Tony enjoys putting words together to make new words. He describes his new puppy as 'nibblynaughty' when he tells everyone about his shoes being chewed.	■ Provide opportunities for talking for a wide range of purposes. For example to present ideas to others as descriptions, explanations, instructions or justifications and to discuss and plan individual or shared activities ■ Encourage children to experiment with words and sounds, for example in nonsense rhymes

DfEE (2000), pages 52–53

Early Learning Goals for mathematical development

By the end of the foundation stage, most children will be able to:

- say and use number names in order in familiar contexts;
- count reliably up to ten everyday objects;
- recognise numerals one to nine;
- use language such as 'more' or 'less', 'greater' or 'smaller', 'heavier' or 'lighter', to compare two numbers or quantities;
- in practical activities and discussion begin to use the vocabulary involved in adding and subtracting;
- find one more or one less than a number from one to ten;
- begin to relate addition to combining two groups of objects, and subtraction to 'taking away';
- talk about, recognise and recreate simple patterns;
- use language such as 'circle' or 'bigger' to describe the shape and size of solids and flat shapes;
- use everyday words to describe position;
- use developing mathematical ideas and methods to solve practical problems.

Early Learning Goals for calculating

Stepping stones	Examples of what children do	What does the practitioner need to do?
Compare two groups of objects, saying when they have the same number	The children were watching the goldfish swim around. Terri said, 'Those two are playing with each other, but that one is all on his own.'	■ Model language that may not be as familiar to children as 'more', such as 'same as', 'less' or 'fewer'
Show an interest in number problems Separate a group of three or four objects in different ways, beginning to recognise that the total is still the same	Alan said, 'if you want to come on our plane, we'll have to put in another chair.' A group of children were acting the story of *Three Billy Goats Gruff*. Charlotte said, 'The big one has gone over the bridge, so there are one, two left. Now he's gone over. Only one left.'	■ Create opportunities for children to separate objects into unequal groups as well as equal groups ■ Pose problems as you read number stories or rhymes, for example. 'How many will there be in the pool when one more frog jumps in?' ■ Model and encourage use of related mathematical language, for example 'share', 'some', 'each', 'more', 'less', 'fewer', 'same as' and number names up to five, then 10

Sometimes show confidence and offer solutions to problems

Find the total number of items in two groups by counting all of them

Use own methods to solve a problem

Say with confidence the number that is one more than a given number

Colin and Ben suggest what might be done about the extra biscuit. 'Someone else can have the extra one.' 'Get one more and then we can both have two.'

Adeola enjoyed picking up as many conkers as she could, grabbing more and working out how many she had altogether. 'Five and four ... nine! That's my best go.'

Jordan was finding out which fruit the children wanted. 'Do you want an apple or banana?' he asked and made a mark on his clipboard. He counted the marks, and said, 'There's six apples and nine bananas ... lots more want bananas.' The practitioner asked, 'how many children have you asked?' Jordan looked at his marks. 'That's nine, then, 10, 11, 12, 13, 14, 15. There's 15 people!'

- Pose more complex problems, for example sharing a number of things when there will be a remainder
- Show interest in how children solve problems and value their different solutions
- Encourage children to count how many there are altogether by moving two groups close to each other if necessary
- Encourage children to record what they have done, for example by drawing or tallying
- Provide experience of reciting number names from starting points other than one, to help children 'count on'
- Make sure children are secure about the order of numbers before asking what comes after or before each number
- Play games where a number of objects are hidden from a group and children guess how many
- Deliberately give the wrong number and ask children to tell you how to put it right
- Model and encourage use of mathematical language, for example 'count', 'count on', 'how many', 'altogether', 'add', 'one less' and 'number before'

In practical activities and discussion begin to use the vocabulary involved in adding and subtracting

Use language such as 'more' or 'less' to compare two numbers

Find one more or one less than a number from one to 10

Begin to relate addition to combining two groups of objects and subtraction to 'taking away'

The children were reading a story and predicting what would happen next. 'If two more come there will be seven, because five and two make seven.'

Singing the sausage song, Tessa said, 'If one more bursts there will be four left.'

Playing the dice game, Ryan thought Luke had miscounted. 'No!' said Luke, 'I had seven and then I threw away three, so that's four. That's right!'

- Discuss with children how problems relate to others they have met and their different solutions
- Encourage children to choose numbers for problems and to make up their own story problems for other children to solve
- Encourage children to extend problems, for example, 'Suppose there were three people to share the bricks between instead of two.'

DfEE (2000), pages 76–77

Early Learning Goals for knowledge and understanding of the world

By the end of the foundation stage, most children will be able to:

- investigate objects and materials by using all of their senses as appropriate;
- find out about, and identify some features of, living things, objects and events they observe;
- look closely at similarities, differences, patterns and change;
- ask questions about why things happen and how things work;
- build and construct with a wide range of objects, selecting appropriate resources, and adapting their work where necessary;
- select the tools and techniques they need to shape, assemble and join the materials they are using;
- find out about and identify the uses of everyday technology and use information and communication technology and programmable toys to support their learning;
- find out about past and present events in their own lives, and in those of their families and other people they know;
- observe, find out about and identify features in the place they live and the natural world;
- begin to know about their own cultures and beliefs and those of other people;
- find out about their environment, and talk about those features they like and dislike.

Early Learning Goals for exploration and investigation

Stepping stones	Examples of what children do	What does the practitioner need to do?
Explore objects Show an interest in why things happen and how things work	Amy is fascinated by a kaleidoscope and wonders at the moving shapes and colours.	■ Provide and encourage children to play with and talk about collections of objects that have similar and different properties, for example natural and made, size, colour, shape, texture, function ■ Provide a range of materials and objects to play with that work in different ways for different purposes, for example egg whisk, torch, other household implements, pulleys, construction kits and tape recorder

Sort objects by one function Talk about what is seen and what is happening	While playing with a toy fire engine, Lucy puts all the hoses and reels into one compartment and all hammers and ladders into another	■ Encourage children to sort objects by different criteria, for example things found on a walk or tools in the design area, as they set tables or organise storage of collections of clothes in the home corner ■ Talk about tools and their effects and objects and how they work, for example a washing machine at home, a teapot or a water wheel
Notice and comment on patterns Show an awareness of change	Some children talk about the changes in ingredients as they mix them together during a cooking activity. They watch, fascinated, as the cake rises in the microwave. Nadia and Masud discuss the rising levels and size of bubbles as they use a whisk in the water tray	■ Provide opportunities for children to notice and discuss patterns around them, for example rubbings from grates, covers, bricks, tree bark ■ Discuss events that occur regularly within the children's experience, for example seasonal patterns, daily routines, celebrations ■ Examine change over time, for example growing plants or looking at photographs of children since birth, and change that may be reversed, for example melting ice
Look closely at similarities, differences, patterns and change Ask questions about why things happen and how things work	Angela investigates why the bike stops when the brakes are pressed. She gets her friend to operate the lever as she looks at the way the brakes touch the wheel	■ Encourage children to observe, comment on and record similarities, differences, patterns and change within their activities ■ Model investigative behaviour and raise questions such as, 'What else could we try?', 'What do you think?', 'Tell me more about', 'What will happen if?', 'What could it be used for?' and 'How might it work?' ■ Encourage children to raise questions and suggest solutions and answers

DfEE (2000), pages 88–89

Early Learning Goals for physical development

By the end of the foundation stage, most children will be able to:

- move with confidence, imagination and in safety;
- move with control and co-ordination;
- show awareness of space, of themselves and of others;

- recognise the importance of keeping healthy and those things that contribute to this;
- use a range of small and large equipment;
- travel around, under, over and through balancing and climbing equipment;
- handle tools, objects, construction and malleable materials safely and with increasing control.

Stepping stones	Examples of what children do	What does the practitioner need to do?
Manage body to create intended movements Combine and repeat a range of movements	Nikki was helping to sweep up after lunch. He looked for a piece of food, went over to it, crouched down, brushed it into his dustpan, stood up, went to the bin and emptied the dustpan. He repeated this until all the pieces were gone.	■ Respect individual progress and preoccupations, allow time to explore and practise movements ■ Use observation and knowledge to know when to intervene with fresh challenges or when to allow children time to perfect a new skill or explore an idea ■ Encourage children to move using a range of body parts and to perform given movements at more than one speed such as quickly, slowly, on tiptoe ■ Encourage body tension activities such as stretching, reaching, curling ■ Celebrate each child's attainment by inviting them to demonstrate it as appropriate to others from time to time
Sit up, stand up and balance on various parts of the body Demonstrate the control necessary to hold a shape or fixed position Mount stairs, steps or climbing equipment using alternate feet	While watching the geese in the park, Olivia tries to imitate them by standing on one leg, sometimes overbalancing	■ Celebrate each fresh accomplishment of each child ■ Provide balancing challenges, for example walking along a chalk line – straight and then twisty or on a slightly raised surface ■ Plan games to encourage children to move and then stop, for example moving like an animal ■ Teach and encourage children to use the vocabulary of controlled effort, for example 'strong', 'firm', 'gentle', 'heavy', 'stretch', 'tense', and 'floppy'

		■ Plan opportunities for children to tackle a range of levels and surfaces including flat and hilly ground, grass, pebbles, asphalt, smooth floors and carpets ■ Provide equipment that offers a range of challenges, such as climbing frame, scrambling net and logs
Manipulate materials and objects by picking up, releasing, arranging, threading and posting them Show increasing control over clothing and fastenings	Winston carefully sprinkled the cress seeds over the tray of compost. Ami fastened the buttons on her coat. 'I can't do my dress buttons because they are at the back,' she said	■ Provide objects that can be handled safely, including 'small world' toys, construction sets, threading and posting toys, dolls' clothes, material for collage and shapes ■ Encourage children to adopt a position in which they can work comfortably and effectively, such as sitting, kneeling or standing at a table or at floor level ■ Give individual children opportunities and encouragement to build up the skills which lead to personal autonomy, such as dressing and undressing and using knives/forks/chopsticks
Move with control and co-ordination Travel around, under, over and through balancing and climbing equipment	A group of children were playing 'Snakes and Ladders'. They shook the dice carefully and rolled them onto the floor in a controlled way. They picked up the counters and moved them skilfully up and down the board. The practitioner had created an obstacle course. Claudette swung along the overhead ladder, hand over hand, crawled through the tunnel, hopped along the bench and rolled sideways across the mat.	■ Talk with children about their actions and encourage them to think about and practise the way they move and use resources, for example carrying a book can be done with one hand, a jug of water may need two, the floor is safe to roll over but a narrow bench may need hands and feet ■ Teach children skills that help them in their actions, for example how to lift and move a chair safely

DfEE (2000), pages 106–107

Early Learning Goals for creative development

By the end of the foundation stage, most children will be able to:

- explore colour, texture, shape, form and space in two and three dimensions;
- recognise and explore how sounds can be changed, sing simple songs from memory, recognise repeated sounds and sound patterns, and match movements to music;
- respond in a variety of ways to what they see, hear, smell, touch and feel;
- use their imagination in art and design, music, dance, imaginative and role play and stories;
- express and communicate their ideas, thoughts and feelings by using a widening range of materials, suitable tools, imaginative and role play, movement, designing and making, and a variety of songs and musical instruments.

Early Learning Goals for exploring media and materials

Stepping stones	Examples of what children do	What does the practitioner need to do?
Begin to differentiate colours Use their bodies to explore texture and space Make three-dimensional structures	The children collect paper and materials for a 'texture wall'. They touch them with their fingers and feel them against their cheeks to get a sense of their properties. Amy holds up a piece of wrinkled shiny paper and is transfixed by the effect of light hitting it.	■ Provide a wide range of materials, resources and sensory experiences to enable the children to explore colour and texture ■ Make time and space for the children to express their curiosity and explore the environment using all the senses ■ Extend children's thinking through sensitive and well-timed and well-considered comments and questions ■ Be aware of health and safety issues as children explore the environment, explaining what is and is not safe to touch and where it is safe to engage in movement

Differentiate marks and movements on paper

Begin to describe the texture of things

Use lines to enclose a space, then begin to use these shapes to represent objects

Begin to construct stacking blocks vertically and horizontally and making enclosures and creating spaces

Alexander is using purple paint, which is his favourite colour. He makes lots of 'spiral' marks and movements on his paper. He repeats this exercise using crayons and again in his lunchtime custard. He goes to the music area and dances round and round to a tape. Emily joins in and they imitate each other's movements.

- Demonstrate, teach and model skills and techniques associated with the things children are doing, for example show them how to stop the paint from dripping or how to balance bricks so that they will not fall down.
- Introduce vocabulary to enable children to talk about their observations and experiences, for example 'smooth', 'shiny', 'rough', 'prickly', 'flat', 'patterned', 'jagged', 'bumpy', 'soft', and 'hard'
- Make suggestions and ask questions to extend children's ideas, for example, 'I wonder what would happen if you used the chalk on its side on that bumpy piece of paper?'

Explore what happens when they mix colours

Understand that different media can be combined

Make constructions, collages, paintings, drawings and dances

Use ideas involving fitting, overlapping, in, out, enclosure, grids and sun-like shapes

Choose particular colours to use for a purpose

Experiment to create different textures

Work creatively on a large or small scale

Melanie tips red and white paint on to her mixing tray and stirs them together. With much delight she announces, 'Look, look, it's gone pink!'

A small group of children were dancing. They circled round and round each other, and went through the spaces between each other.

After watching a television programme about dinosaurs, Philip used lots of boxes to make a large model. He looked for something hard and scaly for the dinosaur's back.

- Support children in mixing colours, joining things together and combining materials, demonstrating where appropriate
- Introduce vocabulary to encourage children to describe their actions and the effects of their actions
- Encourage children to move and use spaces to develop creative ideas
- Support children in thinking through their projects, making suggestions and offering options
- Help children gain confidence in their own way of representing ideas
- Offer constructive feedback and help children to begin to make aesthetic judgements about their work. Ask questions such as, 'Was that how you wanted it to look?', 'Is there any part you would like to change?' and 'Which bit do you like best?'

Explore colour, texture, shape, form and space in two or three dimensions

A small group of children are using large blocks to represent their experience of a visit to the ferry port. Having constructed a large model that covers most of the carpeted area, they focus on the fine detail. After much discussion and negotiation they make arrows for the one-way system and a variety of signs and symbols. They tell the stories of the various people who will go on the ferry and are most concerned as to whether one family will get there on time.

- Provide children with opportunities to use their skills and explore concepts and ideas through their representations
- Support children in making choices
- Help children to express the way they feel about their representations, modelling appropriate words at appropriate times, for example, 'That makes me feel very...'
- Continue to give constructive feedback and support children in making aesthetic judgements

DfEE (2000), pages 120–121

The national curriculum

The national curriculum is a mandatory (compulsory) curriculum for children in all state schools. Privately funded schools are not obliged to follow the same guidelines, but in practice many of them do. The national curriculum is divided into various stages and is set out as follows:

	Pupil ages	Year groups
Key stage 1 (KS1)	5–7 year olds	1–2
Key stage 2 (KS2)	7–11 year olds	3–6
Key stage 3 (KS3)	11–14 year olds	7–9
Key stage 4 (KS4)	14–16 year olds	10–11

At the end of each key stage there are a number of tests that all children must complete. These are the **national curriculum standard attainment tasks (SATs),** and they are used to monitor each individual child's performance as they progress through school.

Key stage 1 includes:

- English;
- Mathematics;
- Science;
- Technology (design and technology, and information technology);
- History;
- Geography;
- Art;

- Music;
- Physical Education.

The attainment targets at the end of key stage 1 are based around the following areas of learning:

English
Speaking and listening
Reading
Writing

Mathematics
Using and Applying Mathematics
Number and Algebra
Shape, Space and Measure
Handling Data

Science
Experimental and Investigative Science
Life Processes and Living Things
Materials and their Properties
Physical Processes

Design and Technology
Designing
Making

Art
Investigating and Making
Knowledge and Understanding

Music
Performing and Composing
Listening and Appraising

For each of the other subjects, teachers make a decision about the level attained based on the range of descriptions set out for each key stage level. Details of these can be found in *Key Stages 1 and 2 of the National Curriculum* (DfEE, HMSO). Your college library will probably stock a copy.

Activity 5.7

If you have a placement in a Year 1 or Year 2 class you are likely to find yourself working with children who are following key stage 1. Note the way in which their learning follows on from the foundation stage. For example, you will find that many of the tasks they are set assume that certain skills have already been learnt.

1 Give an example for the English curriculum.

2 Give an example for the Mathematics curriculum.

3 Give an example for the Physical Education curriculum.

4 Share your examples with others in your group. What additional examples are they able to offer?

Key terms

You should now understand the following key words and phrases. If you do not, read through the chapter again and review them.

appropriate support

avoiding stereotyping and discrimination

evaluating activities

foundation stage curriculum

importance of preparation

importance of using real tools

interest tables

meeting differentiation of need

national curriculum

natural materials

outings with children

play

small world play

standard attainment tasks (SATs)

supervision

Test Yourself

1　In what ways does play help a child develop?

2　What does the term 'holistic' mean?

3　How many points can you think of that need to be considered when planning an activity?

4　What are the six areas of learning in the foundation stage curriculum?

5　When do children normally move into key stage 1 of the national curriculum?

6　Give at least five examples of creative activities.

7　Give at least five examples of how music can be introduced to children.

8　Explain three different ways of enabling children to enjoy books.

9　What is the difference between large scale and small scale construction?

10　In what ways can the role-play corner give opportunities for mathematics development?

11　How can you ensure equal opportunities within role play?

12　When producing a recipe card to use during a cooking activity with young children, what should you include?

13　Give five examples of suitable cooking activities with young children.

14　What is the difference between locomotor and non-locomotor skills?

15　Give at least three examples of equipment to support locomotor development and three to support non-locomotor development.

16　What is malleable play? Give at least three examples.

17　What is small world play? Give at least three examples.

18 Shape sorters and puzzles are both structured activities. How do they help physical development? What other examples of structured activities can you think of?

19 What is an interest table? What sorts of items would normally be included?

20 In what ways do plants and animals offer valuable learning opportunities for young children?

References and suggested further reading

Hobart, C and Frankel, J (1999) *A Practical Guide to Activities for Young Children* (2nd edn), Nelson Thornes

Qualification and Curriculum Authority (QCA) *Early Learning Goals* (2000), DfEE

Tassoni, P and Hucker, K (2000) *Planning Play and the Early Years*, Heinemann

Series

Stepping Stones series by Nelson Thornes. Titles include:
At Home and Far Away
Gardens
Ourselves
Toys
Creatures Great and Small
Food

Journals and magazines

Examples include:
Nursery World
Nursery Education
Nursery Projects
Child Education

Websites

www.qca.org.uk

www.toy-tia.org

6 Care of babies

In studying how to care for babies you will develop your understanding of their growth and development, together with a variety of ways of stimulating them, responding to them, and caring for them. Babies have particular needs regarding supervision and hygiene, and you will need to be aware of them all.

Normal growth and development of babies 0–12 months

Throughout childhood growth is rapid, being particularly so during the first year, with a steadier rate developing from the toddler stage onwards. Infants and young children are measured using the **centile charts** (see illustrations below). These charts enable **health visitors** and **paediatricians** (doctors specialising in the care of babies) to monitor development, and to identify any causes for concern in babies' growth rates. Slight differences in the growth expectations of girl infants and boy infants are expected, with boys, on average, being slightly heavier than girls at birth. The 50th centile line is the central line on the centile charts. It indicates what the average is at each age. The upper and lower lines represent the boundary within which 80 per cent of children will fall. A child who falls outside of these boundaries will be monitored more closely and may need further investigation into their development at some stage.

The pattern (or line) formed as a child's measurements are plotted on the centile chart is known as a 'growth curve'.

In the following centile charts you can see that there are slight differences between the expectations for girls compared to the expectations for boys.

Birth and the neonatal stage (up to one month)

Definition

Neonate
An infant under one month old.

Immediately after birth, each infant is assessed using the **Apgar score**. This gives an important indication regarding the infant's well-being and immediate healthcare needs, and is therefore an important aspect of neonatal care. An illustration and explanation of the Apgar score chart is found in Unit 8.

LINKS TO UNIT 8, pages 321–322.

A centile chart for the weight of a baby girl

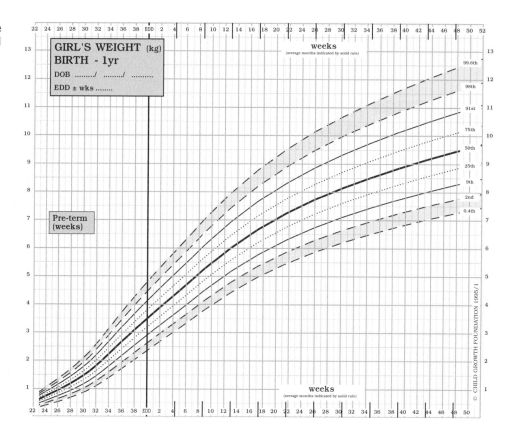

A centile chart for the length of a baby girl

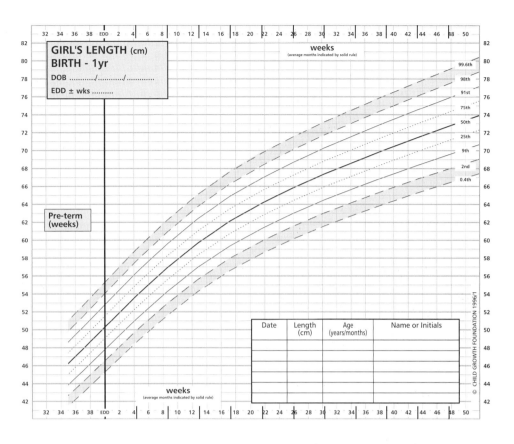

A centile chart for the head circumference of a baby girl

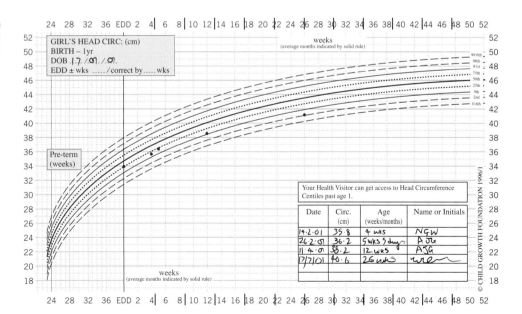

A centile chart for the head circumference of a baby boy

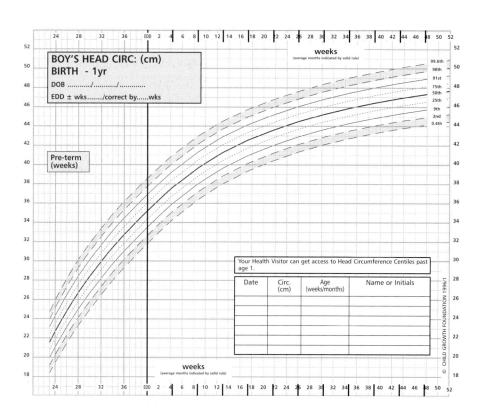

The normal neonate

When an infant is delivered there are many distinct features regarding their skin, eyes, senses and general appearance. You will find more on this in Unit 8, but the following illustration shows the features you will find summarised there.

- Sleep
- Lack of head control
- Vernix caseosa
- Lanuga
- Fontanelles: posterior and anterior
- Flattened or mis-shapened head
- The umbilical 'stump'
- Swelling or bruising
- Sticky eyes
- Unco-ordinated eyes
- Eye colour
- Flexed posture of infants
- Poor circulation
- Swollen genitalia
- Posture

- Effects of mother's hormones
- Infant's stools (faeces)
- Spots and rashes
- Peeling skin
- Neonatal jaundice

Birthmarks
- Port wine marks
- Strawberry naevus (haemangioma)
- 'Stork bite'
- Mongolian blue spots
- CMNs (congenital melanocytic naevus)

Reflexes
- Blinking reflex
- Rooting reflex
- Sucking reflex
- Palmar grasp
- Plantar reflex
- Stepping reflex
- Moro reflex
- Startle reflex
- Asymmetric tonic neck reflex

The senses
- Hearing
- Vision
- Touch
- Smell

Infancy: one month to one year

As the infant grows new skills develop continuously, building on what they have previously achieved. This section outlines those changes and has been divided into three main areas of development. They are:

- physical development;
- cognitive and language development;
- social and emotional development.

Physical development (gross motor skills)

Gross motor skills are the skills that involve whole body movements. The development between the neonatal stage and the infant's first birthday can be summarised as follows:

- the infant's movements initially remain jerky and uncontrolled;
- head lag gradually decreases, and head control is usually achieved by five months;
- rolling over is first seen between four and six months (from back to side), and then from front to back by about eight months;
- reaching for objects usually begins at about four months with the ability to pass toys from hand to hand from about seven months;
- at four months the infant discovers their own feet, and also manages to sit with support;
- sitting alone commences at about seven to eight months, with greater balance gradually developing;
- crawling can start from six months (commando crawling on their tummies) and traditional crawling often from about eight months, while some infants bear-walk or bottom-shuffle;
- some infants miss out the crawling stage, and move straight to pulling themselves up on furniture at around eight to ten months;
- standing alone can occur any time from ten months, but is more usual at around a year, when generally the infant's balance is more established;
- walking is normally achieved by twelve to sixteen months.

Physical development (fine motor skills)

Fine motor skills involve the development of hand and finger co-ordination, gradually developing the ability to control their environment and the objects within it. It can be summarised as follows:

- hand and finger movements gradually increase, from the grasping of adults' fingers in the earliest months, through to playing with their own fingers and toes;
- handling and then holding toys and objects from three to four months;
- everything is explored through the mouth;
- at about seven months, the infant will try to transfer objects from one hand to the other with some success;
- pincer grasp (finger and thumb) begins to emerge;
- by about ten months, pincer grasp is developed;
- the infant will pick up small objects;
- toys are pulled towards the infant;

Crawling can start from 6 months

Walking is normally achieved by 12–16 months

- pointing and clapping are deliberate actions for most infants by ten to twelve months;
- controlled efforts are made when feeding, with some successes.

The infant will pick up small objects

Cognitive and language development

- The infant continues to explore by taking objects to their mouth throughout most of the first year.
- By about four months recognition of an approaching feed is demonstrated by excited actions and squeals.
- Language develops through cooing, gurgling, excited squealing and changing tones of their own voice.
- By five months enjoyment of the infant's own voice is obvious. Chuckles and laughs are evident.
- By about eight months the infant babbles continuously and tunefully, for example, mamamama babababa.
- By nine to ten months the infant begins to understand that an object exists even if it has been covered up. The term used to describe this is object permanence.
- First 'words' may be apparent by a year, usually dada, mama, baba.
- Understanding of simple instructions or statements begins from about nine months, and is clearly evident by a year.

Social and emotional development

- The first social smile is usually seen by six weeks.
- Smiling is first confined to the main carers, and then in response to most contacts.
- The infant concentrates on the faces of their carers.
- Pleasure during handling and caring routines is seen by eight weeks, through smiles, cooing and general contentment.
- Expressions of pleasure are clear when gaining attention from about twelve weeks.

- Social games, involving handling and cuddles, gain chuckles from four to five months onwards.
- Infants enjoy watching other infants.
- Regular sleep patterns begin to emerge from about four months onwards, although these will continue to change.
- From about nine or ten months the infant may become distressed when the main carer leaves them temporarily, losing their sense of security and becoming wary of strangers. This is a normal stage in development.
- Playing contentedly alone increases by one year, but the reassuring presence of an adult is still needed.

Making eye contact

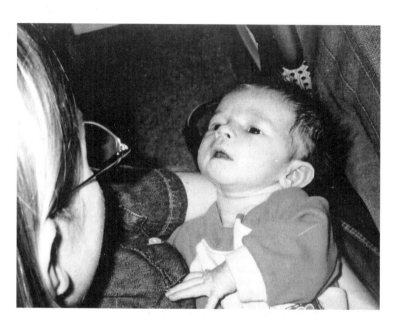

Care routines

The routine of any setting caring for babies needs to be designed to specifically meet the needs of each individual infant in the setting's care, taking into consideration each area of their development. As the carer of a baby you will need to think how you meet a baby's:

- social needs;
- intellectual (or cognitive) needs;
- physical needs;
- language needs;
- emotional needs.

Care routines must be constantly monitored for their suitability, as they will need to be adjusted as the infant gets older, in order to meet their changing developmental needs. These needs will include:

- sleeping patterns, as the infant gradually has longer periods of wakefulness;
- feeding times, incorporating the introduction of weaning;
- amounts of time spent specifically playing with them;
- time for stimulation, involving games, music, outings and so on;
- time for rest and relaxation, sleep, cuddles and books.

Babies need a routine that is not rigid but provides continuity and security for them. A secure baby is usually a settled baby. Babies have periods of wakefulness and periods of deep sleep. They can appear very alert and content at times, and restless and irritable at others. A baby's day needs to include:

- sufficient feeds for their current age, weight and level of development;
- sufficient extended periods of sleep;
- time for love and cuddles;
- stimulation through toys, adult communications and through the general environment;
- regular changes of nappies;
- opportunities for fresh air.

Fostering relationships

Part of the role of the carers of young babies is to develop a secure relationship with them. This gives the baby a secure base developed through familiarity, and also offers constant care and clear understanding of the individual baby's needs. This will also increase the trust and feelings of security of the baby's parents. Most baby rooms within nurseries operate to a key worker system. This means that each baby is linked specifically to one carer, who will take overall responsibility for monitoring their well-being, feeding, changing and generally caring for them.

Parents will also know whom to approach specifically to ask about their baby's well-being and to whom to pass information. This is an important aspect of a setting working in partnership with parents.

Case Study

Happy Hippos Creche

Happy Hippos is a creche catering for children from six weeks up to school age, and is set within a further education college. It is open between 8.50 a.m. and 4.15 p.m. to accommodate parents on a variety of courses. Sanita is three months old and is about to join the creche baby room. Her mother speaks little English and is taking language support classes for a twelve-week term.

1 What routine would you expect Sanita's day to take?
2 How is Sanita's daily routine likely to change over the next three months?
3 How could the creche staff ensure that clear communication takes place between themselves and Sanita's mother?

Definition

Paediatric
Specifically for children

Management of a distressed baby

Babies become distressed for lots of reasons. It may be because they are tired, wet, hungry, uncomfortable, unwell, teething or simply bored. Working out what is the cause of their distress is not always easy. If a young baby is distressed at the same time of day every day, it can often be attributed to **colic**.

Remember!

Every baby is different. Each baby has their own individual personality. Some babies cry much more than others. It is possible to overstimulate a baby, tiring them and causing irritability. Illness must never be ruled out, but will usually be considered when other causes have been eliminated unless additional symptoms are present. Offer support to parents of a constantly crying baby as it can be very draining.

Activity 6.1

1 Research the support group 'Cry-sis'.
2 Prepare a leaflet about Cry-sis that could be given to parents or carers of a regularly distressed infant.

'I'm tired'
Babies become over-tired if they do not have sufficient periods of restful sleep, and a baby who is constantly disturbed may become irritable. It is important to allow babies an extended period of sleep whenever possible.

Colic – 'my tummy hurts'
This is a painful condition, common in the first four months, in which the baby pulls up their legs indicating abdominal pain and is very difficult to console. There is no known cause for colic and it tends to disappear by itself by the time the baby reaches four months old. It is, however, distressing for both baby and carer, and advice from a health visitor is advisable. The baby is usually thriving well in spite of the colic and no other symptoms are displayed.

'I want my nappy changed'
A wet or soiled nappy is uncomfortable, and most babies prefer to be clean and dry. Regular changing of babies helps prevent the development of nappy rash, as does allowing fresh air to their bottoms by leaving them to kick freely at some point each day.

'My gums hurt'
If a baby is unwell or teething they may simply want to be cuddled. For a teething baby, a refrigerated teething ring will help cool down their gums and firm, flexible teething toys will give them something appropriate to chew hard on. Preparations are available to rub on to the gums to alleviate discomfort of the gums. and paediatric paracetamol can be given in times of extreme discomfort.

'Please leave me alone'
Sometimes babies become distressed when being handled, but this is usually a stage that passes quickly. Handling of these babies should be gentle and kept to a minimum until they once again find it more pleasurable.

'I'm too hot'
A baby who is too hot or too cool may also cry in discomfort. Adjusting the temperature of the room or their clothing will usually help.

'I am so bored'
Sometimes, however, babies are simply bored, and so it is important to offer them stimulation. Three-dimensional mobiles over the cot or hanging from the ceiling are ideal visual stimulants and musical toys for them to listen to will stimulate them aurally. Babies also enjoy the company of their carers and will respond with pleasure and recognition from a very early age.

'I want my bottle'
A hungry or thirsty baby is often the easiest to identify as they tend to root for the breast or bottle when picked up or suck on whatever passes their mouth. In a daycare setting it is important to make a note of the time and amount of feed taken by the baby. This helps you to anticipate their next feed time and gives appropriate information to their parents.

Babies become distressed for lots of reasons

Remember! Sometimes babies will simply want a drink in the same way as adults and older children do. Small amounts of cooled boiled water can be introduced to even very young babies, especially in hot weather.

Remember! Babies are best dressed in layers of lightweight clothing that can be taken off or added to as necessary.

Hygiene, health and safety procedures

Caring for the physical needs of a baby includes looking after their skin, hair and tooth care, bathing and nappy changing, rest, sleep and play routines. Particular attention will need to be paid to hygiene, health practices and safety. **Cross-infection** can be minimised by strict handwashing and attention to anti-bacterial cleansing of nappy changing areas, sinks, toilets and so on.

Each baby in a daycare setting should have their own changing items, which are kept separate, therefore helping to reduce the possibility of cross-infection.

Caring for babies' skin

Care of the skin is important because it is the front line area of defence for the body as it comes into contact with the environment. It is necessary to protect the skin from short-term problems:

- discomfort;
- irritation;
- infection.

It is also necessary to protect the skin from long-term problems:

- sunburn;
- sun damage (that can lead to skin cancers);
- scarring from repeated irritation or infections.

Babies have sensitive skin and many of our everyday products are far too harsh for them. It is therefore important to use specially prepared baby products suitable for sensitive skins during all care routines.

Skin types

Skin types vary, as do family practices, and it is important that in any Early Years setting the preferences of parents are taken into account. Most daycare settings ask parents to provide their own products and these are clearly labelled and kept solely for the use of their baby.

An example of individual care practice would be Jerome. Jerome is West Indian and his skin tends to be very dry. His parents rub cocoa butter into his skin after his bath. They also massage his skin with oil, particularly his arms and legs, at each nappy change. They have supplied Jerome's nursery with a bottle of oil, and asked them to continue this practice during the day.

Babies with black skin have a greater tendency to dry skin than those with other skin types.

Remember! Any oil used on babies and young children should be free of nut traces (almond oil used to be popular but is no longer used), as there is concern about links with the increase in nut allergies in young children. Many specialists recommend the use of organic sunflower oil, which is what Jerome's parents use.

Eczema

Definition

Eczema
A dry, scaly, itchy skin condition.

A common skin complaint in young children is eczema. Children with this condition will need particular support during bad phases. Some will need to have prescribed ointments applied during the day. Staff taking on this role should wear disposable gloves to reduce the risk of passing any infection on to the child, and also to prevent themselves from absorbing the ointments or creams (which often incorporate corticosteroids) into their own skin.

Note: Older children with eczema may need to be encouraged to wear gloves during activities such as sand play to avoid exacerbating their condition. They should be taught to wash and dry their skin carefully and thoroughly.

Skin infestations and conditions

From time to time **skin infestations** and infectious conditions can occur in Early Years settings. These can spread very quickly, but preventive measures for cross-infection, which should be standard practice, should help contain them to some extent. There will usually be a policy regarding the admittance of children and babies with an infectious condition. Ask your current placement setting if you can see what is included in their policy. Skin infestations and infectious conditions include:

- scabies;
- impetigo;
- hand, foot and mouth.

Scabies

What is scabies?	Scabies are tiny parasites that burrow into the skin. They are sometimes known as itch mites due to the intense itching they cause, particularly at night. It is an extremely infectious condition, which is passed on by physical contact, either from person to person, or via towels, flannels and bedding.
Identifying scabies	The scabies mites burrow into the skin, leaving thin track marks under the skin where they have passed through. The itching causes redness and sore patches, which may at times be mistaken for eczema.
Treatment	Scabies will not disappear without treatment. A special lotion prescribed by the GP is needed, and each individual who has been in contact with the infected child needs to be treated. This usually includes their whole family and the staff in their care setting who have worked closely with them.

Impetigo

What is impetigo?	Impetigo is an extremely infectious skin condition, which often affects the mouth and nose. It also affects the nappy area of babies. It is caused by bacteria, which enter the body through a break in the skin. As with scabies, it is passed on by physical contact, either from person to person, or via towels, flannels and bedding.
Identifying impetigo	Red skin with tiny blisters is the most noticeable sign. The blisters weep and gradually crust over with yellowish scabs.
Treatment	Antibiotic creams will be needed from the child's GP. It is important to try to avoid cross-infection, and to discourage children from scratching. Babies and toddlers may benefit from wearing cotton gloves at night. Scarring can occur if scratching is intense. Complications are a possibility, causing a general infection of the body, which can affect the child's kidneys.

Hand, foot and mouth

Hand, foot and mouth is discussed in Unit 3. You may find it useful to refer back to that section now.

 LINKS TO UNIT 3, page 147.

Activity 6.2

These are not the only skin problems you might come across when working with babies and young children. What other skin infestations or problems can you find out about?

Case Study

Bluebell Nursery

There is an outbreak of an infestation in Bluebell nursery, and you have been asked to prepare a brief note to be given to parents. You can select whichever infestation you wish for your example.

1 How will you explain the condition to the parents?

2 What advice and guidance could you offer them?

3 What reassurance can you give them regarding the practice of the staff in the nursery?

4 Do you think an illustration would be helpful?

Sun care

Research has shown how seriously our skin can be damaged by the sun's rays, and children and babies should not be exposed to the sun for more than a very short period of time. Babies should be kept in the shade whenever possible (watch out for the sun moving round) and outdoor play in sunny areas should be restricted, particularly around midday when the sun is at its highest point.

Hats should be worn, and each setting should have a policy regarding the application of suncreams. Sunscreen creams and lotions for children and babies should be of the highest factor, or be a total sun block. Written parental permission should be obtained before staff apply cream to any child.

Hair and tooth care

Hair care is needed to prevent infestation from headlice and to encourage good grooming for the future. Again, cultural practices differ. Muslim babies will have their heads shaved within forty days of birth as part of cultural tradition, and many Caribbean parents traditionally weave and plait their babies' hair at a very early age.

Washing the hair of babies can at times be traumatic, as not all babies are happy to have water in their eyes. Hair rings can be purchased, which prevent water from reaching the eyes and can make for a happier bathtime. Hair washing products should always be 'non-stinging' to the eyes. There are plenty of different products available.

Dental care

The brushing of a baby's teeth should commence as soon as the first ones arrive, and definitely when a baby has corresponding teeth top and bottom. Soft baby toothbrushes are specially designed for the delicate gums and first teeth, and their regular use will encourage the baby into a habit of good oral health care for the future. In daycare settings each baby should have their own toothbrush, which should be labelled and kept separately.

It is important to teach children the correct amount of toothpaste to use, and to remember that toothpaste should not be swallowed.

The usual order in which milk teeth appear

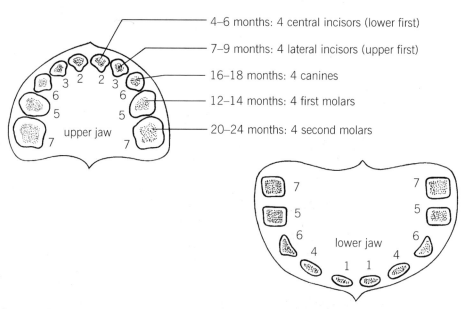

4–6 months: 4 central incisors (lower first)

7–9 months: 4 lateral incisors (upper first)

16–18 months: 4 canines

12–14 months: 4 first molars

20–24 months: 4 second molars

upper jaw

lower jaw

Choosing clothes for babies

Adults need to take responsibility for what the children in their care wear, as young children are not able to make an 'informed' choice for themselves, but those who are able to will state their preferences with no regard to temperature, weather or planned activity.

Clothing for babies needs to:
- be easy to put on and take off;
- have room for them to grow;
- allow unrestricted movement;
- be suitable for the time of year and temperature of the environment they are in;

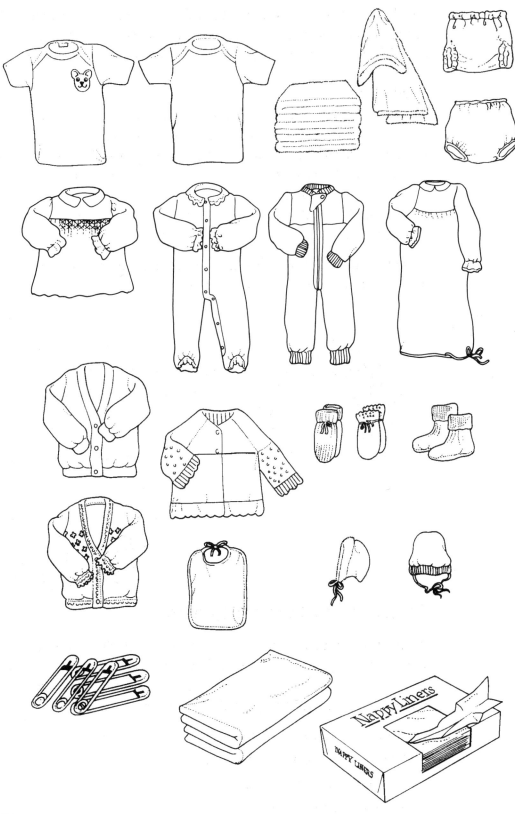

A baby's clothing

- avoid cramping of their toes (for example in all-in-one suits);
- be free from long ties or ribbons (to avoid choking);
- be free from loose buttons or poppers (another choking hazard);
- be free from looped edgings on seams that may catch their fingers;
- avoid lacy designs that may also catch small fingers;
- be easy to wash and dry;
- be made of natural materials such as cotton to allow the baby's skin to breathe;
- not involve fluffy materials or wools such as mohair as this can irritate noses and get in hands and mouths;
- be of a suitable length for dresses not to get caught when toddling or crawling;
- be washed in non-biological powders to avoid reactions to the harsh detergents in many modern washing agents.

Remember! It is better for babies to wear several layers of clothes that can be removed or replaced according to temperature, than one warmer layer that offers no opportunity for adjustment, as babies are not able to control their body temperature and could therefore become overheated.

Babies' footcare

Babies' feet are very delicate and their bones are still forming, therefore they should not be given shoes before they are walking, as this can hinder the natural growth and development of their feet, leading to deformity. Socks, all-in-one suits and bootees should all have sufficient room for natural movement and growth.

Remember! When a baby is ready to have their first pair of proper shoes it is important to have their feet measured and shoes fitted by a footcare specialist.

Bathing and nappy changing

Hygiene must always be a top priority when dealing with body fluids of any kind. This includes nappy changes. In daycare settings the use of disposable gloves is now the norm, whereas in a home setting good personal hygiene practice should be sufficient.

Babies are usually topped and tailed in the mornings, and bathed in the evening before being put to bed. **Topping and tailing** involves washing the face and refreshing the top half of the body, together with changing the nappy.

Topping and tailing

Preparation

Get everything ready in advance. You will need:

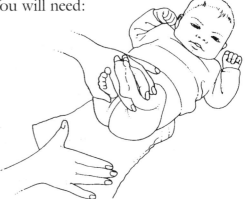

- towel;
- changing mat;
- bowl of cooled boiled water;
- bowl of warm water;
- cotton wool;
- barrier cream (if using);
- a clean nappy;
- a fresh set of clothes;
- access to a nappy bucket (for towelling nappies); or
- a nappy sack (if using disposables);
- access to the laundry basket for clothes.

Method

1 Place baby on changing mat and undress to their vest and nappy.

2 Using the cooled boiled water, wipe each eye from the nose corner outwards, using each piece of cotton wool only once.

3 Repeat two or three times for each eye.

4 Dry gently with the corner of a clean towel.

5 Gently clean ears and around the face using moistened cotton wool, ensuring that you reach all the creases, particularly under the chin and behind the ears. Dry gently.

6 Using a larger piece of moistened cotton wool, freshen up the baby's armpits and hands, removing all fibres collected between the fingers. Dry gently.

7 In newborn babies check that the umbilical stump is clean, but do not clean it unnecessarily. Whenever possible, it should be left alone. (They tend to shrivel up and drop off seven to ten days after birth.)

8 Remove soiled nappy and place in bucket or nappy sack.

9 Clean the nappy area thoroughly, with warm water (or baby wipes if used), ensuring that you clean all creases, wiping from the front to the back.

10 Put on clean nappy (applying barrier cream if used), dress and have a cuddle!

Remember!

Cleansing of a girl's nappy area should always be by wiping from the front to the back to avoid any infection from the bowels passing into the vaginal area. Cleansing of a boy's nappy area does not necessitate the pulling back of the foreskin. Excessive cleaning can actually cause irritation and infection, rather than preventing it.

Changing nappies

Parents and carers today have a vast array of choices regarding the type of nappies they use. Disposable nappies are extremely absorbent and can be easy to use, but they are expensive and are a significant environmental concern. Towelling nappies are cheaper to use, but they have to be washed and dried. In many areas there are nappy laundering services. These are expensive to use, but sometimes appeal to the environmentally conscious parent, who does not want to bother with the extra washing themselves. Towelling nappies can be bought ready 'shaped', or as squares that need to be folded. If folding the nappy yourself there are a number of ways to do this, as shown below.

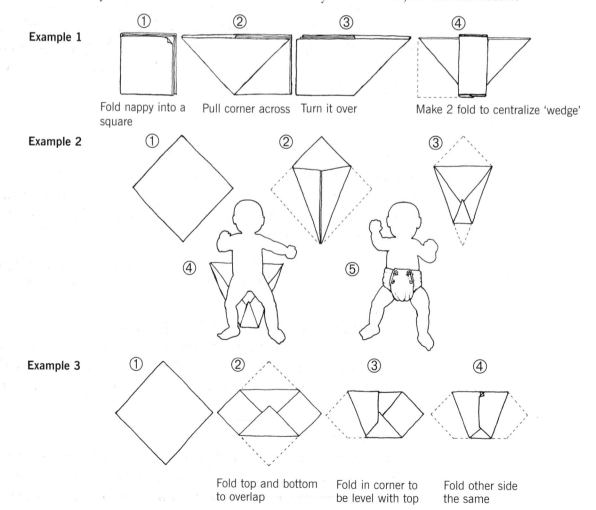

Example 1

① ② ③ ④

Fold nappy into a   Pull corner across   Turn it over   Make 2 fold to centralize 'wedge'
square

Example 2

① ② ③ ④ ⑤

Example 3

① ② ③ ④

Fold top and bottom   Fold in corner to   Fold other side
to overlap   be level with top   the same

Activity 6.3

1 Within your group, plan, research and carry out a debate on the benefits and drawbacks of towelling nappies and disposable nappies. Remember to consider issues of cost, convenience and the impact on the environment.

2 Back up your debate with evidence.

Bowel and bladder problems in children

Definition

Dehydration
Where the water content of the body falls dangerously low.

Minor bowel and bladder problems

All children suffer from diarrhoea and constipation at some point. These are usually due to a gastro-enteritis, a viral infection (diarrhoea) or changes in the diet (constipation). They are unpleasant conditions, but rarely serious.

Diarrhoea

Avoiding food, and drinking plenty of clear fluids, usually helps a child remain hydrated, until the virus has passed. If, however, a child suffers from vomiting and diarrhoea for a considerable length of time, they may begin to dehydrate, particularly babies and toddlers, and medical attention will be important to ensure that their body is rehydrated. More information on gastro-enteritis and other common illnesses in children can be found in Unit 3.

LINKS TO UNIT 3, page 148.

Constipation

Usually, increasing the child's consumption of roughage (fruits and vegetables in particular) will reduce the problem, and improve their health in general too. If the problem continues, advice from a health professional may be needed.

Remember! Laxatives should never be given to a child without medical advice.

More serious bowel and bladder problems

Children with certain chronic conditions suffer from either intermittent or constant bowel problems. This includes children with cystic fibrosis and coeliac disease. Both of these conditions are regularly diagnosed by the toddler stage.

Cystic fibrosis (CF)

This is a condition that is mostly associated with respiratory problems, due to the sticky secretions that build up in the lungs, but is a serious digestive condition too. The obstruction in the bowel associated with

CF is often found shortly after birth. An outline of its main symptoms can be found in Unit 3, on page 98.

Coeliac disease

Coeliac is a condition affecting the lining of the small intestine. It is an intolerance of the protein gluten, which is found in wheat, barley, rye and oats.

Symptoms indicating coeliac begin to show once foods containing gluten are introduced to the infant's diet. Suffers of this condition fail to thrive in the usual way, by not putting on weight and being continuously low on the centile growth charts. Children are lethargic and pass pale, unpleasant stools. The condition can be confirmed through blood tests or a biopsy of the jejeunum (part of the small intestine).

The only way to control the symptoms of coeliac is for a gluten-free diet to be adopted. This will be necessary for life. Advice will be given to the family from a dietician, as gluten is found in many everyday foods, and establishing what is suitable and what must be avoided can take time.

If coeliac remains untreated it can lead to iron deficiency anaemia and possible long-term problems with bone density. Calcium supplements are often given throughout life.

Bathing

Bathing young babies is usually very pleasurable, and can be carried out by either the 'traditional' method or the 'modern' method. Early Years professionals need to be able to carry out both methods, to meet with parental preferences.

Traditional method

Prepare everything in advance, ensuring that the temperature of the room is suitable (at least 20°C/68°F) with no draughts, and that all windows and doors are closed. All that you will need must be to hand, and the bath should be in a safe and secure place. A special bath stand or a firm surface is ideal, but many people choose to place the baby bath in the family bath or on the floor. Any of these options are acceptable.

You will need:

- bath, with water at 37°C – *always check* this before putting the baby in (using your elbow or preferably a bath thermometer);
- changing mat;
- towels;
- cotton wool;

The traditional method for bathing a baby

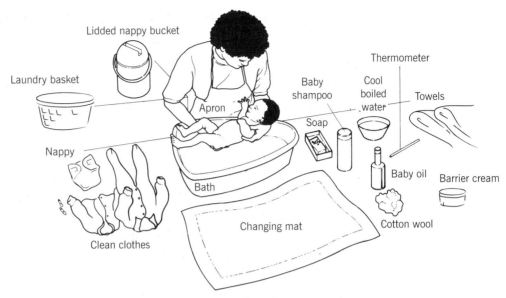

- bowl of cooled boiled water (for the eyes);
- shampoo (if using);
- soap;
- barrier cream (if using);
- a clean nappy;
- a fresh set of clothes;
- access to a nappy bucket (for towelling nappies); or
- a nappy sack (if using disposables);
- access to a laundry basket for clothing.

How to do it

1 Undress baby to just their nappy and wrap them in the towel with the top corner folded away from you.

2 Wash eyes and face as in topping and tailing guidelines above.

3 Hold baby over the bath (still wrapped in towel) under your arm, resting on your hip.

4 Gently wet their hair all over.

5 Add shampoo or soap and rub in gently but firmly.

6 Rinse their hair by leaning baby backwards over the bath, towel drying their hair with the folded over corner of the towel.

7 Lay baby across your lap and remove nappy, cleansing away excess faeces.

8 With your spare hand gently wet and soap baby all over, turning them by pulling them over towards you, holding shoulder and thigh, and on to their tummy. When their back and bottom are also soaped, turn again in the same way (always towards you).

273

9 Supporting the baby's head and neck with one hand and their bottom with the other, lower them into the bath.

10 Gently rinse baby all over, continually supporting the head and neck with your wrist, and holding their shoulder and arm.

11 When ready to be dried, lift baby on to your lap, wrap in towel and cuddle dry!

12 Apply nappy and clothing as before.

13 Brush or groom hair as appropriate.

14 Trim nails as necessary using blunt baby scissors (with parents' permission).

Remember! Always keep hold of the baby, by firmly holding the arm and shoulder furthest away from you. Even very young babies can move suddenly.

Other points to remember

1 Babies usually have a feed after a bath and are then put down to sleep.

2 Only use talcum powder if parents insist. It has been suggested that it may link to the development of asthma in early childhood.

3 Cultural practice regarding hair care, use of oils and creams should be adhered to.

4 *Never* poke cotton buds into ears, noses and so on.

5 Babies need total supervision by a responsible adult at all times when being bathed.

Babies need supervision at all times when being bathed

Modern method

How to do it

1 Bath water, clothing and so on needs to be prepared in the same way as with the traditional method.

2 A bathing preparation is added to the water.

3 The baby is lowered into the water after the eyes and face have been washed.

4 Soaping of the baby is by using the 'bubble bath'.

5 Process then continues as the traditional method.

Remember !

Using a bathing preparation can make the water (and baby) quite slippery, so particular care is needed in holding the baby securely.

If a bathing preparation causes irritation of the baby's skin do not continue its use. Some preparations irritate a baby's skin in the early weeks but can be used without problems later on.

Bathing older babies

From seven or eight months onwards, babies can progress into the family bath, although some babies will prefer the security of the baby bath for far longer. They are usually much more active by this time and the additional room for splashing is appreciated. They are often able to sit alone quite well, but remember that the water will make them buoyant and you will need to be ready to support them if they slip.

Other points to remember

The same precautions are needed regarding temperature, preparation and supervision as with younger babies.

- Ensure that the baby cannot touch the hot tap, which remains hot for some time after use.
- Do not have the water too deep, or the baby will float.
- Sitting on a rubber mat can help them feel more secure.
- A range of containers and bath toys will be enjoyed.
- Many babies enjoy bathing with a parent.

Fearful babies

At times a baby may become fearful of water. This may be due to an incident such as:

- slipping in the bath;
- disliking water getting in their eyes;
- stinging eyes from soaps or shampoos.

You should ensure that you:

- always hold babies securely when in the bath;
- never allow babies to try and stand in the bath;

- always use non-stinging products, especially designed for babies' delicate skin;
- use a hair ring to keep water out of their eyes, if they dislike the sensation;
- do not make a big issue of bathing if it becomes a battle – often if you omit the bath or the hair wash for a couple of days, the issue will go away, as the baby 'forgets' it was a problem.

Remember ! Although most parents and carers like to freshen their babies at the end of each day with a bath, it is not absolutely essential. A good wash using the top and tail method can also maintain good health care.

Preparation of bottle feeds and weaning foods

Feeding and nutritional needs

For the first four months most babies will need only milk feeds, either breast or bottle, giving them all the nutrients they need to support their growth and development.

Breast feeding

Breast milk offers a degree of natural immunity to the infant through the mother's own immunity, and it is considered to be nature's 'designer food', because as the infant grows, the mother's breast milk changes to meet her child's developing needs. The colostrum-rich early milk offers some protection against common infections and is particularly important to newborn infants. Even when mothers are not intending to breast feed long term, they are encouraged to do so for the first few days.

For **breast feeding** to be successful the mother needs to eat well and drink plenty of fluids. The more the baby feeds, the more milk is produced, working on a supply and demand basis. Once the initial stages of breast feeding are passed, and any soreness or discomfort has been overcome, breast feeding is usually considered a pleasurable part of mothering.

Definition

Engorgement
Painful, over-full breasts.

Babies vary considerably in the length of time they suckle. Some will take all they need in just a few minutes, whereas others will suck for far longer. Letting the baby decide the length of a feed will maintain a balance and help prevent engorgement of the breasts. At each feed the baby will initially receive the 'fore' milk, which offers satisfaction in the short term, but the richer 'hind' milk that follows often gives satisfaction for a longer period. It is usual for babies to feed from alternate breasts at alternate feeds.

Expressing breast milk

Many mothers choose to express some of their breast milk, which can then be given in a bottle or cup, and this can be a useful answer to continuing to breast feed when returning to work. Breast pumps can be either manual or mechanical and they produce a vacuum that draws out the milk in much the same way as the baby's sucking. Hand, battery or mains operated pumps are far quicker to use than expressing by hand, and are suitable for expressing significant quantities.

Expressed milk can allow other family members to enjoy the process of feeding the baby, and it can give the mother some time for herself. It can also remove any issues of embarrassment or cultural indiscretions regarding feeding in front of other people.

Expressed milk needs to be kept in sterile containers and refrigerated until needed. Breast milk can be frozen (ice-cube trays are useful for this) and used in preparing solid food when the baby reaches the onset of mixed feeding. Usual sterilising procedures are needed. These processes are discussed on page 279.

Breast-feeding mother's diet

As well as eating well, a lactating mother needs to be aware that whatever she eats will be passed on to her child. This includes alcohol, spicy food, medication and the effects of smoking, so no medication should be taken without checking that it is safe for the breast-feeding child too. This applies to cough and cold remedies as well as prescribed items.

Breast feeding

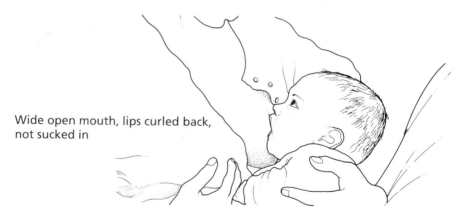

Wide open mouth, lips curled back, not sucked in

Checklist

1 Feeding on demand allows babies to satisfy their hunger.

2 If a baby sleeps well in between feeds it usually means they are getting sufficient nutrients.

3   Regular weighing of babies allows mothers to monitor the sufficiency of their milk production and gives peace of mind.

4   Green, slimy stools may indicate that a baby is not getting enough and longer or more frequent feeds may need to be encouraged.

5   The breast-feeding mother needs to sit comfortably, supporting her back. The baby sucks with lips curled back and takes the whole of the areola into the mouth.

6   Eye contact is made between mother and child during a feed, enhancing bonding, and the developing baby also pats the mother's breast contentedly.

Definition

Areola
The ring of pigmented skin around the nipple.

Formula feeding

Formula milk is an extremely good alternative to breast milk, but no artificial milk can ever be as ideal for a baby's stomach as breast milk. As the baby's nutritional needs change, parents need to make any changes to the formula they use. This is linked to the growth rate of their baby and their levels of hunger. In Early Years settings babies' feeds will usually be supplied ready prepared by the parents and stored in a refrigerator until needed.

In early years settings baby feeds will usually be supplied ready prepared

Remember! Each baby must have their feeds labelled clearly. The feeds must be stored separately to avoid confusion or cross-infection.

Preparation of formula feed

You will need:

- formula feed;
- bottle;
- teats;
- knife;
- kettle – pre-boiled.

Remember!   Wash your hands thoroughly before you handle any feeding equipment. Prepare feeds on a cleaned surface. Have spare teats handy in case you drop one!

Method

1 Boil the kettle in advance.
2 Remove bottle from steriliser unit and rinse with boiled water.
3 Pour sufficient cooled boiled water into the bottle for the feed required (1 fl oz boiled water for each scoop of formula).
4 Check the level is accurate.
5 Open the tin of formula.
6 Using the scoop enclosed in the tin, add the correct number of scoops to the bottle. Remember to level each scoop off with a flat knife.
7 If using straight away, put on the teat, ring and lid, and shake gently to dissolve the formula.
8 The feed is ready for use after checking the temperature is OK.
9 If storing the feed for later, put a disc and ring on the bottle and shake gently to mix.
10 Remove disc and replace with upside-down teat (*do not* allow formula to touch the teat, as bacteria could begin to form).
11 Cover with disc and lid and refrigerate until needed.

Checklist

1 It is important that the scoops of formula are level.
2 Heaped scoops or 'packed' down scoops lead to over-feeding, and over-feeding can lead to weight gain, high levels of salt intake and possible kidney strain.

3 Insufficient scoops of formula to the number of ounces of water leads to under-feeding, and under-feeding can lead to poor weight gain and a hungry baby.

4 A baby needs 75 ml of formula per 500 g of body weight (2½ fl oz per lb) in each twenty-four hour period.

5 It is easier to make up enough feeds for the day in one go if suitable refrigeration is available.

6 This is particularly useful for families with twins or other multiples.

Activity 6.4

Calculate the amount of formula needed in each bottle for the following babies.

1 Clyde weighs 6 kg and is having seven feeds in each twenty-four hour period.

2 Josh weighs 9 kg and is having six feeds in each twenty-four hour period.

Giving a formula feed

It is important to be prepared in advance with all that you might need to hand. You should be seated comfortably and able to give the baby your full attention. Often a baby will be more comfortable having their nappy changed prior to feeding, but individual routines will vary.

Remember! Wash your hands thoroughly before feeding a baby or handling feeding equipment.

Method

1 Have all equipment together and suitably covered.

2 The bottle can be kept warm in a jug of hot water while you settle with the baby.

3 Hold the baby close to you, offering a sense of security and pleasure.

4 Test the temperature of the formula against the inside of your wrist. It should feel warm, not hot.

5 Check that the milk is flowing at the appropriate rate for the baby you are feeding. Several drops per second is usual, but rates do vary from baby to baby.

6   Encourage the onset of feeding by touching the teat against the baby's lips before placing the teat into the mouth.

7   Milk should always cover the whole teat to stop the baby taking in excess air and becoming frustrated at not receiving enough milk at a time.

8   If the baby is reluctant to suck, pull the teat gently, as the tension of this will often give them the impetus to suck harder.

9   About half-way through the feed, stop and wind the baby (see below).

10   Wind again when the feed is over and settle the baby down to sleep. They may need another nappy change.

11   When a baby has finished feeding, any remaining formula should be discarded and the bottle washed thoroughly, before placing in a steriliser.

Remember!   Always throw away left over milk and *never* use the same bottle twice without sterilising.

Winding

Winding a baby is the process of helping them release any trapped air taken in during the feeding process. They are best held in an upright position to allow the air to 'rise'. Useful positions for this include the following:

- sitting the baby forward resting against your hand allows you to rub or gently pat their back with your other hand;

Winding a baby

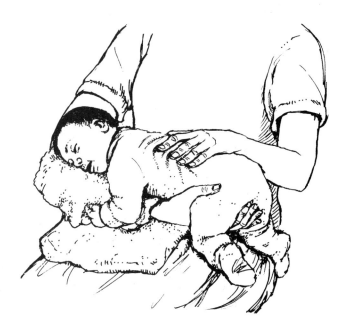

- placing the baby on your shoulder and, again, rubbing or gently patting them;
- resting baby along your forearm (very young babies only) and rubbing their back;
- for some babies lying them prone across your lap and rubbing their back works well.

Remember ! It is always useful to have a cloth handy as many babies posset (regurgitate) some milk during the winding process. The head and neck of young babies should always be well supported.

Activity 6.5

You have been asked to prepare a leaflet on formula feeding for GCSE pupils at the local school who are learning about the responsibilities of parenting.

1 Set out the instructions clearly.
2 Make specific reference to health and safety practice.

Sterilising methods

Bottles and all other feeding utensils need sterilising to prevent illness occurring due to the growth of bacteria. There are various methods to choose from:

- cold water sterilisers;
- steam sterilisers;
- microwave sterilisers;
- sterilising by boiling.

Cold water sterilisers

This method of sterilising uses chemicals either in solution or tablet form. The steriliser needs to be filled to the required capacity and the solution added (or sterilising tablet allowed to dissolve), before adding bottles and other feeding equipment. Each washed bottle, teat or other item needs to be fully submerged, and held under water by a 'float'. Sterilising takes thirty minutes from the time the last piece of equipment has been added. The solution needs to be replaced every twenty-four hours and most tanks hold a large amount of feeding equipment.

A steam steriliser

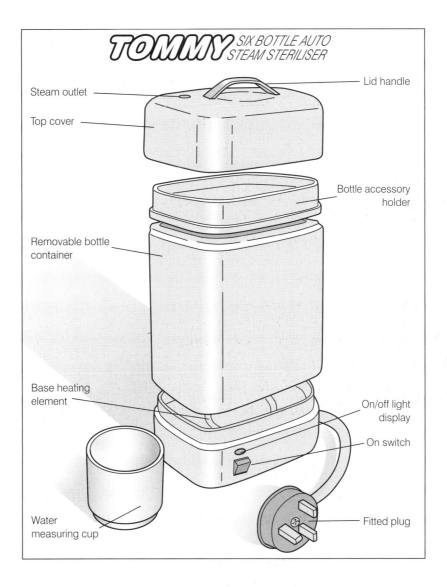

TOMMY SIX BOTTLE AUTO STEAM STERILISER

- Steam outlet
- Top cover
- Lid handle
- Bottle accessory holder
- Removable bottle container
- Base heating element
- On/off light display
- On switch
- Fitted plug
- Water measuring cup

Remember! Fully submerging items such as bottles means ensuring that all air bubbles are released, as any air bubble leaves an area unsterilised, and therefore is a potential source for bacteria growth.

Steam sterilisers

The steam sterilising method is quick and efficient, but is expensive, and once opened the bottles need to be prepared within a short period of time, as opening the steriliser allows the potential for bacteria growth. There is a risk of scalding from the release of steam if the unit is opened while still very hot, so care must be taken. Steam sterilisers usually hold six or eight bottles at a time. They are ready for use within approximately twelve to fifteen minutes from switching on.

Microwave sterilisers

This method works on the same principle as the steam steriliser. The units usually only hold four bottles, but the method is quick. Metal objects cannot be placed in the microwave steriliser.

Boiling method

Boiling feeding equipment is a cheap, but no longer popular choice. It has considerable potential for accidents due to the use of large quantities of boiling water. It can, however, allow reassurance that equipment is sterile if another form of sterilising is not possible. This method only needs ten minutes of boiling time to be ready. All equipment must be fully submerged, as with the cold water method.

A microwave steriliser

Activity 6.6

In pairs, choose one of the following topics and prepare a short presentation for the rest of your group. Select from:

1 the advantages and disadvantages of breast and formula feeding;

2 different methods of sterilising feeding equipment;

3 the preparation and storage of formula feeds;

4 supporting mothers who are breast feeding.

Weaning

Babies grow at their fastest rate during their first year and it is important that they are given a healthy and varied diet. This means a good balance of calcium, protein, carbohydrates and fats, together with a range of vitamins and minerals.

Definition

Weaning
The introduction of solid food to an infant's diet.

From about four months onwards, babies begin to be less satisfied with what they receive from breast or formula milk and an introduction to solid food becomes appropriate. It is usual to introduce solids to them before they reach six months. This transition into mixed feeding is called 'weaning'. Breast and formula milks do not have sufficient iron for continued healthy development, and prolonged (exclusive) milk feeding will not provide enough of this important mineral. Up to four months of age the baby has sufficient stocks of iron taken from their mother during pregnancy, and below four months the baby's digestive system is not usually mature enough to cope with the components of solid food.

Babies can be
introduced to solids
before 6 months

Weaning should be a pleasurable experience for both carer and child, encouraging the infant to explore new tastes over a period of time. It should not be a situation of stress or tension. At times it can be difficult to get a baby interested in trying to take solids from a spoon, but it is important to keep on offering it to them, without worrying about regular refusals. The baby will get there in time and in the early stages of weaning the baby will still be having all of their milk feeds and so will not be losing out nutritionally.

Do not introduce weaning (or a new food) when the baby is unwell or tired.

Offering half of the milk feed before the solids and half afterwards works well for most babies, but each baby is different and they will soon indicate their preference!

The four main food groups are:
- proteins, which help growth, development and tissue repair;
- carbohydrates, which provide energy;
- vitamins, minerals and fibre, for general good health and the prevention of illness;
- dairy products, which are high in calcium, enhancing and maintaining bones and teeth.

Also, there are fats and oils, higher energy giving foods, which are essential to children, but should be consumed sparingly by adults.

Remember ! Milk remains an important part of the baby's diet until they are at least a year old. The aim of weaning is to introduce babies to a variety of textures, tastes and experiences to integrate them fully into family mealtimes.

As the level of solid food intake increases, the milk feeds will decrease until the baby is having sufficient solid food at a 'mealtime' to be satisfied with a drink of water to accompany it. The table on page 286 sets out a sample programme for weaning a baby.

Remember ! Weaning is an important part of development, both socially and physically. Research from Bristol University has shown that babies who are not introduced to mashed (rather than puréed) food by ten months of age are likely to be fussier eaters later on in their lives. It is not usually beneficial to an infant to hold back the start of weaning for any length of time, even if they still seem content with their milk feeds.

The following table shows the estimated average requirements (EARS) for energy in the UK (per day). As the infant becomes more active, their energy levels increase, and again this indicates the need for solid foods to complement the nourishment of the milk feeds.

Age range	Males		Females	
	MJ	kcal	MJ	kcal
0–3 months (formula fed)	2.28	545	2.16	515
4–6 months	2.89	690	2.69	645
7–9 months	3.44	825	3.20	765
10–12 months	3.85	920	3.61	865
1–3 years	5.15	1230	4.86	1165
4–6 years	7.16	1715	6.46	1545
7–10 years	8.24	1970	7.28	1740

Overcoming feeding difficulties and food allergies

At times babies can repeatedly refuse solid foods. It is important during these periods to consider the following questions.

- Is the child unwell?
- Are they teething?
- Are you giving them too many new foods too quickly?
- Are you offering food at the right consistency?
- Are you feeling anxious about the weaning process, and possibly passing your anxiety on to the child?

It is important to make sure that you:

- make mealtimes a pleasure, not a battle;
- make gradual changes to the consistency of foods;

A suggested weaning plan

Age/months	4 months	4½ months	5–6 months	6–7 months	7–8 months	9–12 months
On waking	Breast- or bottle-feed	Breast- or bottle-feed	Breast- or bottle-feed	Breast- or bottle-feed	Breast- or bottle-feed	Breast- or bottle-feed/cup
Breakfast	1–2 teaspoons baby rice mixed with milk from feed or with water; breast- or bottle-feed	2 teaspoons baby rice mixed with milk from feed or with water; breast- or bottle-feed	Bay rice or cereal mixed with milk from feed or with water or pureed banana; breast- or bottle-feed	Cereal mixed with milk from feed or water; fruit, toast fingers spread with unsalted butter	Cereal, fish or fruit; toast fingers; milk	Cereal and milk; fish, yoghurt or fruit; toast and milk
Lunch	Breast- or bottle-feed	1–2 teaspoons pureed or sieved vegetables or vegetables and chicken; breast- or bottle-feed	Pureed or sieved meat or fish and vegetables, or proprietary food; followed by 2 teaspoons pureed fruit or prepared baby dessert; drink of cooled, boiled water or well-diluted juice (from cup)	Finely minced meat or mashed fish, with mashed vegetables; mashed banana or stewed fruit or milk pudding; drink of cooled boiled water or well-diluted juice in a cup	Mashed fish, minced meat or cheese with vegetables; milk pudding or stewed fruit; drink	Well-choped meat, liver or fish or cheese with mashed vegetables; milk pudding or fruit fingers; drink
Tea	Breast- or bottle-feed	Breast- or bottle-feed	Pureed fruit or baby dessert; breast- or bottle-feed	Toast with cheese or savoury spread; breast- or bottle-feed	Bread and butter sandwiches with savoury spread or seedless jam; sponge finger or biscuit; milk drink	Fish, cheese or pasta; sandwiches; fruit; milk drink
Late evening	Breast- or bottle-feed	Breast- or bottle-feed	Breast- or bottle-feed, if necessary			

- only offer one new food or new consistency at a time;
- only offer new foods when the infant is well and content;
- offer a new food alongside a familiar food, to ensure that at least part of the meal is eaten.

Babies experimenting with feeding themselves

Babies enjoy trying to feed themselves. They can usually cope with finger foods from eight months onwards, and suitable foods would include rusks, fingers of soft bread, pieces of pear and slices of banana.

When the infant shows an interest in trying to handle the spoon, give them a spare one. You will then remain in control of the feeding process, while satisfying their curiosity and skill development.

Remember! Feeding can be messy, so feed babies in a suitable environment. Babies need to try to feed themselves in order to learn. Happy mealtimes will encourage a positive attitude to food and eating later on.

Complying with parental wishes relating to feeding babies

When working in care settings you will need to be aware of a variety of dietary needs. These can be for:

- medical needs, for chronic conditions such as lactose intolerance, gluten intolerance or food allergy;
- cultural needs, heeding the forbidden or restricted foods and food combinations of some cultures;
- social needs/family choice, which would include diets such as being vegetarian or vegan.

Parents' wishes regarding their child's diet need to be valued. It is perfectly acceptable to seek their advice regarding meeting their child's needs. Most parents will be pleased that you have shown an interest and taken the time to ensure you are providing for them appropriately. You may find it helpful to refer back to the chart of food related customs in Unit 3.

LINKS TO UNIT 3, page 87.

Creating a safe and stimulating environment

Caring for a baby's environment

Room temperature and suitable levels of ventilation are an important factor in looking after a baby, and any room where a baby spends much of their time should be a constant 20°C (68°F) day and night.

A room thermometer should be placed on the wall in the baby room of any Early Years setting and should be checked regularly, adjusting the heating accordingly.

Overheating of babies is thought to be a contributory factor in sudden infant death syndrome (cot death), and recommendations are that babies should not be piled high with blankets, just a sheet and two layers of blankets will normally be sufficient.

Duvets and baby nests are no longer recommended, as they do not allow for temperature regulation. Cot bumpers are also advised against as they add extra warmth to a baby's cot, as well as having the potential for suffocation.

Having a well-ventilated room will help to prevent cross-infection and make the working or living environment a more pleasant place to be, both for the baby and for their carers.

Remember !   A blanket folded in half counts as two layers.

Checklist

1   You can check if a well baby is too warm or too cool by feeling their abdomen. If it feels warm and clammy then they are hotter than necessary. An abdomen that is slightly cool to touch is usual.

2   Removing a layer of clothing should be sufficient to keep them at a more comfortable temperature.

3   Cool hands and feet do not automatically indicate a 'cold' baby.

4   The circulation of young babies is not as fully developed as adults and older children, and many babies have cool extremities, especially before they become mobile.

5   If you are concerned that a baby is unwell or has a raised temperature, always check it with a thermometer and seek medical advice as necessary.

Normally body temperature is between 36 and 37 degrees centigrade

A high temperature (pyrexia)

Normal body temperature is between 36 and 37°C. A temperature above 37.5°C indicates **pyrexia** (fever). Young children's temperatures are often a sensitive indicator of the onset of illness and a raised temperature should never be ignored.

Check for overheating in the first instance by:
* removing clothing or a layer of bedding;
* reducing the temperature of the room;
* sponging the child with a cool flannel.

If fever is suspected:
* take the child's temperature and record the outcome;
* remove clothing or a layer of bedding;
* sponge with a cool flannel;
* offer plenty of fluids;
* use a fan to circulate cool air around them;
* observe the child carefully, particularly very young babies.

Febrile convulsions

* **Febrile convulsions** can occur in some children when their temperature rises, involving loss of consciousness, flickering of eyes and general jitteriness.
* A child who has one febrile convulsion is more likely to have another. It does not however mean that they have developed epilepsy.
* Medical advice should be sought if a febrile convulsion occurs.
* The child should be placed in the recovery position when the convulsion is over while medical advice is sought.
* The child needs reassurance and rest following a febrile convulsion.

Remember ! Parents should always be informed if a child has become unwell, even if they appear well again by the time they are collected.

Maintenance and cleaning in the nursery

- Carpeted surfaces should be vacuumed regularly.

- Washable (non-slip) floors should be cleaned with a mop (disinfected).

- All surfaces used for making up, or standing feeds upon, should be thoroughly
  cleaned with an anti-bacterial product.

- All general surfaces should also be kept clean with an anti-bacterial product.

- Soft toys should be washed regularly.

- All toys should be cleaned regularly with an anti-bacterial product.

- Thermometers must be checked regularly to ensure that rooms are kept at an
  appropriate temperature (18–20°C/65–68°F).

- Lighting must be adequate for safe working practice.

- Good ventilation reduces the risk of cross-infection.

- Ventilation points need to be kept clean, to avoid a build-up of dirt and bacteria.

Safety equipment suitable for the development stages of babies

In any setting that cares for babies and young children there should be an awareness of safety marks, and the need to buy toys and equipment that have been tested and safety marked whenever possible.

Safety equipment needed for the different stages of a baby's development includes:

For newborn infants:

- a safe surface on which to change the baby
- a cat/insect net
- a sturdy cot, Moses basket or carry-cot that conforms to current safety standards
- a suitable mattress, again that conforms to current safety standards and is the correct size for the cot
- avoid cot bumpers, quilts and duvets, which have been linked to the overheating of young babies that can contribute to cot death
- an appropriate (rear-facing) car seat.

When the baby sits up:

- be aware of new areas that can be reached by the baby
- flexes should be kept out of reach
- hot food should not be placed in front of the infant, in case they topple on to it
- harnesses are definitely needed in chairs, prams and strollers
- do not change the baby's car seat round until they reach the correct weight (as indicated on the car seat).

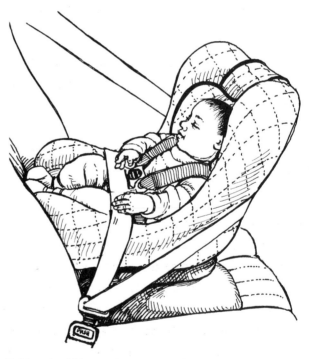

Babies should be put in an appropriate car seat

When the baby can crawl:

- play pens can be useful
- fire guards prevent the baby accessing fires
- electric socket covers should be used
- a video guard can be bought
- safety gates at top and bottom of stairs, and possibly needed across the kitchen too
- toilet lid catches can be useful
- trailing leads need to be secured
- sharp corners need to be protected with transparent 'corners'
- safety glass (or a special safety film) should be placed in all full-length glass doors
- remove overhanging tablecloths
- keep cleaning fluids up high, preferably shut away out of sight
- hot drinks should be kept out of the baby's reach
- be aware of pet food and pet water bowls
- be aware of loose carpet fibres, which can cause choking if swallowed
- strong netting is needed over garden ponds.

When the baby is standing, climbing or toddling:

- cooker bars help to protect from saucepan spills
- keep cooking handles turned inwards at all times
- a fridge lock may be needed
- catches are needed on windows, doors and drawers
- safety glass, or safety film on doors, and low windows, and on glass coffee tables.

General safety points:

- smoke alarms should be installed
- safety mats in baths are important
- slam stoppers on doors, to prevent fingers being trapped, are extremely useful
- razors, chemicals and medicines should be kept locked away securely
- cold water should always be added to baths before hot water
- toys should be checked regularly to ensure they are whole, undamaged and clean.

Safety marks

Mark	Name	Meaning
	BSI Kitemark	Indicates a product has met a British safety standard and has been independently tested
	Lion Mark	Indicates adherence to the British Toy and Hobby Association Code of Practice and ensures a product is safe and conforms to all relevant safety information
	Age Warning	Indicates: 'Warning – do not give the toy to children less than 3 years, nor allow them to play with it' Details of the hazard, e.g. small parts, will be near the symbol or with the instructions
	BEAB Mark of the British Electrotechnical Approvals Board	Indicates that electrical appliances carrying this mark meet a national safety standard
	BSI Safety Mark on gas appliances, light fittings and power tools	Indicates the product has been made and tested to a specific safety standard in accordance with the British Standards Institute
	Safety Mark on upholstered furniture	Indicates upholstery materials and fillings have passed the furniture cigarette and match tests – a lighted cigarette or match applied to the material will not cause the article to burst into flames
	Low Flammability labels	Children's pyjamas, bathrobes made from 100% Terry towelling and clothes for babies up to 3 months old must carry a label showing whether or not the garment has passed the Low Flammability Test. Either of these two labels is acceptable. Always look for these labels when choosing such garments.
	Keep Away From Fire label	Indicates the garment is not slow burning and has probably not passed the Low Flammability Test. Great care must be taken anywhere near a fire or flame

Case Study

Narindar

Narindar is a young mum with a small baby. She has recently returned to work, leaving three-month-old Vikram in the care of the baby room at her company's workplace nursery.

Vikram's key worker is Shumilla who has already built up a good relationship with Narindar and they chat easily each evening when Vikram is collected.

Shumilla is rather concerned that Narindar seems unaware of some of the safety precautions needed when caring for a baby. For example, Narindar has referred to leaving Vikram 'lying happily on the sofa' while she makes tea.

1 How could Shumilla raise Narindar's awareness of safety issues further, without causing offence?

2 What are the safety issues regarding having a baby of Vikram's age?

Toys and play equipment suitable for the developmental stages of babies

When planning play for babies and toddlers an important consideration is the positioning of visual stimuli around the room. Because of the different physical stages of a baby's development, they need visual stimulation when they are lying on their backs (supine), lying on their tummies (prone), when sitting, either propped up with cushions or in a chair and also while moving around. This will ideally be achieved through the positioning of objects of interest at different levels, including:

- at skirting board levels (for example, safety mirrors);
- on windows and on walls (for example, pictures, designs, areas of colour);
- on the wall behind and immediately above a sofa (a great place for a safety mirror);
- objects hanging from ceilings (mobiles, balloons and windchimes are favourites);
- attachments to prams, cots, highchairs etc. (for example, music boxes, soft toys and wobbly objects).

Stimulating play environments

Stimulating play is an essential part of a child's daily experience and as an Early Years professional you will be responsible for providing the children in your care with a range of stimulating opportunities, both indoors and outside.

Careful positioning of stimulating objects, as suggested above, is just the first stage of planning a stimulating environment. Very young babies initially obtain most of their stimulation from interactions with their mother or main carers, through feeding, care routines, gentle rocking and soothing and the calming tone of their voice. By about six weeks babies demonstrate that they have become much more visually alert, are usually smiling and focusing on the faces of their carers and familiar objects. They are already using all of their senses to learn about their world, and will be showing clear enjoyment of stimuli that hold their attention such as mobiles, which are usually brightly coloured and three-dimensional. Many have a musical element, which adds further to the stimulation.

Stimulating play is an essential part of a child's experience

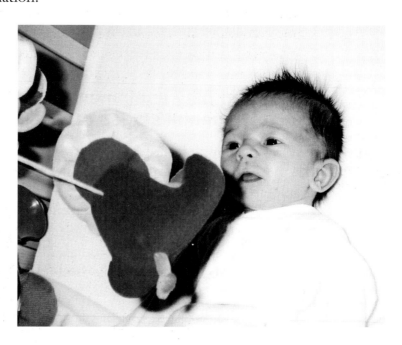

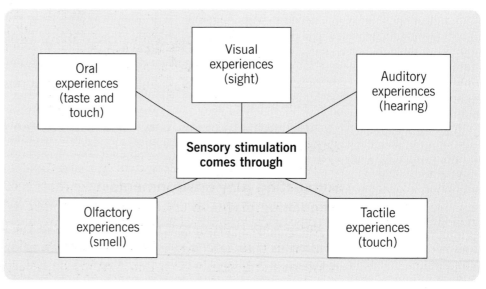

Activity 6.7

1 Select ten play items from a baby setting you are familiar with.
2 Make a note of which senses each item will stimulate.
3 Compare your ideas with those of another student. Did you both agree?

From around six weeks babies benefit from an activity frame or something similar that can be placed above them, encouraging them to focus visually and aurally on the items hanging in front of them and enjoying tactile experiences too, as they come into contact with the items during their natural body movements. Eventually, these movements become more intentional, and repeated actions will be observed, often in response for the 'reward' of a noise or visual 'experience' (movement, reflection or fluttering of material). Opportunities to play at bathtime or when having their nappy changed gives freedom from the restriction of clothes, allowing full leg mobility, and should be encouraged whenever possible.

An activity frame encourages babies to focus visually and aurally

Outside

Babies enjoy being outside watching the leaves on trees fluttering and taking in the sounds and smells of the garden. Fresh air is good for them, but they should never be left unsupervised. Care should be taken to ensure that prams are not positioned in the sun, as a baby's delicate skin burns extremely easily. Whenever possible allow a baby to lie out of doors in warm weather without a nappy on, as exposure of the nappy area to fresh air is healthy and stimulating for their skin too. Although most professionals agree that taking a baby out each day is a good idea, this does not apply if the weather is particularly cold, or is foggy.

Remember! Babies absorb information from all around them and will benefit from as wide a range of experiences as it is possible to give them.

Stimulating play for older babies

As they develop, older babies will be interested in a range of household articles. Sturdy boxes can be handled easily, being passed from hand to hand from about six months onwards and knocked together as manipulative control is developed. They will also enjoy banging things in order to make a noise. A useful item for this is a wooden spoon on a saucepan lid or the tray of their high chair. Babies enjoy activities that enable them to explore by themselves through all of their senses. An excellent resource for this is a **treasure basket**.

Treasure baskets

Infants from about six months of age will enjoy exploring a treasure basket. They ideally need to be able to sit up securely in order to benefit from the freedom to explore. A treasure basket includes a range of objects that are made of natural materials that can be easily handled by the infant. They should be selected carefully to stimulate all the senses, and they should be completely safe. The infant should be allowed to focus on the objects they are handling without distraction from the adult or older children.

Nothing in a treasure basket should be made of plastic or any man-made materials.

From about the age of 6 months, a baby will enjoy eploring a treasure basket

Activity 6.8

You have been asked to prepare a treasure basket for the eight-to-ten-month-old babies in the baby room where you are on placement.

1 What will you include in your basket?

2 What senses will each item stimulate?

3 What health and safety issues will you need to take into consideration?

Remember!

The objects included in a treasure basket need to be kept very clean. They should not have sharp or rough edges or be at risk of 'coming apart', and none should be small enough to be swallowed, or put up noses. The infant will need supervision while exploring their treasure basket, but not direct adult intervention. The adult's role is to provide, to oversee and to allow freedom of exploration.

Some older children with a special need may also benefit from exploring a resource prepared along the lines of a treasure basket.

Importance of praise and encouragement to promote development

Children respond well to praise and encouragement, and this applies to babies too. When interacting with babies you can make them feel wanted and valued as a person by remembering to:

- give them your full attention;
- mimic their actions, showing pleasure;
- make eye contact with them;
- offer objects to them and accept objects when they offer them to you.

Bonding

A bond is a child's secure two-way relationship with a carer or carers. It is discussed in Unit 2 in the section on emotional development. One very pleasurable way of developing a bond with a baby is through baby massage.

LINKS TO UNIT 2, page 55.

Baby massage

Baby massage is a popular and important means of communication between a parent and baby, as it enhances the parent's understanding of their baby's needs. Baby massage involves eye contact, touch, smiling and other pleasurable facial expressions, and as it involves such close contact, interaction between parent and baby is heightened. Baby massage is also used by therapists to help mothers who are suffering from post-natal depression. It strengthens their contact with their baby and encourages the bonding process.

Baby massage provides a means of communicatiion between baby and parent

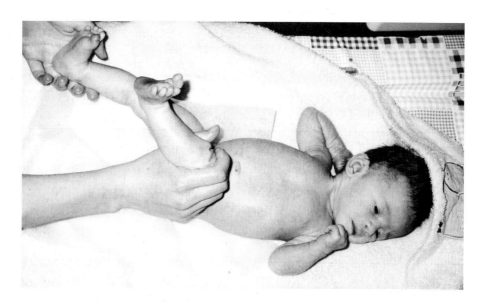

Remember! The role of a carer is significant to the baby and their development, but within a care setting, it is not usual for staff to carry out massage with the babies. Their relationship with each infant is built on familiarity, stability and continuity of care.

Communication with babies

Communication with babies can be both verbal and non-verbal. The pattern of language development in babies and young children is described in Unit 4. You may find it useful to refer back to that section now.

 LINKS TO UNIT 4, page 160.

Role of the carer in language development

Taking time to observe an adult with a young baby will give you an example of how you can 'converse' with a baby in the earliest weeks.

This is known as pre-verbal communication, as the adult encourages the baby to take a share in the conversation, asking them questions and supplying them with answers or making reaffirming comments following a pause in which the infant adds their own vocalisations. Welcoming the vocal sounds of babies encourages them to vocalise further. Responding to babies and watching them respond to you will enhance their communication with you. This 'turn-taking' between carer and infant was identified by Stern in the 1970s, who put forward the theory that infants learn the basis of their social interactions in this way.

Motherese

The term 'motherese' is what we often call baby talk. Motherese speech:

- has a higher pitch than that used with other people;
- is slower, with simplified words and phrases usually being employed;
- includes frequent pauses, to facilitate the turn-taking;
- mostly consists of key words linked to the current situation, for example, naming words if playing jointly with a toy (nouns), or action words (verbs) when moving the infant or referring to a specific action.

Examples could include 'Here is teddy' or 'Up you come for a cuddle'.

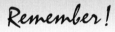 **Remember!** Adults communicate with babies in many ways. The following checklist lists some of the most important ones.

Checklist

- Eye contact during breast or formula feeds.
- Turn-taking vocally or visually.
- Initiating 'conversations' with babies as you play.
- Observing the needs of babies through their body language or facial expression.
- Responding to their cries.
- Encouraging them to vocalise.
- Showing appreciation of their vocalising.
- Giving praise.
- Calling to them when out of their visual range.
- Stimulating them aurally.
- Stimulating them visually.

| Case Study | **Mary** |

Mary works in the baby room. She is preparing a formula feed for William, who is six months old. William is in his chair, and Mary is currently out of his line of vision as she gets his bottle ready. She calls to him in a sing-song voice, pausing to hear him make a noise in response, before calling him again. When she brings his feed to him, Mary takes him out of his chair and cuddles him on her lap while he is fed. He watches her face, and she smiles at him, talking quietly to him all the time.

1 Which forms of communication listed above do you consider that Mary used?

2 Do you think there were opportunities for any other form of communication to have taken place?

3 What might be the outcome for a baby who does not have opportunities for communication?

Key terms

You should now understand the following key words and phrases. If you do not, read through the chapter again and review them.

Apgar score
baby massage
bowel and bladder problems in children
breast feeding
care routines
caring for a baby's environment
caring for babies' skin
centile charts
choosing clothes for babies
colic
communication with babies
cross-infection
dental care
febrile convulsions
feeding difficulties
formula feeding
fostering relationships

health visitors
management of a distressed baby
motherese
neonate
paediatricians
post-natal
pyrexia
safety equipment for different stages of a baby's development
skin infestations
sterilising methods
stimulating play
topping and tailing
treasure basket
weaning
winding a baby

Test Yourself

1 Describe the common features of the neonate.

2 At what age do babies usually start to roll over?

3 By what age can babies usually pull themselves to standing?

4 Between what ages is walking normally achieved?

5 Define what is meant by the terms gross motor and fine motor skills.

6 What is the pincer grasp?

7 What is object permanence?

8 By what age is the social smile usually seen?

9 At around what age is it usual for an infant to become distressed when their main carer leaves them?

10 Why do the care routines for babies need to change as they get older?

11 What different reasons can you think of why an infant might be distressed?

12 What specific skin care might a black-skinned baby need?

13 In what order do a baby's teeth usually appear?

14 What is meant by the term 'topping and tailing'?

15 What is the maximum temperature for a baby's bath?

16 What positions for winding a baby can you think of?

17 What are the ideal first weaning foods for babies?

18 How many types of dietary need can you think of?

19 What is normal body temperature?

20 What is motherese?

References and suggested further reading

Dare, A and O'Donovan, M (1998) *A Practical Guide to Working with Babies* (2nd edn), Nelson Thornes

— (2002) *A Practical Guide to Child Nutrition* (2nd edn), Nelson Thornes

Green, S (2003) *Baby and Toddler Development Made Real*, David Fulton Publishers

Meggitt, C and Sunderland, G (2000) *Child Development. An Illustrated Guide*, Heinemann

Sheridan, M (1991) *From Birth to Five Years: Children's Developmental Progress* (revised edn), Routledge

Walker, C (1998) *Eating Well for the Under Fives in Child Care*, The Caroline Walker Trust

Websites

www.babycentre.co.uk

www.pampers.com

www.bounty.com

www.nctpregnancyandbabycare.com

www.capt.org.uk

7 Working in partnership with parents

This unit covers:

- Working in partnership with parents and families
- Boundaries of responsibility when working with parents
- Sharing information with parents
- The carer as a member of a team

Considering **parents as partners** in the care and education of their children has always been part of a good Early Years setting's ethos, but the Children Act 1989 included a directive for all settings to draw up a 'Parents as partners policy', which has now made this the norm everywhere. Working in partnership with parents not only shows respect for the parents as the main carers of their children, but also enables the most effective care of individual children to be put into place. If Early Years staff do not communicate with, ask questions of, and receive relevant information from, children's parents, they will not be fully prepared to respond to children's individual needs, identify potential points of crisis for them, or have the awareness to help them to cope with new or worrying situations. Also, an understanding of cultural values and family needs is important, and should be respected within the boundaries of each setting's equal opportunities ethos.

There is a Special Educational Needs (SEN) Code of Practice in which Chapter 2 of the code is specifically linked to working in partnership with parents. The emphasis on involving parents in decisions about their child's education is seen as critical in achieving the most effective programme for any child, but is particularly important if the child has an additional need.

Remember! Parents are usually the people who know their children best. Early Years settings play a supporting role in their care and development.

Working in partnership with parents and families

Parents new to an Early Years setting will understandably worry about their child, particularly if it is the first time they have placed them into daycare. They need to know that they can trust the staff to care for them well, and staff must take on the role of supporter, as well as carer, reassuring them of the care and attention their child will receive, offering opportunities for parents to check on their child's progress by telephone or other means when they feel they need to, and by keeping them fully informed of all issues relevant to their child. This is part of building a positive relationship with parents.

A welcoming entrance creates a positive impression

Difficulties that can arise

Not all parents find it easy to interact with staff, and some may not easily build up relationships with other parents linked to the setting either. This can be for a variety of reasons. For example, parents may:

- be shy;
- have a low self-esteem and consider that others are not interested in what they do, or what they have to say;
- not know what to say to people they do not know, naturally keeping to themselves;

- have faced prejudice and discrimination in the past and therefore avoid new situations where they are unsure of how they will be regarded;
- not have the language skills to interact with others easily;
- feel socially excluded by others attending the setting;
- lack the time to stop and chat, therefore missing out on opportunities to get to know people;
- at times be embarrassed about the reason their child attends the setting, perhaps attending on the direction of social services.

Case Study

Cathy

The Dawson family have had a troubled couple of years, involving eviction due to noise and violence (Mr Dawson was drinking heavily and becoming very aggressive), a temporary separation of the parents and social services investigations regarding the possible neglect of the two children, Paula (three years) and Stevie (one-and-a-half years).

The family have recently been rehoused and Mr Dawson is trying hard to keep off alcohol. The two children are always pale and seem unsure how to play. Theirs is a small community, and Mrs Dawson, Cathy, is aware that everyone knows of their problems. She is very embarrassed by this, but determined to improve the situation for her family and develop her skills as a parent.

Social services have arranged for Cathy to bring Paula and Stevie to the family centre three days each week. The centre has both a pre-school group and a parent and child group. Cathy, Paula and Stevie attend both.

1 How could staff help Cathy to feel welcome and relaxed do you think?

2 How might staff help the children in their play?

3 How could attending the centre with her children help Cathy in her parenting?

Parents' wishes

Care of a child that positively reflects parents' wishes can only be achieved if it is based on good communication and interpersonal skills. The interpersonal skills you need as an Early Years worker involve an understanding of how your words, attitudes and actions are likely to be interpreted by the families you work with. This includes issues of discrimination, prejudice and stereotyping. Each of these is discussed in detail in Unit 1. You may find it helpful to return to that section now.

LINKS TO UNIT 1, pages 5–9.

There will be times when you do not agree with a family's parenting methods, and there will also be some parents with whom you are able to build a better relationship than others. What is important to remember is that all parents have a right to the respect, time and interest of the staff who are caring for their child. This includes you as a student too.

Activity 7.1

1 What examples can you think of where a parent has been shown respect by the staff at their child's Early Years setting?

2 In what ways have you seen staff at your placement give their time to the parents of the children on an individual basis?

3 In what ways have staff at your placement shown an interest in parents?

4 Have you seen instances where respect, time or interest has not been shown to parents? If yes, why do you think this was? What else should have been done?

Settling children into the setting

Before looking at this topic, it will be helpful to remember your own feelings about 'settling in'.

Activity 7.2

1 Think back to your own childhood, and try to recall how you felt when you started at a new school or, if your memory allows, a nursery or playgroup setting.

2 How do you feel today as an adult, when you start somewhere new or different, for example, going to an interview, starting a weekend job or perhaps your first day at college?

3 What words would you use to describe those feelings? Unsure? Scared? Confused as to why you are there and what you should do?

These feelings will be similar for a young child, but without the adult understanding of time, care giving and safety that we know are in place within Early Years settings.

Parents also feel anxious, and this sometimes transfers itself on to their children too. It is therefore important that parents are encouraged to be involved in a suitable settling-in routine for their child when they start at a

Care needs to be taken
to settle a child into
a setting

new setting. For some children this will simply mean a few minutes of reassurance at the start of the first couple of sessions, but for others it will need a greater degree of sensitive handling from both staff and parents.

Many settings now operate a home visit policy as standard practice, and this enables the child and their parent/s to start building a relationship with the person who will be the child's key worker. This home link is usually followed closely by a visit to the Early Years setting by the child with their parent.

Children need time to learn to trust their new carers, and parents have to learn to let go of their child a little. This is hard for them both to do. Staff should never underestimate the difficulty parents feel in leaving their child for the first time. It is an important milestone in both of their lives. Many parents walk away in tears, often more distressed than their child.

Settling-in policies

Most settings have a **settling-in policy** for children. This should be discussed with parents prior to the child starting to attend. It usually includes issues such as:

- key worker details – their name, role and where they can be found;
- guidance on time spent with the child – first-time parents often need to be guided by the experience of staff, but, of course, every child is different;

- activities that will help a child feel secure – some activities such as sand play can be very soothing and absorbing, and are often ideal 'settling in' activities;
- methods of keeping in touch with the setting during those early days, where concern and anxiety are highest – staff should check that they have the correct contact details for the parent, and also invite them to phone for reassurance if they wish;
- guidance on collecting the child early during the initial stages – explaining to parents that collecting a child a little early can help avoid the child becoming anxious if they see other children leaving.

It is important that parents work in collaboration with staff, letting them know when they are ready to leave, so that a member of staff can be involved with their child directly if appropriate, or available to step in immediately if they become distressed.

Case Study	**_Rhona_**

Rhona

Rhona finds it very hard to leave two-year-old Reece at nursery. She holds him to her anxiously before she says goodbye, and is crying even before she has left the room. This often unsettles Reece, who has usually been contentedly playing.

How could staff help reassure Rhona about Reece's welfare in her absence?

Boundaries of responsibility when working with parents

Parents' wishes

Parents have rights, and the Children Act 1989 recognises that parents have their own specific needs and are entitled to be involved in any decisions made regarding their child. Early Years settings need to remember this.

The particular wishes of parents will vary from family to family, and culture to culture. They may be linked to diet, sleep provision, clothing, personal care routines or behaviour management. Specific parental needs or wishes must be identified, discussed with them and acted on in an appropriate manner.

Although parents' wishes are to be valued and acted upon whenever possible, there will be times when these wishes are in conflict with the ethos of the setting. For example, a parent may request a behaviour management strategy that would not normally be used by staff within the setting. The settings policy on behaviour management would therefore need to be explained to the parent, and reasons given as to why staff cannot carry out their wishes. Parents will then make the decision as to whether this is the setting for their child.

At no time should an Early Years setting compromise its policies or uphold a practice that could be detrimental to a child or to other children in the setting. Honesty and tact are needed at these times in discussing alternatives and their benefits to parents. This would be a role taken on by the setting manager or a child's key worker. It is not an appropriate role for a student. An example might be a parent asking for their child to be refused a snacktime biscuit because they have not eaten their breakfast, or alternatively a parent who requests that their child is not to interact with another child, for whatever reason.

Communication

Communicating appropriately with parents involves:

- greeting parents warmly on arrival;
- key workers being available to parents on a regular (ideally daily) basis;
- showing respect for all family members;
- respecting issues of confidentiality and privacy;
- giving equal time to all parents as needed;
- using suitable methods of presenting information to parents, verbal, written and visual;
- ensuring that parents are informed of all procedures within the setting when they take up a place for their child;
- keeping parents informed of their child's progress;
- bringing to parents' attention specific areas of interest shown by their child;
- sharing information regarding a child's health.

Remember! Staff with good communication and interpersonal skills will build better relationships with parents. This, in turn, will help secure a safe and happy environment for the children.

The safety of children

At all times the responsibility of every Early Years setting is to the **safety of children** within their care. This includes acting upon any concerns regarding a child's safety and well-being when they leave the setting for home. A child protection policy that sets out the procedures to be taken if there are any concerns will help parents understand how the setting will act, when the setting will act and why the setting will act.

Activity 7.3

Ask to see the child protection policy at your current, and any other, setting you attend. Find out the following:

1 Are all parents given a copy to read automatically?

2 How do staff ensure that parents understand the policy?

3 Are parents asked to sign to say that they have read and agree with the settings policies?

4 Do you understand the policy? If not, ask your placement supervisor to explain it to you.

When a referral has been made by the setting following concern about a child's safety or well-being, the relationship between staff and parents can come under strain. If a parent is the direct subject of the concern, there will most likely be embarrassment and awkwardness between staff and parent while any investigation takes place. If the parent had been unaware of the situation involving their child that raised concern, or had felt powerless to stop it, again embarrassment is likely, together with deep distress.

Early Years staff need to remember that at times parents need help and support too, and staff can be part of this support by being a good role model in how they work with the children, demonstrating clearly the most appropriate ways of managing a child's behaviour, and trying to maintain communication in some way with the child's parent, whatever the circumstances. Communication may only be maintained through a welcoming smile or a nod of acknowledgement initially, gradually building up once again as the parent feels more able to communicate directly again. If the referral came from the setting they may well feel very hurt and angry with staff, especially if the concerns have been unfounded, and staff will need to absorb this anger as best they can. This again raises the importance of all parents being familiar with the setting's child protection policy, and its implications if a concern is raised.

Once an 'unfounded' concern has been cleared up, most parents will appreciate that staff were acting in the best interests of the child and relationships will usually begin to thaw once again. To refresh your understanding of referral procedures in child protection you may find it helpful to return to Unit 2.

 LINKS TO UNIT 2, page 68.

Sharing information with parents

The importance of **sharing information with parents** that is accurate, relevant and presented in an appropriate manner cannot be over-emphasised. Information given should include personal contact, written material and visual material. At times there may also be a need to have contact by telephone. Examples would include:

- initial enquiries about the provision;
- parents asking questions prior to taking up a place for their child;
- making arrangements for home/setting visits;

- the setting manager informing parents of illness or an accident involving their child.

The 'parents as partners' policy underpins all information exchanges. It should ensure that parents are kept informed about:

- admissions procedures;
- administrative procedures;
- health and safety procedures;
- curriculum planning procedures;
- assessment procedures;
- complaints procedures.

Many settings also have regular parent surveys to help staff evaluate the quality of the provision they make for the children in their care.

Remember ! Parents will have different levels of literacy skills, due either to different heritage languages, limited education and, at times, learning difficulties. Staff need to find ways to provide parents with information in alternative formats appropriate to their needs.

Activity 7.4

How could you provide the following information, using a variety of formats?

1 Information regarding the time a coach is leaving for the nursery outing.

2 Information explaining to parents that there has been an incidence of an infectious illness in the setting, for example, chicken-pox or headlice.

3 Information requesting parents to supply sun-hats during hot weather.

4 Information regarding the warning signs for meningitis.

5 Information regarding an increase in the fees for the setting in the near future.

Access to files

Each child will have a file within the setting and parents have a **right of access to those files**. This allows parents to see how and when their child has been observed and assessed, by whom, and any notes made about their development and progress. It is therefore important that staff back up any concerns they have with evidence, and talk to parents whenever they have a concern. It would be very inappropriate for a parent to find out about a staff member's concern regarding their child's development or behaviour by reading the child's file.

Access to files should be limited, applying only to staff who need to have access, the manager of the setting and the child's parents. This is all part of a setting's commitment to confidentiality.

Confidentiality

Confidentiality within the setting should always be maintained appropriately. At times staff will be privy to information regarding a family that would usually have been kept private. The trust placed upon such staff should be respected, and only transferred on a needs to know basis. Confidentiality includes:

- respecting a family's privacy;
- finding an appropriate place to speak to a parent when conversation is clearly of a sensitive nature;
- **working on a 'needs to know' basis**;
- keeping parents informed of any concerns;
- limiting access to children's records.

When a child's welfare is of concern

If there is concern that a child is suffering abuse, or their well-being is of general concern, information can be passed on to other professionals as is felt appropriate. This would be the role of the setting manager or the designated person for child protection. Parents would usually be informed that this has taken place.

Confidentiality as a student

At times during your course of study, you will need to observe children and may make notes. You will need to have permission from your placement supervisor to do this. If these observations are then recorded into your portfolio or professional practice log you must ensure that no child can be identified. Even initials are often unnecessary, but these can be used if it helps you.

Remember! Children with unusual names can often be identified by their initials too!

If your observations raise any concerns about a child with you, speak to your placement supervisor, not other staff members or students – work on a 'needs to know' basis.

Case Study

Denni

Denni is a student on placement at the Little Saplings pre-school. Another student in her group at college has told her that she saw a child from Little Saplings being smacked very hard by a man out in the street at the weekend. The little boy was cowering by the wall and sobbing.

1 Should Denni treat this as just gossip, or should she be concerned?

2 If she is concerned, whom should Denni talk to about this?

The carer as a member of a team

Early Years workers can be employed in a variety of different roles, and although some aspects of all posts will be the same, some will undoubtedly be 'job specific'. The individual attitudes and skills that contribute to a good team are discussed in Unit 1. You might find it helpful to look back at that section now.

 LINKS TO UNIT 1, page 20.

The role of the nanny/childminder

As a nanny, parent helper or childminder you will:

- work within a home setting;
- have shared responsibility for the child with the parents;
- need to observe parents' wishes regarding their child's care;
- need to discuss and have a mutual understanding of what you each consider to be safe practice with young children;
- need to reach an agreement regarding mealtime behaviour, the types of food to be prepared and provided, and parents' views on sweets and treats;
- need to discuss the ways in which they manage their child's behaviour, and agree how this will continue under your care.

Remember! You should never compromise your beliefs in what constitutes appropriate strategies for the management of behaviour.

You will also:

- need to plan a daily routine suitable for the ages of the children in your care, in agreement with their parents;
- need to plan an appropriate programme of activities and outings for the ages of the children in your care, negotiating with parents any additional costs that may be involved;
- need to reach an agreement regarding the boundaries of your responsibilities for the children, for example, who takes them to the doctors, the dentist, for hospital appointments and so on;
- observe confidentiality and the privacy of the family at all times;
- liaise as appropriate with outside bodies and professionals as relevant to the children in your care, for example, portage workers, speech therapists, physiotherapists;
- communicate sensitive information to parents immediately you are aware of a problem or issue, for example, a medical concern, a behavioural issue or information a child may disclose to you;
- need to ensure that you meet the requirements of any regulatory body relevant to your role, for example, Ofsted inspection regulations if you are registered as a childminder.

Remember !   Portage is a daily home-teaching programme for children with a particular need in which the portage worker develops an individual programme for the child and the parents continue to implement it on a daily basis. The portage worker makes regular, usually weekly, visits.

Whatever your role with parents within a family situation it is important that you respect the parents as the main carer of the child, encouraging them to:

- ask questions about their child's day;
- be involved in sharing their child's enjoyment of activities and outings;
- contribute ideas, and share outings on occasions when possible;
- expect and appreciate feedback on their child's time with you.

The role of the Early Years worker within a group setting

As part of your role as an Early Years worker within a group setting you will:

- read through, and carry out the duties associated with your role in line with the objectives and policies of the setting;

- ensure that you talk to parents and other team members in an appropriate manner, recognising the expertise and experience of others, and acknowledging that there can be more than one way to do most tasks;

- encourage parents to ask questions and contribute ideas and skills to the setting;

- adhere to the boundaries of confidentiality by following the appropriate practice for the setting at all times;

- carry out instructions and requests by parents in line with the ethos and boundaries of your role within the setting;

- pass on information promptly and accurately, to the appropriate persons;

- be expected to give accurate and positive feedback in response to a variety of circumstances;

- at times need to deal with conflict, which should ideally be dealt with assertively, never aggressively – conflicts with parents can often be resolved using the policies and procedures of the setting as a point of referral;

- need to learn how to prioritise – this applies to all aspects of your role, but health and safety must always be a top priority;

- develop an understanding of team management, to help you see how the whole team works together and how parents should be considered part of the team that jointly works for the best interest of their child;

- contribute to the evaluation and changes of procedures within the setting, through putting forward ideas, contributing to appraisals and being involved in any development of new policies;

- refer any enquiries that are not the responsibility of the care setting to appropriate people, or give parents the contact details if you have them.

Report writing and record keeping

Whatever setting you work within there will be a need to keep records and write assessments on children, recording information about their development and any concerns that may be raised by staff.

Records usually include the following information:

- child's full name;
- home address and telephone number;
- date of birth;
- parents' details, including any work contact details;
- any alternative emergency contact details (grandparent, neighbour etc.);
- child's medical details – name, address and telephone number of GP;
- any specific medical details, for example, asthma, any allergies, chronic conditions needing regular medication;
- religion (if any) – this could be relevant in the case of an accident;
- relevant information regarding language needs or situations the child may find particularly worrying.

At times records will also need to include sensitive information such as restrictions regarding access to a child by an estranged parent.

Self evaluation

As your role within an Early Years setting progresses, it will be important to undertake self-evaluation, to:

- review your own strengths and weaknesses;
- consider what further development would benefit you;
- reflect on your interpersonal skills.

Activity 7. 5

Using the following headings evaluate how you feel you have progressed so far. You may find it useful to return to these questions again at a later date to reassess how you are developing professionally.

How well have you progressed regarding your:
1 Use of initiative and self-direction?
2 Ability to adapt to an ever-changing environment?
3 Attitude to other people?
4 Ability to work within a team?
5 Ability to identify personal development needs?
6 Development of knowledge and understanding?
7 Development of self-management skills?
8 Ability to problem solve?

Key terms

You should now understand the following key words and phrases. If you do not, read through the chapter again and review them.

access to files

boundaries of responsibility when working with parents

communicating appropriately with parents

confidentiality

parents as partners

report writing and record keeping

role of an Early Years worker within a group setting

role of nanny or childminder

safety of children

self-evaluation

settling-in policy

sharing information with parents

working on a 'needs to know' basis

Test Yourself

1 List at least three reasons why working in partnership with parents is important.

2 How can an anxious parent new to the setting be reassured during the day?

3 List at least five reasons why parents may not find it easy to build up relationships with staff or other parents.

4 How can your interpersonal skills affect your relationships with parents?

5 How can a child be helped to settle into a new setting?

6 What is meant by a home visit?

7 What is likely to be included in a settling-in policy?

8 Give as many examples as you can of how staff should communicate with parents.

9 What is the main benefit of good staff/parent relationships?

10 Why is it important for parents to be familiar with the setting's child protection policy?

11 In what ways should settings present information to parents?

12 Give at least four examples of procedures that should be underpinned by the setting's 'Parents as partners' policy.

13 Why is it important to provide visual as well as written information for parents?

14 Who are the only people that should usually have access to a child's file at an Early Years setting?

15 Give three examples of upholding confidentiality in an Early Years setting.

16 How could a student's observations accidently breach confidentiality?

17 Give at least eight examples of the role of a nanny or childminder.

18 When working as a nanny or childminder how could you keep parents informed, making sure they feel valued and respected as the child's main carer?

19 What would usually be included in a child's records within an Early Years setting?

20 List aspects of your role that a good Early Years worker reflects on regularly.

References and suggested further reading

DfEE (2001) *Special Educational Needs Code of Practice*, HMSO

Green, S (2003) *BTec National Early Years*, Nelson Thornes

Hobart, C and Frankel, J (2003) *A Practical Guide to Childcare and Education Placements*, Nelson Thornes

Hobart, C and Frankel, J (2003) *A Practical Guide to Working with Parents*, Nelson Thornes

Sadek, E and Sadek, J (1996) *Good Practice in Nursery Management*, Nelson Thornes

Whalley, M (1994) *Learning to be Strong: Integrating Education and Care in Early Childhood*, Hodder & Stoughton

— (1997) *Working with Parents as Partners in Education and Care*, Hodder & Stoughton

Websites

www.capt.org.uk

8 Post-natal care

This unit covers:

- Principles of development
- Key principles of infant care and feeding
- Relationship with the child's mother

This chapter focuses on the period of time immediately after birth, from both the perspective of the infant and that of the newly delivered mother. Physical changes and development for them both are discussed, together with the support that they need from those caring for them or working with them. This unit will be of particular interest to anyone wishing to work in post-natal care, either in the home, within the post-natal ward of a maternity unit or through going on to study at a higher level, working towards maternity nursing or midwifery.

Principles of development

The normal neonate

Definition

Neonate
An infant under one month old.

The first month of life is known as the neonatal stage, and the infant is referred to as a **neonate**. Most infants are born at full term and thrive well, settling quickly into a routine with their mother and other carers. This settling-in period involves many new experiences and the beginning of body processes not previously experienced. In the neonate these include breathing, circulation and digestion of new forms of nutrition (milk).

Definition

Lactation
The production of milk by the breasts.

In the mother this includes the onset of **lactation**, healing from the trauma of birth and the resettling of the uterus.

Each of these are normal processes, but each can also present problems.

Birth

Birth is a traumatic experience for both mother and child. The length of labour and the type of delivery can affect the level of distress experienced by the infant, and therefore how well they are at birth. All infants are assessed immediately after delivery using a benchmark known as the **Apgar score**. This is a process of assessment that was devised by Dr Virginia Apgar in 1953, which sets out the vital signs of initial health, indicating whether an infant needs resuscitation or any other form of medical treatment. The five features of the assessment are as follows.

- Heart rate: how fast is the infant's heart beating?
- Respiration: how well is the infant breathing?
- Muscle tone: does the infant appear limp and floppy?
- Response to stimulus: does the infant respond when stimulated?
- Colour: does the infant's skin colour indicate good circulation?

Each feature is scored after one minute, and then again at five minutes, continuing at five-minute intervals as necessary until the infant is responding satisfactorily and the medical team are happy.

Definition

Pre-term
Born before thirty-seven weeks of pregnancy.

The higher the infant scores, the less likely it is that they will need any treatment. Most healthy infants score 9 at one minute. They often lose a score due to discoloration of their hands and feet. This is a common occurrence, and is due to their circulation not yet working fully. Infants who are **pre-term**, of a low birth weight or who have experienced a difficult delivery are more likely to have a lower Apgar score, and a score below 5 would indicate a very poorly baby. The infants who fall into this category make up a large percentage of those who do not survive or who will have ongoing problems.

A premature, difficult or traumatic birth, particularly if either mother or baby are ill and in need of special care, can also have an effect on the bonding process, due to separation and lack of physical contact, for example through the baby being placed in a special care baby unit (SCBU). Health professionals work hard to encourage and maintain links between mothers and their babies in these circumstances. Bonding is discussed in Unit 2, and its links to post-natal depression are discussed towards the end of this unit. You may find it useful to refer to those sections now.

LINKS TO UNIT 2, page 55.

The Apgar score chart

Sign	0	1	2
Heart rate	Absent	100 beats per minute	100 beats per minute
Respiration	Absent	Slow, irregular	Good, regular
Muscle tone	Limp	Some flexion of extremities	Active
Response to stimulus (stimulation of foot or nose)	No response	Grimace	Cry, cough
Colour	Blue, pale	Body oxygenated Bluish extremities	Well-oxygenated Completely pink

What to expect to see in a neonate

At delivery babies are wet and covered to some degree in mucus, maternal blood and body fluids. Their skin colour will vary due to both their ethnic origin and their state of health, with black babies appearing pale at birth, as the skin pigmentation melanin does not reach its full levels until later on. Most infants are delivered on to their mother's abdomen, and the umbilical cord is clamped and cut shortly after birth. Depending on the type and duration of the delivery, infants vary from being alert and wide awake, to drowsy and unresponsive. Medication given to the mother during labour can have an effect on this.

The neonate

General appearance of the neonate

Sleep

At birth the infant will sleep most of the time, mostly waking for feeds and nappy changes. They often fall asleep during the process of these routines too. Sleep patterns change as the infant develops, gradually remaining awake for longer periods.

Head lag

There will be a lack of head control due to under-developed neck muscles, and support is needed during handling. This is often referred to as head lag.

Vernix caseosa

Vernix caseosa may be present. This is a creamy white protective substance, which covers the body of an infant during the latter stages of pregnancy. It is usually seen in pre-term infants, and is often present in full-term infants too. It lubricates the skin and should be left to come off on its own, rather than be washed or rubbed.

Lanugo

A soft, downy hair covering the infant while in the uterus may also be present. It is called lanugo and traces are often found on the back, shoulders and ears at birth.

Fontanelles

There are two fontanelles on the infant's skull. The posterior fontanelle is a small triangular area near to the crown, which closes within a few weeks of birth. The anterior fontanelle is near the front of the head and is diamond shaped. It usually closes over by eighteen months of age and pulsates at the same rate as the infant's heartbeat. Fontanelles are areas of the skull where the bony plates of the skull meet. They enable some movement of the skull during the birth process. Fontanelles giving a sunken appearance can indicate that the infant is not getting sufficient fluids, whereas a bulging appearance can indicate a high level of pressure around the brain, or an infection, and this should always be investigated. An illustration of where the fontanelles are positioned on the crown of the skull can be found in Unit 2.

LINKS TO UNIT 2, page 32.

Mis-shapen skulls

Newborn infants often have a flattened or mis-shapen head due to the pressure of passing down the birth canal, or as a result of a forceps or a ventouse suction delivery. In a multiple birth it can occur due to lack of space and it can take some weeks for the natural shape of the skull to realign itself.

Umbilicus

The most well-known sign of the neonate is the umbilical 'stump'. The umbilical cord is clamped and cut at birth, and the clamp will be left to drop off on its own, usually seven to ten days after birth. The stump needs to be kept dry and clean, although actual cleaning of it is not usually recommended.

Swelling and bruising

Some infants show signs of swelling or bruising, normally due to a difficult birth. This tends to ease off within a few days.

Sticky eyes

Sticky eyes are common in the first few days and unco-ordinated eyes are usual. All babies are born with dark eyes and their permanent eye colour is not established until much later on.

Posture

The posture of infants is very flexed and movements tend to be jerky. The extremities (feet and hands) are often bluish in colour due to poor circulation. This soon settles down.

Genitals

Genitalia appear to be swollen in both boys and girls and blood loss from the vaginal area in girls is quite common. Both are caused by the mother's hormones crossing the placenta.

Breasts

The breasts of both boys and girls may be swollen and leak a little milk. Again, this is due to the mother's hormones crossing the placenta and can be seen regularly in both sexes.

Breasts may be swollen and leak a little milk

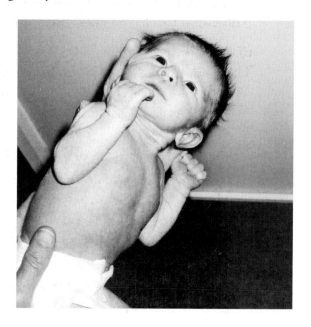

Stools

The stools (faeces) of the neonate are a dark, greenish black. This is due to it containing a tarry substance called meconium, which is also very sticky. The colour and consistency of the stools changes within a few days, as the mother's milk comes in or formula feeding is established.

Spots and rashes

Spots and rashes are very common in the first few days but the infant's skin soon settles down. A particularly common type of spots are 'milia', which are tiny white spots often known as milk spots.

Peeling skin

Peeling skin is quite common on the hands and feet but again this usually only lasts two or three days, and soon settles down.

Neonatal jaundice

Some infants suffer from neonatal jaundice where the skin and eyes become yellowish due to the infant's immature liver function and a subsequent rise in levels of bilirubin.

Bilirubin

Definitions

Sepsis
Blood poisoning.

Phototherapy
Exposure to ultra-violet light.

Bilirubin is formed when red blood cells break down and the liver is unable to cope with its workload. It usually occurs (if it is going to) on about day three after birth. Jaundice occurring before three days old needs particular investigation as liver disease or sepsis may be present and the infant's life could be in danger. On occasions, jaundice can be a sign of the condition galactosaemia (a metabolic disorder), rubella virus (German measles) or cytomegalovirus (herpes). Some infants with raised bilirubin levels require phototherapy, and some jaundice in breast-fed babies is normal. Liver function problems are monitored by nurses who check the colour of the stools and urine of each infant.

Birth marks

There are various types of **birth marks**, including the following.

- Port wine marks: a permanent, dark red mark, often on the face or neck. In the past they were often a permanent disfigurement, but with modern day technology many of these marks can now be successfully removed or depleted by laser treatment.

- Strawberry neavei: quite common. These are raised marks full of blood vessels. They are not actually present at birth, but develop in the first few days or weeks. They have usually disappeared by eight years of age. The full name for this type of neavei is haemangioma.

- Stork bites: quite common. These are tiny red marks found on the eye lids, the top of the nose and on the back of the neck. They gradually disappear and are not usually a problem.

Birthmarks

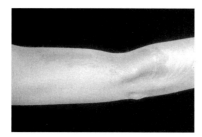

A port wine mark

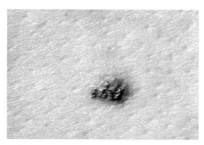

A CMN (congenital melanocytic naevus)

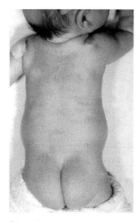

Strawberry naevus

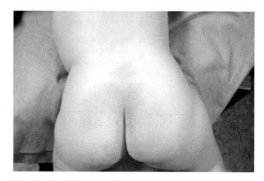

Mongolian blue spot

- Mongolian blue spot: dark marks found at the base of the spine on non-Caucasian (non-white) infants. On occasions these marks have been wrongly attributed to physical abuse. They are usually 'mapped' by health professionals in the early weeks to prevent unfounded concerns being raised. Early Years workers need to be aware of these marks.

- Moles: most people have moles, but some moles can be large and unsightly, for example CMNs (congenital melanocytic naevus). These moles get progressively darker as the infant grows, but they can sometimes be successfully removed or depleted with laser treatment or plastic surgery.

Primitive reflexes

Physically the neonatal stage includes the primary reflexes, the infant's posture, gross movements, visual and other sensory responses. The term primary reflexes means 'automatic body reactions to specific stimulation' (Bee, H, 1992, page 105). These reflexes include the following.

- Blinking: the neonate reacts to sudden lights, noises or movements in front of the eyes.

- Rooting: this is where the neonate turns their face towards their mother to locate the breast.

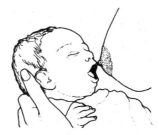

- The sucking reflex: infants will usually suck a clean finger, placed gently in their mouth.

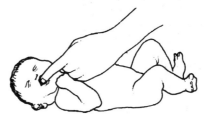

- The palmar grasp: this response is where the infant holds firmly to whatever touches the palm of their hand (gently stroking the back of the hand will usually release the grasp).

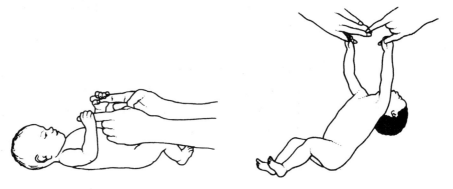

- The plantar reflex: touching the sole of the infant's foot with a finger will result in the flexing of their toes towards your finger.
- Stepping reflex: the neonate's foot responds to contact with a firm surface, resulting in a small 'step' being taken.

- The moro reflex: a sudden movement of the neck is interpreted by the infant as falling. They will throw out their arms with open hands and reclasp them over their chest.

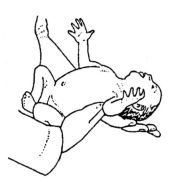

- The startle reflex: again the infant throws out their arms at a sudden noise or movement, but the fists remain clenched.
- The asymmetric tonic neck reflex: when the infant's head is turned to one side they will respond by straightening the arm and leg on the same side, while flexing the limbs opposite.

Some reflexes stay with us for life, for example, blinking, but some are lost after the first few weeks (the primitive reflexes). The presence of reflexes are an indicator of how well an infant's nervous system is functioning (their neurological well-being). As the brain gradually takes over the body's responses, these primitive reflexes disappear. If the primitive reflexes are still present for longer than is considered usual (they start to diminish at six weeks, to be replaced by more deliberate actions), it can indicate that there is a developmental problem with the infant, which may need to be investigated. Their progress will be monitored, together with the usual planned screening procedures.

All infants are usually assessed by a doctor at six weeks of age.

Case study

Connie and her twins

Connie has just given birth to twins, Amy and Max. They are two days old. You are on placement on the maternity unit and have been asked to assist Connie in caring for her babies.

Connie is concerned that Max appears to have swollen breasts.

1 What is the cause of Max's swollen breasts?

2 What other features may Connie see in her babies?

3 In what ways will you be able to support Connie as she learns to care for her babies?

The senses

Hearing	• The hearing of infants is acute (sharp) • They blink in response to sound • The neonate can identify the voice of their main carer almost immediately • Noisy objects can only roughly be located • Sudden noises distress the infant • Infants respond to soothing rhythmic sounds
Vision	• Newborn infants are sensitive to both light and sound • Vision is diffused and limited initially to objects within about a 30-cm (12-in) radius. • Eyes initially do not work together and they will often 'cross' or 'wander' • Eye-to-eye contact with the main carer (usually the mother) is an important means of establishing a bonding relationship • Infants show a preference for human faces • Infants will turn towards a light
Touch	• Skin-to-skin contact is important to the bonding process, and for breast-feeding • Most infants are delivered on to their mother's abdomen • Contact and handling usually soothes a distressed infant, but may be less welcomed by a premature baby • The temperature control of infants is ineffective
Smell	• Infants can identify their mothers by smell • Research has shown that infants can distinguish their mother's milk on a breast pad
Posture and motor skills	• Immediately after birth, many infants naturally curl into the foetal position with their head to one side • Limbs are kept partly flexed and are hypertonic (they have tension) and they tend to display jerking movements • The head and neck are hypotonic (weak) and there is no head control, so full support of the head and neck area is needed whenever the infant is handled

The foetal position

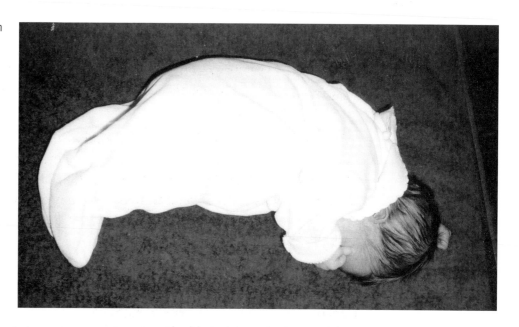

Remember! Research outcomes recommend that infants are always placed on their backs to minimise the risk of sudden infant death. Cot death prevention leaflets are published by the Department of Health. You may find it useful to acquire a copy.

Factors affecting development

Any woman planning to have a baby needs to consider the **factors affecting the development of the foetus**:

- diet;
- level of exercise;
- smoking habits;
- alcohol consumption;
- use of drugs (prescribed as well as recreational);
- social life;
- stability in her relationship.

Planning for a pregnancy in advance can enable a woman to give up smoking or the use of drugs before conceiving, and also reduce or eliminate her intake of alcohol. It can give her time to assess if her relationship is stable, and to begin to eat a healthier diet, eliminating foods that are not considered to be completely 'safe'. If a woman knows that she is unprotected against rubella (German Measles) it is wise for her to become vaccinated, but she should then avoid becoming pregnant for at least three months after having the vaccination. Any unprotected pregnant woman should try to stay clear of children who might have the rubella virus, particularly in the first twelve weeks of pregnancy, as contracting the virus can seriously damage her unborn child.

Women with long-standing medical conditions or disorders should consult their doctor before planning a pregnancy, to ensure that any medication they need to take regularly will be safe for the developing child too. Doctors may need to make changes to their medication, either because it could harm the foetus or because it could make conception more difficult to achieve.

Foods to avoid in pregnancy

Food	Possible outcome
Soft cheeses	Listeria, which can cause miscarriage
Pate	Listeria, which can cause miscarriage
Raw eggs	Salmonella, which causes food poisoning
Raw meat	Toxoplasmosis, which is a mild infection in adults but can cause serious harm to an unborn child

Folic acid

In recent years taking a supplement of **folic acid** has been recommended for women from before conception, up until twelve weeks into the pregnancy, as this contributes to the optimum (best) development of the baby's central nervous system. It helps to prevent problems such as spina bifida occurring. For an overview of this condition look at Unit 3.

LINKS TO UNIT 3, page 107.

Genetic effects on development

The **effects of our genetic inheritance** is an important aspect of our overall development as a person. This is also discussed in Unit 3. It may be useful to refresh your understanding by reading that section now. It covers autosomal recessive transference, autosomal dominant transference and X-linked transference, giving examples of disorders caused by each type of genetic occurrence. Genetic counselling can help parents weigh up the genetic risk of them having a child with an inherited disorder, and can be obtained through a referral from the couple's GP.

 LINKS TO UNIT 3, page 97.

Screening in pregnancy

Some conditions can be identified during pregnancy and the process for carrying out these tests is known as **screening**. They are referred to as antenatal tests and include the following.

Blood tests

Routine tests on blood can screen for low iron levels, venereal disease and rubella (German measles). Low iron levels may need to be boosted by supplements, and venereal disease will be treated as appropriate. A pregnant woman who is not immune to rubella will be advised to avoid contact with the infection during the early months of her pregnancy.

Ultra-sound scan

An **ultra-sound scan** is a usual procedure at around twenty weeks' gestation to note the development levels and measurements of the foetus. Measurements are taken of main bones such as the femur (thigh bone), and the head circumference is noted and the heart chambers carefully examined. Further scans are carried out if considered necessary by the midwife or obstetrician. Specific tests are offered to some women depending on circumstances. For example, older mothers or women with a family history of certain inherited disorders will be offered additional screening.

A scan of a
20-week foetus

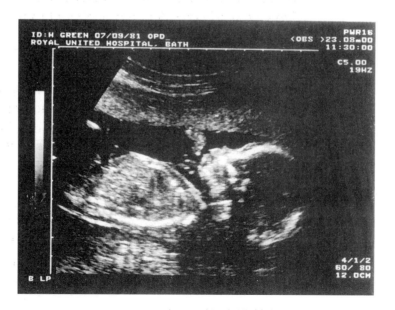

The foetus shown above is developing within the normal range. The measurements and examinations made included the:

- thigh bone;
- head circumference;
- spine;
- heart chambers;
- brain;
- amniotic fluid.

The outcome showed that the foetus (now named Jasmine) was developing well within normal limits, as Jasmine's mother's pregnancy was at 19+3 weeks, according to her dates, and the outcomes were as follows:

bone development 19 + 5 weeks
head circumference 19 + 5 weeks
amniotic fluid 19 + 1 week

Serum alpha-fetoprotein (SAFP)

This test is used to identify the possibility of the foetus having spina bifida. It is taken at sixteen weeks' gestation and is offered to women who are considered to be at risk.

The triple blood test

This triple blood test takes into consideration the mother's age, and measures the levels of human chorionic gonadotrophin (HCG), Serum alpha-fetoprotein (SAFP) and the placental hormones (oestriols). The combined outcome gives an assessment of the risk of the foetus having Down's syndrome. Again it is offered to women in the high risk group, usually mothers over 35 years.

Amniocentesis

This test checks for chromosome disorders, such as Down's syndrome. It usually takes place between sixteen and eighteen weeks' gestation and it involves the sampling of the amniotic fluid from the amniotic sac, while linked up to an ultrasound machine. There is a slight risk of miscarriage occurring with this procedure.

Chorionic villi sampling (CVS)

This CVS test involves the removal of a tiny amount of tissue directly from the placenta. It is usually carried out between eight and eleven weeks' gestation and it can help identify a range of inherited disorders, but, as with amniocentesis, it carries a small risk of miscarriage.

Ongoing screening

Screening programmes continue throughout life. In children they include:

- neonatal screening, during the first months (particularly the first fourteen days);
- infant screening, at six weeks, eight months and around eighteen months;
- childhood screening, pre-school, together with ongoing assessments as necessary.

Environmental effects on foetal development

Even before birth an infant can be affected by environmental influences, as development can be affected antenatally, as well as directly by the environment into which they are born and raised. Examples of this include the effects of alcohol, smoking and both illegal and (some) prescribed drugs. The use of any illegal substance by the mother can affect the developing foetus. On occasions the use of certain prescribed drugs has also had a detrimental effect.

Alcohol

Foetal alcohol syndrome (FAS) results from the mother continuing to consume alcohol, usually in considerable amounts, throughout her pregnancy. It was declared as the leading cause of 'mental retardation' in the US by researchers in 1991. It affects the development of the infant, causing delay, deformities and learning difficulties. Pregnant women are now advised against drinking alcohol altogether, as even a moderate amount can carry a risk to the infant and judgement can become impaired by alcohol, leading to accidents.

Smoking

Smoking (tobacco as well as illegal substances) affects birth weight due to the release of nicotine and any other substances into the body. It can also lead to learning difficulties. There is a suggestion that infants born

Infants born to smokers are at higher risk of sudden infant death syndrome

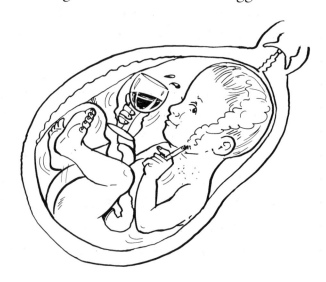

to smokers are at a higher risk of being affected by sudden infant death syndrome (also known as SIDS and cot death), and of developing respiratory conditions later on. Passive smoking is also thought to contribute to respiratory problems in infants and older children, and also to glue ear.

Drugs

Any non-essential drug should be avoided during pregnancy. Illegal drugs, such as crack cocaine, cause low birth weight and developmental delay, and babies who are born addicted suffer withdrawal symptoms after birth, and are in great distress. Many of these babies suffer all-round development problems and some develop epilepsy.

Prescribed drugs are only issued to pregnant women with extreme care, as some have been known to cause deformity and developmental problems. The most notorious incident of this kind was the effects of the Thalidomide drug, which caused severe limb deformity in some children born in the 1960s. The mothers of these children were prescribed the drug in good faith to combat severe vomiting in pregnancy.

Remember !

Cough and cold remedies are also drugs, and should be treated with the same caution as any other medication. A pregnant woman should always check their suitability with their GP or a pharmacist before taking them.

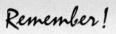

Case Study

Carla

At the age of thirty-eight, Carla is considered to be old (medically) to be having her first baby. Carla had her pregnancy confirmed by her GP and registered with her midwife as soon as she knew she was pregnant.

Carla and her partner had been trying to conceive a child for a few months and Carla had done her best to prepare her body as a 'healthy environment' for her (hoped for) baby to develop within. She gave up smoking almost a year ago, and has reduced her alcohol consumption to just a glass of wine at the weekend. Carla takes no drugs except the occasional paracetamol for a headache, but she began to take the supplement folic acid about five months ago, as she heard it was recommended.

1. How has Carla helped her unborn infant's chances of a healthy development so far?
2. What tests will Carla be likely to be offered during her pregnancy?
3. What are the benefits (and any drawbacks) of the tests?
4. Which of the tests are offered routinely for all pregnant women?

Breast feeding

The mother's own breast milk contains protective substances that help to keep her newborn infant free from infection. For a pre-term infant (under thirty-seven weeks of pregnancy), the mother's milk has a higher protein content, which is particularly beneficial to the baby's well-being. Breast milk is often referred to as being nature's 'designer food', a nutritious option that develops with the infant and adjusts to their needs as they grow. Although modern day formula feeding is an excellent alternative to breast milk, there is no product so ideally suited to each individual baby. It provides for their total nutritional needs for the first months of life.

Throughout the first year there is a need for a high intake of milk to ensure that the infant receives sufficient calcium. This supports the development of healthy bones and teeth.

Basic anatomy of the breast

A woman's breasts begin to develop at puberty, influenced by the sex hormones. Each breast has a range of lobules, which each have ducts (called lactiferous ducts). These link to lactiferous sinuses, which in turn lead directly to the nipple, allowing the milk to be secreted to the sucking infant.

The structure of the breast

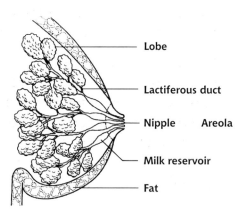

The nipple is surrounded by an area of skin known as the areola. The pigmentation of this area of skin darkens during pregnancy. The areola has a number of glands called Montgomery's tubules, which become larger during pregnancy. The fluid produced within them during pregnancy helps to keep the nipples supple.

Physiology of lactation (milk production)

Lactation occurs following a hormone 'trigger' from the brain following birth. This sends signals to the mother's breasts to start the lactation process. Initially, the breasts secrete a thick, creamy substance called colostrum. This is very rich in protein and is produced in the later stages of pregnancy and for the first few days after birth, prior to the onset of the main milk supply (two to four days after birth). The high protein level in the colostrum is particularly beneficial to newborn infants as it is very nutritious and a small amount can supply the infant with sufficient energy needs in the early days when they sleep a great deal. Mothers are encouraged to breast feed for the first few days, even if they intend to change over to formula feeding.

As breast feeding becomes established, the colostrum gradually lessens until the mother produces only the mature breast milk. This looks thin and watery and often has a bluish appearance. The nutritional quality is not however reduced; it has simply adjusted to the needs of the infant.

Fore milk and hind milk

Lactation produces two stages of milk production. The **fore milk** is the milk the infant receives initially, which satisfies the initial thirst and hunger, whereas the **hind milk**, which is the richer type of milk, due to its higher fat content, offers longer term satisfaction for the infant.

Breast feeding provides sufficient nutrition for an infant up until aged four to six months. By this stage, the iron stores within the mother's milk, which were built up during pregnancy, have been used up and the process of weaning needs to begin. Weaning helps the infant develop a healthy attitude to food for the future, as well as replenishing the iron supplies that have now been reduced, and nourishing the body in general.

Normal changes and common breast-feeding difficulties

For most women the process of breast feeding is a natural action, which after any initial minor issues settles down into a pleasurable routine, offering closeness and an ideal opportunity for bonding. For a few women, problems can occur, both prior to breast feeding and once it has commenced.

Problems that can occur include the following.

Inverted nipples	Some women have nipples that are not raised in the usual way and sometimes there is a need for the nipple to be 'drawn out' with finger and thumb on a daily basis for several weeks prior to the date of delivery. This helps prepare the nipple(s) for breast feeding.
Sore or cracked nipples	Soreness and cracked nipples often occur towards the end of pregnancy, and both cracking and soreness can occur in the early days of breast feeding. These problems can be helped by ensuring that the infant is positioned to the breast correctly, and by regular washing, drying and moisturising the nipple area. Exposure to air can also be beneficial.
Leaking breasts	The woman's body responds to the sound of her child, and her breasts will often produce milk automatically at the sound of her infant stirring. Breast pads can be used to soak up any surplus milk. Again, keeping the nipple area dry and moisturised will help.
Engorged breasts	This is a painful experience in which the breasts become over-full. It can be due to incorrect positioning of the infant on the breast or insufficient emptying of the milk supply. Allowing the infant to feed on demand will often help regulate the milk flow. It is important that breast-feeding women wear a well-fitting and supportive bra at all times.
Blocked ducts	The main cause of blocked ducts is incorrect positioning of the infant when feeding, or lack of regular feeding taking place.
Mastitis	This is an inflammation of the breast or part of the breast. It is a very painful condition, and is often accompanied by fever. It can be due to the breasts becoming over-full or through insufficient feeding by the infant. The mother needs to relieve the painful breast first at each feed, until it improves, and offer frequent feeds until the situation has settled down. In severe cases, the mother may need antibiotics to relieve the inflammation. At times she might be advised to avoid feeding from the affected breast, but to express the milk by hand regularly to lessen the build-up and to continue the stimulation of the milk supply.
Insufficient milk supply	This can occur if breast feeding is regularly replaced by formula feeds, by incorrect positioning of the infant when feeding or if the mother is poorly nourished. It is important that all breast-feeding mothers have a nutritious diet and a high fluid intake.

Key principles of infant care and feeding

When caring for a newborn infant, a number of decisions need to be made. One of the most important is the choice of infant feeding. Research shows that breast feeding is by far the best option for the infant, although formula milks are an excellent alternative. However, breast feeding is not always the best choice for the mother, and this has to be taken into account too. The wishes of the mother, and any medical or social difficulties this may present for her, will need to be balanced against the nutritional needs of the child. For many people it comes down to personal choice, and as an Early Years professional you must respect the choice each individual makes. If asked for your opinion you should be able to outline the advantages and disadvantages of each. They can be described as follows.

Breast feeding or formula feeding?

Advantages of breast feeding:	Advantages of bottle feeding:
• the balance of breast milk nutrients is perfect for the infant • the milk 'matures' with the baby, constantly meeting their needs • breast milk offers a degree of immunity against infection in the early weeks • breast milk protects against eczema, asthma and jaundice • breast feeding helps the mother to regain her figure more quickly • breast fed babies have less gastro-enteritis and fewer chest infections • the baby has less smelly nappies • there is a lower risk of diabetes later on • breast milk is always 'on hand' • breast milk is cheaper – the milk is free!	• feeding routines can be shared • siblings can be more directly involved • can be less tiring for the mother • mother can leave her baby for a while, knowing that their feeding needs will be met • it can now be bought ready made up • it is easy to see how much milk the baby has had

Disadvantages of breast feeding:	Disadvantages of bottle feeding:
• only the mother can feed, lessening the opportunities to involve siblings and others • mother can become over-tired as she has to cover all the night feeds too • there is no record of how much milk the infant has had; you judge by contentment • always a possibility of feeding problems such as mastitis, sore nipples etc. • mother needs a good healthy diet • mother needs support/feeding bras • breast pads may need to be bought	• formula milk lacks the immunological qualities of breast milk • always a risk of bacterial infection from teats, bottles etc. • making up feeds correctly is vital to ensure a correct balance is achieved over-diluting a feed = hungry baby over-concentrated feeds can harm baby • formula feeds need to be bought • a range of equipment is needed for both feeding and sterilising

For information on how to make up a formula feed, or how to sterilise feeding equipment, refer back to Unit 6.

LINKS TO UNIT 6, pages 275–283.

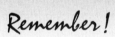

Remember ! A mother has the right to choose the feeding method that suits her needs. At times you may be asked for information on feeding options, but you should not try to influence a woman's decision.

Case Study | **Sita**

Muna is two-and-a-half weeks old and his mother, Sita, has opted to breast feed. Muna has sucked strongly since birth and Sita's milk supply is good.

In the last few days Sita's nipples have become sore and her breasts are very full and lumpy. The milk seems very watery and Sita wonders if it is nutritious enough for her son.

The health visitor is due to visit today, and Sita intends to ask her about her concerns.

1 What might be the cause of Sita's soreness?

2 How could the health visitor advise Sita on reducing the fullness of her breasts?

3 Should Sita be concerned about the nutritional content of her milk?

Supporting a mother in the care of a neonate

Providing care for a neonate

In the earliest weeks, mothers of newborn infants need:

- support;
- encouragement;
- care;
- rest.

Support

This will be needed from family, friends and the primary health team – midwife, health visitor, GP. It will involve emotional support as well as practical support.

Encouragement

This will be particularly essential if the baby is hard to settle, or feeding is difficult to establish. The mother will need reassurance that she is coping well and doing things right.

Care

The newly delivered mother usually needs some care herself. She has had a physically traumatic time – the birth, and has also been on an emotional roller-coaster – the highs regarding the birth of her child, and the lows of feeling daunted by the new responsibilities.

Rest

Looking after a newborn baby can be exhausting, particularly when breast feeding, as the mother has to be 'on duty' for all feeds, day and

Rest is essential when feeding a newborn baby

night. Whenever possible, the mother should be enabled to rest without interruption. This will be important to her milk production (if breast feeding) as well as to her general well-being.

When supporting a new mother, it is important that respect is shown for her cultural practices and her personal choices. Your relationship should maintain a professional manner at all times, ensuring that you avoid:

- directing her actions;
- influencing her choices;
- becoming over-familiar.

You should always:

- respect her privacy, and that of her family;
- maintain confidentiality at all times;
- be willing (and know how) to provide information if asked.

Safety of the newborn infant – summary

- General health and safety practice should be upheld at all times when working with young babies.
- Careful handling and appropriate support of newborn infants is of utmost importance.
- Strict adherence to preventive measures regarding cross-infection is needed, both in the home and in daycare settings.
- Supervision of infants when in their prams is necessary, particularly if cats are around.

Safe practice includes:

- use of cat/insect nets;
- use of baby alarms;
- use of disposable gloves to prevent cross-infection;
- placing moses baskets, baby chairs, car seats etc. on safe surfaces (ideally on the floor);
- maintaining all baby equipment appropriately;
- ensuring that car seats are properly secured and meet all safety standards.

Moses baskets should always be placed on a safe surface

Security in the care environment

- In a care setting, strict monitoring regarding who has access to babies is important.
- Visual and/or audio monitoring of sleeping infants should be in place.

- Standard measures regarding the prevention of strangers into the setting should be established.
- Infants should only be handed over to the persons specified in advance to the setting.

Relationship with the child's mother

Relationships between Early Years staff and parents need to be built on:

- respect – there is a need for both carer and parent to respect each other's knowledge, experience and culture;
- trust – there should be mutual trust that each of you has the best interests of the infant at heart;
- understanding – it should be understood by you both that new skills are being learnt, and that time may be needed to perfect them.

In caring for an infant you will automatically be involved with their family to some degree, and in post-natal care units you will support mothers in a variety of ways, including:

- the development of correct feeding positions and techniques with their babies;
- demonstrating or carrying out the changing and dressing of babies;
- demonstrating how to 'top and tail' babies;
- demonstrating how to bath babies;
- demonstrating how to respond to babies by your own actions and responses.

Stress

Wherever you work in the community, within a family centre or in a nursery you may identify signs of stress in the mothers of new babies. Clearly, a new baby takes up a great deal of time and places extra pressures on parents, and a degree of stress appears in many families at this time. However, at times this becomes a far more serious issue and stress can develop into **post-natal depression**.

Post-natal depression as a general term

It is important that all Early Years workers have an awareness of the early signs and symptoms of post-natal depression. The post-natal period is the first two months following birth and involves the mother:

345

- settling into her new role of motherhood;
- building a bond with her child;
- recovering from any birth trauma or ill effects of pregnancy, for example, haemorrhoids, cuts and tears, iron deficiency;
- adjusting to the feeding and sleeping demands of the new infant.

Post-natal depression is a general term often used to (inaccurately) describe both the mild symptoms of the 'baby blues', and the more serious symptoms of actual post-natal depression.

The 'baby blues'

The most commonly associated signs of the 'baby blues' occur on around day five after birth, once the initial exhilaration of giving birth has passed, and the reality of responsibility begins to set in. It is linked to the various hormonal changes that take place in the woman's body. The feeling of the blues is experienced by nearly two-thirds of all mothers. It is in a sense an anti-climax after all the waiting, and most women become tearful and often feel overwhelmed, wondering if they will cope. The symptoms usually only last two to three days, and they are fine from then onwards. The support and encouragement of family and carers helps significantly here.

Serious post-natal depression

A more serious depression is experienced by around 10 to 15 per cent of mothers, and it can last for several weeks. The woman feels constantly tired and restless, but often cannot sleep. Her appetite is usually poor during this time and many women in this category may face additional stress factors such as:

- financial problems;
- relationship problems;
- being a single parent;
- being a first-time mother;
- a previous personality disorder, which may become heightened.

The depression often clears up on its own as the weeks go by, when the mother realises that she is actually coping fine, but occasionally her GP may prescribe anti-depressants to help her. Again, support and encouragement can play an important part in her recovery.

Depressive psychosis

The rarest, and most severe, form of post-natal depression is known as puerperal psychosis, and signs of it usually begin to be seen two to three weeks after the arrival of the baby. Symptoms include:

- severe mental confusion;
- feelings of worthlessness;
- rapid mood swings;
- threats of suicide;
- concerns by the mother that she will harm her own child.

Treatment of this type of depression is long term and needs careful handling. Ideally the mother will be admitted to a special unit for post-natally depressed women, where she can be treated for her illness while still caring for her baby. The illness is a product of having given birth, so it is illogical to treat the mother without her baby. Trained counsellors and family therapists are often involved alongside the medical staff. The condition can last for a considerable length of time.

Sadly, there are limited numbers of these special units and many mothers have to be treated within general mental health units, or through primary health care support. It should be clearly understood that there is no one 'type' of person who is more likely to suffer from post-natal depression than any other. It is experienced by mothers who have brought up children previously without any problems, as well as first-time mothers. It is experienced by women from all walks of life and from all cultures. It also does not automatically follow that a mother who has suffered depression after one birth, will experience the same following subsequent births.

Support and encouragement by family and carers is vital here, but often the depressive feelings of worthlessness remain with the affected mother, despite their reassurances.

The first ten days following birth

While still under the care of the maternity unit or hospital, the mother will be examined daily for:

- blood pressure;
- the healing of any stitches;
- the position of her womb (it gradually moves back to its original site within the abdomen).

She will be questioned about her bowel and bladder movements, and whether she is suffering any pain. As the womb contracts, pain similar to that experienced by many women during their period is present. This tends to be more marked following second or subsequent births.

The infant will be monitored regarding:

- the passing of urine;
- the consistency and colour of their stools;
- any skin problems;
- how well established feeding is;
- their weight;
- the measurement of their head circumference.

Before being discharged from the unit or hospital a paediatrician will examine the neonate by:

- checking their reflexes;
- checking their mouth to ensure the palette is intact;
- checking their hips for secure joints and their ability to rotate;
- checking the spine to ensure it looks healthy and straight;
- examining their abdomen to ensure all internal organs feel appropriate in size and position;
- listening to the heart sounds.

Once the mother and infant have been declared fit to go home, their care will be passed to their local midwife.

The role of the midwife after the birth

The midwife will visit each day until the infant is ten days old (occasionally longer if the umbilical cord is still intact, or there is a

Weight should be recorded regularly

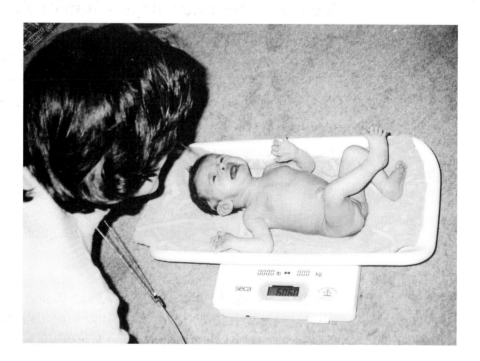

significant problem). He or she will weigh the infant regularly, monitoring the normal weight loss and subsequent regaining of weight, recording it on the centile charts in the infant's health record book. They will also continue to monitor skin, stools, urine etc.

The midwife also follows up on the mother's health and general well-being, monitoring the contraction of the womb, blood loss and any feeding problems.

The Guthrie test

At around seven to eight days a heel prick test (known as the **Guthrie test**) is carried out. This tests the infant for a rare inherited disorder called penylketonuria (PKU), which is seen in about 1 in every 10,000 births. It requires an extremely strict special diet throughout life to ensure that the effects of the untreated condition (learning disability, skin problems and a shortened life span) are avoided. For more on this condition, see Unit 3.

LINKS TO UNIT 3, page 99.

The blood test for hypothyroidism is also carried out. It is known as the thyroid stimulating hormone test (TSH). If an infant tests positively following TSH they need to take a hormone supplement throughout their life to alleviate symptoms of the condition.

Eleven to fourteen days – health visitor

Between day 11 and 14 the **health visitor** will arrange to call. Again the infant will be weighed, the general well-being of both mother and infant will be talked through, and general safety issues in caring for a new baby will be discussed. This includes sensitive issues such as cot death and the recommended measures to help prevent it.

The health visitor will often call weekly initially to ensure that mother and baby are coping well. They will then be invited to attend the health clinic regularly. The health visitor can often build quite a close relationship with a mother, as they see them quite often. They are one of the front-line health care professionals who look out for signs of depression.

Death among newborn infants

Sadly, even with modern day health care a small number of infants still die. Their deaths are categorised as follows.

Stillbirth	An infant who dies before birth, any time after 24 weeks of pregnancy, is termed as being stillborn.
A perinatal death	This refers to any infant who dies within one week of birth. The perinatal mortality rate also includes the numbers of babies who have been stillborn.
Neonatal death	This term refers to infants who die within the first 28 days of life.
Post-neonatal death	The death of any child after the first 28 days have passed, but before they reach 1 year old, is placed in this category.

Six weeks – paediatric checks

At the six-week assessment, the GP (often a paediatric specialist) will check the following:

- the size and shape of the baby's skull, measured with a special tape measure;
- skin, checking for any blemishes, irritations or birth marks;
- the spine, again checking that it is straight.

Check that the baby's spine is straight

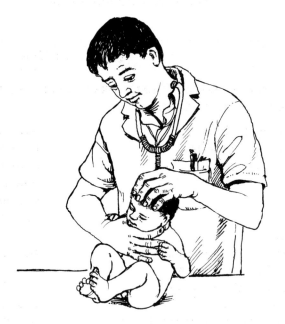

- muscle tone, checking that the infant moves symmetrically (not lop-sided), and that their head is in line with their body when held forward;
- baby's heart and breathing will be assessed and listened to;
- the abdomen will be checked again, assessing the correct positioning of liver, spleen, kidneys and bladder;

- the umbilicus, ensuring that the area has dried up well;
- eyes are examined for signs of cataracts, glaucoma and high pressure;
- the infant's sucking reflex will be assessed by a clean finger placed in the mouth;
- the palette is checked to ensure it is complete;
- the mouth is examined for signs of tongue tie (a restriction on the movement of the tongue);
- pulses in the main arteries are assessed to ensure that a strong blood supply is circulating the body;
- feet and legs will be assessed for 'inward turns' or club foot;
- the penis of a boy is examined for correct positioning of the hole at its tip;
- testicles are carefully felt for within the scrotum. Occasionally the testes have not descended, and this will be monitored further. They usually descend before the age of three months;
- gentle examination of the vulva in a girl is carried out, checking that all is correctly sized;
- hips are rotated and pressed outwards to ensure that 'clicking hips' (a dislocation) are not a problem.

Key terms

You should now understand the following key words and phrases. If you do not, read through the chapter again and review them.

advantages of bottle feeding	lactation
advantages of breast feeding	neonatal death
anatomy of the breast	neonate
Apgar score	paediatric checks
birth	perinatal death
birth marks	physiology of lactation
breast feeding	post-natal depression
common breast-feeding difficulties	post-neonatal death
effects of genetic inheritance	pre-term
environmental effects on foetal development	primitive reflexes
	providing care for a neonate
factors affecting the development of a foetus	relationships with the child's mother
	role of the midwife after the birth
folic acid	safe practice
fore milk and hind milk	screening in pregnancy
general appearance of the neonate	senses
Guthrie test	stillbirth
health visitor	ultra-sound scan

Test Yourself

1 What primitive reflexes can you explain?

2 What is vernix caseosa?

3 What is the usual cause of neonatal jaundice?

4 What does the Apgar score measure?

5 What effects can the mother's hormones crossing the placenta have on the neonate?

6 Which birth mark is only found on dark-skinned infants?

7 Which fontanelle closes by eighteen months of age?

8 Why are black infants usually pale at birth?

9 What factors can you think of that can affect the developing foetus?

10 Why is folic acid considered to be important for pregnant women?

11 How many screening processes during pregnancy can you explain?

12 Why is breast milk best for babies?

13 What is the difference between fore milk and hind milk?

14 Why is weaning usually introduced at about four months?

15 Explain the advantages and disadvantages of breast feeding.

16 Explain the advantages and disadvantages of formula feeding.

17 Give examples of safe practice when caring for young babies.

18 What are the 'baby blues'?

19 What does the midwife monitor during the infant's first ten days?

20 What does a paediatrician check for at an infant's six-week assessment?

References and suggested further reading

Baston, H and Durward, H (2001) *Examination of the Newborn. A Practical Guide*, Routledge

Bee, H (1992) *The Developing Child* (6th edn), Allyn & Boston

Dare, A and O'Donovan, M(1998) *A Practical Guide to Working with Babies* (2nd edn), Nelson Thornes

Green, S (2003) *Baby and Toddler Development Made Real*, David Fulton Publishers

Keene, A (1999) *Child Health. Care of the Child in Health and Illness*, Nelson Thornes

Phillips, C (1996) *Family-Centred Maternity and Newborn Care* (4th edn) Mosby Publishers

Websites

www.babycentre.co.uk

www.pampers.com

www.bounty.com

www.parentlineplus.com

www.nctpregnancyandbabycare.com

Glossary of terms

ABC of behaviour strategy	When considering a pattern in behaviour, it stands for the antecedent, the behaviour and the consequence of situations
ABC of resuscitation procedures	A sequential emergency first aid process: open the airway; breathe for the injured person; help circulation to be restored
Accident book	A book in which staff record all accidents or injuries that occur in the workplace
Anonymity	Ensuring that an individual's identity remains unknown
Apgar chart	The chart noting the health score given to a baby at birth
Area child protection committee (ACPC)	A group of professionals who meet to discuss individual child abuse or protection cases
Artificial ventilation	Breathing for another person, when they are unable to do so for themselves
Associative play	Children playing with the same activity, but who are not yet playing co-operatively
At risk	A significant concern regarding a child's welfare, or potential welfare, has been identified
Aural stimulation	Stimulation through sound (hearing)
Baby massage	A pleasurable form of physical contact that aids relaxation, and can help the bonding of parents and child
Barriers to communication	Any obstruction to understanding between individuals
Behaviour management	Strategies for setting boundaries for children's behaviour
Behaviour policies	Written agreements setting out the behaviour management of an Early Years setting
Body language	The non-verbal signals given out by our bodies, including facial expressions and gesture
Bonding	The close relationship formed between a child and one or more of the child's main carers
Care of the environment	Considering the safety needs of the Early Years setting
Care order	A legal order in which a child is placed in the care of the local authority
Caudal	Referring to the lower parts of the body
Causes of ill health	The range of reasons why individuals become ill
Centile	A mark used for the measurement of growth in infants and young children (also known as percentile)

Cephalo	Referring to the head
Chest compressions	An emergency first aid procedure
Child assessment order	A legal order applied for in court when a child is considered to be at risk or already suffering significant harm
Child protection register	A computerised list, kept by a local authority, of children who are considered to be 'at risk'
Children Act 1989	A major piece of legislation, bringing together a range of laws to do with the rights and well-being of children
Children in need	A child who is unlikely to achieve a reasonable standard without intervention or specific support. The term is used within the Children Act 1989 in reference to disabled children
Chromosome	Part of human genetic make-up
Colic	Acute spasmodic abdominal pain, common in young babies
Colostrum	The milk initially produced by the breast – rich in nutrients
Communication	The means of passing and receiving information
Confidentiality	Keeping information to yourself. Not passing on information inappropriately. Respecting the privacy of others
Containment	Helping a child to express his or her emotions safely
Continuity of care	Routine and familiarity, which helps children feel secure
Cooled boiled water	Water that has been boiled and allowed to cool. Used to prepare formula feeds, and to cleanse the eyes of newborn babies
Co-operative play	The stage of play when children play with each other, sometimes taking on simple roles or making simple rules for their games
COSHH	Regulations: Control of Substances Hazardous to Health (1994)
Cradle cap	A crusty secretion on the scalp of a baby
Cross-infection	The passing of infection from one person to another
Cycle of disadvantage	The process whereby the experiences of one generation of a family have an effect on the next, continuing some or all of the problems they face
Development	The changes that take place as an individual grows
Developmental delay	The term often used when a child's development falls behind the pattern of averages
Developmentally appropriate	What is expected of a child for that stage of development
Direct contact	Cross-infection through contact with an infected individual
Disclosure	Telling someone about abuse suffered, either currently, or in the past
Direct discrimination	Telling an individual that they cannot do something because of their race, sex, situation or disability

Discrimination	The unfair treatment of an individual, group or minority, based on prejudice
Distal	A distance away from the central point of the body
Diversity	Being different or varied
Droplet infection	A common cause of cross-infection
Dysfluency	Being unable to speak words fluently, stammering. A common (temporary) occurrence in young children
Early Learning Goals	The aims of the six areas of learning that make up the foundation stage curriculum. Most children achieve them before they enter key stage 1 of the national curriculum
Emergency protection order	An order of law, applied for through the courts to help protect children from harm
Emotional abuse	The continual rejection, terrorising or criticism of an individual
Emotional disturbance	Evidenced by behaviour that causes concern and needs professional intervention (when serious or long term) or sensitive handling by parents and carers (for temporary or common problems such as tantrums)
Environmental factors	Any influences from around an individual that could have an impact on them in any way
EPOCH	The organisation End Physical Punishment of Children
Equality	The state of being equal, of having an equal opportunity
Evacuation procedures	The planned process of removing children from an unsafe situation to a safe environment
Evaluation	Reflecting on and giving consideration to a past event, action or project
Evidence	Supportive material or information
Exploratory play	Play in which a child is able to find out by experimentation and discovery
Eye contact	Looking directly at an individual when talking to or explaining something to them
Febrile convulsion	A slight 'fit', which can be caused by a raised temperature in a child
Fine motor skills	Hand/eye co-ordination and hand manipulation
First aid	The emergency actions taken following an accident or sudden illness
Foetal alcohol syndrome (FAS)	Physical and cognitive abnormalities often found in babies born to alcoholic mothers
Fontanelle	An area of an infant's skull where the bony plates meet. They enable some movement during the birth process
Food-related customs	Acceptable and unacceptable foods linked to culture
Formula feed	A bottle of milk made for a baby using powdered formula and cooled boiled water
Foundation stage curriculum	A Government-led curriculum for children from the age of three years

Free play	Play that is undirected
Genotype	The complete genetic inheritance of an individual
Good-enough parenting	A term used to refer to parenting that is adequate, although may not be considered to be ideal by many people
Gross motor skills	Large body movements, balance and co-ordination
Growth	Increasing in size, height, weight and so on
HASAWA	The Health and Safety at Work Act 1974
Health	The state of well-being
Health visitor	A specially trained nurse who is part of the primary health care team. Part of the health visitor's role is to support children's healthy development
Heritage language	What used to be called mother or parent tongue; the language spoken at home
Heuristic play	Play in which a baby explores objects, e.g. in a treasure basket
Holistic model	Taking an all-round consideration
Hygiene	Good practice regarding cleanliness, handling food and personal care
Imaginative play	Play in which children take on roles and use their imagination
Immunisation programmes	A series of vaccinations for children to prevent illness and to help eradicate certain conditions from society
Incest	Sexual intercourse between two relatives who are too closely linked to legally be able to marry
Indicators of abuse	Signs and symptoms that may be seen in children, which could suggest that abuse has taken place
Indirect contact	Cross-infection where there is no specific contact with an infected individual
Institutional discrimination	The policies or practice of an organisation, which systematically discriminates against a minority group or groups
Interpersonal skills	Communicating with others in a positive (good skills) or negative (bad skills) manner
Key worker	An individual who has specific responsibility for a child or group of children, being a known link between parents and the setting
Laissez-faire model	Taking an approach involving unrestricted freedom or indifference, e.g. the adult lets the child play without restriction and little or no guidance
Lifestyle factors affecting health	How choices we make about the way we live our lives, such as smoking, have an impact on health
Long-term effects of abuse	The ongoing effects suffered by an individual following abuse
Managing unwanted behaviour	Methods to lessen undesirable behaviour in children
Manipulative play	Play that enables children to practise their fine motor skills

Marginalise	Treating someone or something as insignificant or unimportant. To place at the edge (of importance)
Maturational	To do with maturity
Meeting differentiation of need	Providing activities which support all children's development, incorporating additional guidance for those who need it and opportunities for extension for those children who are more able
Milk teeth	The first set of twenty teeth that an infant has (deciduous teeth)
Multi-cultural	Referring to a varied range of cultural and ethnic backgrounds
Nappy rash	A red, sore rash on a baby's bottom and sometimes the thighs
National curriculum	The curriculum followed by children in all state schools
Negative images	Illustrations or descriptions that portray limitations or negativity regarding individuals
Neglect	A form of abuse where the care of a child is insufficient or inappropriate
Neonatal jaundice	A problem with the function of the liver during the first weeks of life
Neonate	An infant under one month old
Non-verbal communication	The messages that are given through body language and facial expression
Objectivity	Without bias
Observation skills	The ability to carry out appropriate methods of observation, knowing when to use them and how
Palmar grasp	Grasping an object using the whole hand
Paramountcy principle	A main principle of the Children Act 1989 where the welfare of the child must be the first and most important consideration
Parents' expectations	What parents expect of an Early Years setting, when they leave their child in the care of the setting
Partnership with parents	Active involvement of parents by the setting
Perception	Gaining insight or awareness
Personal safety	Being responsible for one's own safe working practice
Phenotype	The visible arrangement of characteristics inherited by an individual from his or her parents
Physical environment	The surroundings (building, room layout, lighting, ventilation and so on)
Pincer grasp	Grasping an object with the first finger and the thumb
Placement log	An ongoing record charting a student's experience in a range of placements
Play therapy	The use of play to help alleviate some of the effects of abuse or other traumas experienced in childhood
Police protection	Legal protection for a child from harm

Positive images	Illustrations or descriptions that positively portray all the individuals included within them
Positive reinforcement	Rewarding good (behaviour), rather than responding to undesirable (behaviour) in children
Potential hazard	Any situation that has the potential to cause harm
Prejudice	An opinion formed in advance, a pre-judgement
Primary socialisation	The impact of immediate family and social groups on a child
Primitive reflex	An automatic response. Many examples are seen in newborn infants
Principles of diet and nutrition	The basis of healthy eating
Professional	A person who is qualified, competent and experienced at what they do
Pro-social	An innate (born with) predisposition to relate to other people
Proximal	Close to the central point (of the body)
Pyrexia	A high temperature, fever
Quality assurance	A set standard, achieved when specified criteria have been met
Racism	The belief that some races have cultural characteristics that make them superior (or inferior) to others
Recovery order	A legal order enabling the police to take into their possession a child who is the subject of police protection or an emergency protection order, if the child is missing, has run away, or has been abducted from the person responsible for his or her care
Recovery position	The position individuals are placed in following an accident or sudden illness, after their situation has been stabilised, while they await further medical treatment (for example following an accident) or rest (for example following an epileptic fit)
Referral procedures	The process of reporting concerns about a child's safety
Reflexes	An involuntary response to a stimulus, for example blinking
RIDDOR	Reporting of Injuries, Diseases and Dangerous Occurrences Regulations 1995
Rights	Our entitlements as individuals
Role model	A person who is considered to be setting an example to others
Routines	A set procedure that should meet the needs of all concerned
Safety marks	National standards regarding safety, printed on the packaging of objects, to guide consumers as to their suitability for the intended use or recipient. For example, on toys, baby equipment, electrical appliances
Screening	The process of examining a whole population to identify who is showing signs of a disease, or may be predisposed to develop it
Secondary socialisation	The impact of social contacts on a child, outside the child's immediate family and social group. This would include teachers, Early Years professionals and so on
Sensory impairment	A lack of full experience of sight or hearing

Separation anxiety	When an infant is distressed due to being apart from his or her main carer
Sequential	Occurring in a sequence
Setting boundaries	Stating acceptable limitations
Short-term effects of abuse	Effects that take place immediately, for example physical pain, injuries or infection
Signed language	Communication without the necessity of speech
Skin care	Appropriate care of different types of skin
Small world play	Any toys that are a scaled-down version of real life
Social and economic factors affecting health	Health problems linked to issues such as poverty
Social constructivist theory	Learning by exploring a range of experiences and objects from everyday life
Social learning theory	Learning by observing and copying others. A theory often associated with Albert Bandura and the Bobo dolls
Solitary play	Playing alone, a normal stage of development in young children
Spontaneous play	Play that is unplanned, undirected and allows freedom
Stages of play	The changes in how children's play develops, usually linked to age
Standard attainment tasks (SATs)	Tests carried out at regular intervals during formal schooling
Stereotyping	Categorising, taking away individuality
Sterilising techniques	Methods of ensuring that utensils (bottles, teats and so on) used for babies are free from bacteria
Stimulate	To arouse curiosity, interest and development
Stimulating play	Activities or objects that stimulate
Stools	Another term for faeces, body waste
Structured play	Play that is pre-determined or has specific constraints. For example, completing a jigsaw puzzle
Supervision order	A legal order in which a child is under the supervision of the local authority, but where the authority does not have parental responsibility
Suppressed immunity	Where the immune system is impaired in some way, leaving an individual susceptible to infection
Symbolic play	The use of objects to represent other objects in play
Teamwork	Working co-operatively with a group of colleagues
Theories	Ideas, philosophies
Tokenism	Making only a small effort, or providing no more than the minimum, in order to comply with criteria or guidelines

Topping and tailing The washing of the facial area of a baby, together with a nappy change

Transmission model An approach in which the adult controls the learning process, often suppressing the child's own initiative

Treasure baskets A small basket of natural objects ideal for babies from about six months of age to enable exploration of a range of natural materials, smells and shapes, for example, a natural sponge, a wooden spoon

Turn-taking Responses made by young babies to adults when they make 'conversation' with them. This can be an expression, a movement, a smile or a sound

UN Convention on Children's Rights This 'national constitution' was adopted by the United Nations assembly in 1989 to uphold agreed rights for children whenever possible

Visual stimulation Stimulation through sight

Vocational Learning through practical experience as well as theory

Weaning The introduction of solid food to young babies

WHO The World Health Organisation

Zone of proximal development (ZPD) A theory in which the child is lifted to a level of achievement they would be unlikely to reach without additional support from an adult. The theory was initiated by Lev Vygotsky

Index

Page numbers in italics indicate figures, charts or tables.